T3-BSD-743

Photo-Textualities

Photo-Textualities

Reading Photographs and Literature

EDITED BY MARSHA BRYANT

DELAWARE

Newark: University of Delaware Press
London: Associated University Presses

© 1996 by Associated University Presses, Inc.

All rights reserved. Authorization to photocopy items for internal or personal use, or the internal or personal use of specific clients, is granted by the copyright owner, provided that a base fee of $10.00, plus eight cents per page per copy is paid directly to the Copyright Clearance Center, 222 Rosewood Drive, Danvers, Massachusetts 01923. [0-87413-551-6/96 $10.00 + 8¢ pp, pc.]

PR
478
.P 45
P 46
1996

Associated University Presses
440 Forsgate Drive
Cranbury, NJ 08512

Associated University Presses
16 Barter Street
London WC1A 2AH, England

Associated University Presses
P.O. Box 338, Port Credit
Mississauga, Ontario
Canada L5G 4L8

Library of Congress Cataloging-in-Publication Data

Photo-textualities : reading photographs and literaturé / edited by
Marsha Bryant.
        p.   cm.
    Includes bibliographical references and index.
    ISBN 0-87413-551-6 (alk. paper)
    1. English literature—20th century—History and criticism.
    2. Literature and photography—Great Britain—History—20th century.
    3. Literature and photography—United States—History—20th century.
    4. American literature—20th century—History and criticism.
    5. Photography, Artistic—History and criticism. 6. Realism in
literature. I. Bryant, Marsha, 1960–
    PR478.P45P46   1995
    820.9′356—dc20   95-44280
                                                          CIP

The paper used in this publication meets the requirements
of the American National Standard for Permanence of Paper
for Printed Library Materials Z39.48-1984.

PRINTED IN THE UNITED STATES OF AMERICA

9 3996 - 11

I found her words opening a way back to the photo, a way that I thought had been closed to me for good.

—Richard Powers, *Three Farmers on Their Way to a Dance*

Contents

Acknowledgments

THIS PROJECT BEGAN WITH A SPECIAL SESSION that Corey K. Creekmur and I cochaired at the 1989 MLA Convention; the number of people submitting proposals and attending the session convinced us of the need for *Photo-Textualities*. Some contributors read earlier versions of their essays at The University of Oklahoma's conference, "Cultural Studies in the 1990s," in a session Carol Shloss chaired. I would like to thank several people whose suggestions proved helpful to my work on the anthology. Caryl Flinn, Robert B. Ray, Timothy Sweet, and Gregory L. Ulmer read early versions of the introduction. The students in my graduate seminar on documentary books gave me valuable insights on how photo-textuality affects reading. I am grateful to Elizabeth Langland and Stephen Watt for sharing their expertise in anthology editing. Finally, I would like to thank Camden Pierce for his support and patience. Some of my work on the anthology was supported by a Research Development Award from the University of Florida.

Introduction

Marsha Bryant

LITERATURE AND PHOTOGRAPHY HAVE BEEN crossing each other's representational borders ever since Edgar Allan Poe acclaimed the invention of the daguerreotype in his essays of 1840.[1] Their imbrications occur even in the language we use—from the etymology of the word *photography* (writing with light) to the current term *visual literacy*. Both in popular and in academic culture, people often think of one representational form in terms of the other. Recently, Ellen Goodman has characterized Ann Beattie's novel *Picturing Will* as "a series of literary snapshots" forming a "photo album," while Andy Grundberg has declared that Walker Evans's album *American Photographs* should be read "the way one reads a novel."[2]

Occasionally the academy has brought together photography and literature in comparative studies of individual artists; for example, a comparison of Evans's documentary photographs and Jorge Luis Borges's story "The Aleph" appears in the collection of Logan Grant Essays on Photography, *Multiple Views*. And border crossings within a single artist's career have received some attention, as the publication of Eudora Welty's photographs demonstrates.[3] Yet despite the broad cultural interaction of photography and literature, their crossings within individual books have not received much critical inquiry. This collection of essays focuses on books that juxtapose photographs and literary language and on the implications that such border-crossing texts hold for critical practice. While most of the contributors work in literary studies, *Photo-Textualities* includes insights from contributors in visual studies. Crossing academic disciplines, the dialogue we initiate moves critical inquiry on what Jefferson Hunter calls "photo texts" beyond the boundaries of traditional textual criticism.[4]

As literary practice continues to negotiate with photographic practice, criticism has begun to map out this interaction. Some of these critical inquiries occur within the wider terrain of image/text studies—including questions about the theoretical status of words and images across the representational spectrum (most notably in W. J. T. Mitchell's *Iconology*), as well as questions about the photo-text's relation to other intertextualities among verbal and visual arts, and its position within the history of book illustration.[5] *Photo-Textualities* contributes to this larger dialogue by acknowledging the multiple and competing ways in which the visual and verbal components of photo-texts interact. Unlike most comparative studies of literature and photography, *Photo-Textualities* does not focus its inquiries on photography's general influence on writing.[6] Yet *Photo-Textualities* does not ignore larger cultural contexts, including photography's relation to other visual arts.[7]

Photo-Textualities's tightened focus allows us to consider an expanded array of photo-textual dynamics in books composed of photographs and words. More broadly focused discussions often limit photo-texts to "classic" examples such as Alvin Langdon Coburn's collaborations with Henry James on the New York Edition, or James Agee and Walker Evans's *Let Us Now Praise Famous Men*.[8] In fact, the textual genres these books represent—the novel and the documentary, respectively—dominate most inquiries on photo-texts. *Photo-Textualities* expands the photo-textual novel's domain by reaching back to Hawthorne's *The Marble Faun* (a precursor to the James-Coburn collaboration), which has not received the critical attention of *The House of Seven Gables* and its fictional daguerreotypist. At the same time, *Photo-Textualities* reaches forward to Richard Powers's postmodern novel (*Three Farmers on Their Way to a Dance*), which empowers its frontispiece photograph in ways inconceivable to James. This anthology also breaks with conventional configurations of photo-textuality and documentary. Unlike some recent work in both literary and photographic studies, *Photo-Textualities* does not privilege the documentary book as the most productive site in which the two representational forms enter negotiations with each other. Moreover, we open up new possibilities for documentary by recovering alternative models from the 1930s (*Men at Work, Letters from Iceland, Three Guineas*), by interrogating post-thirties models (*A Seventh Man* and *After the Last Sky*), and by including examples outside American culture.[9]

The contributors to *Photo-Textualities* address a wide range of literary and photographic genres, as well as hybrid forms and texts which elude traditional genre classification. Besides fiction, literary genres include nonfiction forms such as biography and autobiography, as well as travelogue and documentary. The range of photographic genres extends to landscapes, portraiture, documentary, tourist snapshots, and media images as well as to the standard photo-textual forms of published album and photo-essay. Some contributors find that photo-textuality lends itself to hybrid forms such as novel/travelogue (Hawthorne's *The Marble Faun*), novel/history (Powers's *Three Farmers on Their Way to a Dance*), documentary/children's book (Hine's *Men at Work*), and documentary/travelogue (*Letters from Iceland*). Still other contributors suggest that photo-textuality presents an alternative form outside the boundaries of genre. Carol Shloss proposes that we see Berger and Mohr's *A Seventh Man* as a "constellation provided by the photographs and texts which, taken together as a system, operate according to a discernable syntax." In their essay, Julia Duffy and Lloyd Davis

find that the combination of photographs and words in Woolf's *Three Guineas* "disrupts conventions of syntax, signification, and genre." In short, the plural form of this collection's title is deliberate: we investigate the richness of photo-textualit*ies*.

The academy's marginal attention to photo-texts seems especially surprising given photographic studies' and literary studies' growing interest in cultural contexts. In his introduction to *Multiple Views*, Alan Trachtenberg points out that the new photographic studies have abandoned the search for "an intrinsic identity for photography" and have turned their inquiries toward "concrete studies of what the medium *does*—the cultural and ideological work it performs within specific conditions and circumstances."[10] Similarly, new directions in literary studies—especially cultural studies—have called for examining literary texts within broader cultural frameworks than an individual writer's career, artistic movements, or the literary canon. As Lawrence Grossberg, Cary Nelson, and Paula A. Treichler note in their introduction to *Cultural Studies*, the new interpretive strategies depart from literary studies' traditional assumptions "that texts are properly understood as wholly self-determined and independent objects."[11] *Photo-Textualities* shares this interest in the cultural work that representations perform—whether these be literary, photographic, or a combination. The contributors bridge contemporary methodologies with the close readings and comparisons of more traditional textual and inter-art studies. Since the photo-text is already a culturally loaded form—marking intersections of the human and the mechanical, the verbal and the visual, the literary and the popular, the book and the cinema—it offers us a unique site for assessing how literature and photography work with and against each other to shape strategies for representation and reading.

Traditionally, photo-texts have been read in terms of the image/caption model or the collaboration model; the form seems to invite dualistic ways of thinking. Yet each of these models can limit our understanding of photo-texts. While the image/caption model appears to present a particular kind of collaboration, it actually operates as a binarism privileging one textual component over the other. When *caption* functions as the valued term, photography is subordinated to the role of "illustration"; as contributor Kevin G. Barnhurst puts it, "The caption eliminates all the potential narrative frames but one, the depicted content." Roland Barthes reflects the prevalence of this discursive hierarchy when he interrogates the image/caption model in "Rhetoric of the Image": "Does the image duplicate certain of the informations given in the text by a phenomenon of redundancy or does the text add a fresh information to the image?" Note how neither alternative allows the possibility of the photograph adding "fresh information" to the verbal text; nor can the verbal text be redundant.[12] We can see the limitations of this model in scholarly assessments of Virginia Woolf's *Three Guineas:* some of them go so far as to *invent* the text's photographs, assuming that those in the original edition depict the photographic images Woolf describes verbally.[13] The image/caption model can also reverse the hierarchy, further limiting our interpretations of photo-texts. When "image" functions as privileged term, then language occupies that most physically marginal of verbal forms, the photo caption.[14] Perhaps this binarism arouses both Hunter's concern when he calls Agee's portion of *Let Us Now Praise Famous Men* an "enormously expanded, limit-defying caption working against the Evans photographs" (78), and Archibald MacLeish's when he labels his *Land of the Free* "a book of photographs illustrated by a poem" (89).[15] William Stott points out that initial reviews of American documentary books often emphasized their photographs.[16] Yet such applications of the image/caption model would miss the significance of *Men at Work*'s preface and captions to Hine's construction of masculinity in this photo-text. A more productive model would, in Hunter's words, present "no question of passages being pressed into captioning or, on the other hand, pictures being pressed into illustration."[17]

Alternative strategies of representation have challenged our habit of pitting images and captions against each other. For example, postmodern photographer Richard Prince's Cowboy series has appropriated the photographs in Marlboro advertisements through "rephotography"; by cropping out the words, Prince releases

these images from the confines of image/caption layout.[18] Even the "classic" photo-text *Let Us Now Praise Famous Men* shows the model's inadequacies. Agee and Evans subvert image/caption layout by physically separating their respective contributions from one another (Evans's photographs appear in the photo-text's opening pages, comprising "Book One"). As several critics have pointed out, Agee provides few direct cross-references to Evans's photographs; yet he does offer several passages which function as deferred captions. Consider this photo-textual crossing that represents Squinchy Gudger. In Evans's untitled photograph, the covered child and pallet comprise most of the frame—contrasting sharply with the dark wooden floor in the background, and divorced from other human figures or home furnishings.[19] On the other hand, Agee's verbal representation integrates child and surroundings by presenting his photographic

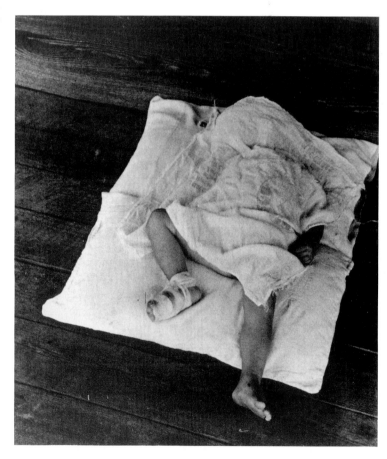

Untitled, by Walker Evans. From Let Us Now Praise Famous Men *(1941; reprint, Boston: Houghton Mifflin, 1988).*

descriptions as Squinchy's "earliest and profoundest absorptions":

> And on a pallet a baby lies, spread over with a floursack against infringement of flies, and sleeps and here a moving camera might know, on its bareness, the standing of the four iron feet of a bed, the wood of a chair, the scrolled treadle of a sewing machine, the standing up at right angles of plain wood out of plain wood, the great and handsome grains and scars of this vertical and prostrate wood. . . . (149)

Although the book's format physically separates these representations, photographs and words in *Let Us Now Praise Famous Men* refuse to reside on their respective sides of the image/caption border. Textually and culturally, they spill into one another. Just as Agee's words reach across to photography—another description of weathered boards stresses that "all these are visible at once" (145)—Evans opens his photographs to include writing. Both crossings reflect larger negotiations about literature's and photography's respective positions in an increasingly visual and technological culture. Agee's "moving camera" marks his response to a question that Miles Orvell finds central to American modernist writers: "How does the writer achieve aesthetic authenticity, how does one reproduce 'reality itself' in a world in which modes of vision have been radically affected by technologies of perception?"[20] Evans's photograph also signals this perceptual shift. A closer look at the image of Squinchy reveals a faint trace of writing on the rumpled flour sack, and the blanket beneath the child suggests a screen.[21] Read allegorically, the photograph might say that as writing recedes from our view, the outlines of the child's body become more clearly visible.

Rather than conceive of the visual and verbal portions of this photo-text as images and captions, we might turn to Mary Ann Caws's model of *interference:* "The mutual interference of two objects, a visual and a verbal one, involves a dialogue, which the reader or observer enters into and sponsors, and which with other dialogues forms part of a more general conversation."[22] Conjuring up the metaphor of radio transmission—in which two simultaneously received stations are both distinguishable and inseparable—

this model avoids what W. J. T. Mitchell calls our culture's "compulsion to conceive of the relation between words and images in political terms, as a struggle for territory, a contest of rival ideologies."[23] Unlike the image/caption model, interference neither marginalizes one textual component, nor draws rigid boundaries between literature and photography.

The collaboration model would seem a desirable alternative to the image/caption model, but it requires some revision in order to aid in our investigation of photo-textualities. While the latter model's binary oppositions can make it counterproductive, the collaboration model's privileging of authorship and homogeneity can also limit approaches to photo-texts. Hunter reaches this interpretive impasse when he defines successful photo-textual collaboration as "discovering similar artistic predilections, using analogous techniques, drawing on the strengths rather than the weaknesses of each mode, and in general finding common ground."[24] Describing collaboration as a marriage is problematic in two ways: it presupposes that photo-texts are the product of two identifiable artists, and it suggests a blending into textual oneness that ignores the purposeful disruptions shaping our responses to photo-texts. First, constructing a marriage of "artistic predilections" limits inquiries to stylistic features that particular writers and photographers share. While this interpretive strategy may prove useful in assessing such texts as *Let Us Now Praise Famous Men*, it excludes a number of important photo-texts in which the issue of authorship is not so clearly defined (for example, *The Marble Faun* and *Three Guineas* each have verbal texts by a single, canonized writer and visual texts by photographers indeterminable in name and number). Moreover, the collaboration model can prove problematic by assuming that all images in photo-texts are artistically ambitious. *Photo-Textualities* considers the work of such canonized photographers as Lewis Hine and August Sander, but it also investigates W. H. Auden's snapshots and other photographs that, in contributor Timothy Sweet's words, "do not ask to be considered as works of art in themselves." Second, the marriage-of-artists approach implies a homogeneity that can impose too great a stability on photo-texts. As Thomas Jensen Hines explains, "When we confront a composite work, we experience most immediately the effects of the 'collaboration of the arts' rather than the acts of collaboration of the artists";[25] thus our reading of photo-texts often makes us more aware of photography's and literature's different signifying strategies. For example, contributor Stephen Watt points out that "photographs in a biography serve . . . as a standard against which one assesses the interpretive constructions of the biographer," asserting the productiveness of such photo-textual tensions. Charting a course between the extremes of the image/caption and collaboration models, this collection opens up more possibilities for photo-textual interferences. We push critical inquiry far beyond the interpretive and generic boundaries established by the New York Edition and *Let Us Now Praise Famous Men*.

Part 1: "Photo-Textual Transformations," shows how traditional assumptions about both textuality and interpretation are unsettled when literature and photographs cross their respective boundaries to form a single text. As contributor Corey K. Creekmur points out, for example, inserting photographs into novels displaces the literary reading convention of suspending disbelief because "a photograph offers us apparently objective proof and so reason to believe." Conventions for interpreting photographs are equally questioned; Warehime shows how Lartigue thwarts photography's memorializing tendency with images "frozen in the seemingly infinite potentialities of an incompleted gesture." The photo-texts examined here range from *The Marble Faun* (in which an established novel is transformed through photographs) to *Three Farmers on Their Way to a Dance* (in which a canonized photograph is transformed through fiction).[26] By considering photographs as both autonomous *and* collaborative components of these texts, the contributors in part 1 move beyond the "illustration" and image/caption models that subjugate a text's photographs to its verbal component.

The first essay in part 1 addresses the textual and cultural impact of photographs on a literary text first published with no graphic accompaniment. In "Photography and the Museum of Rome in Hawthorne's *The Marble Faun*," Timothy

Sweet assesses two photo-textual transformations of Nathaniel Hawthorne's literary text and their complicity in cultural appropriations of the Eternal City. Reconstructing the book's history of publication, Sweet shows how Italian booksellers and the American publishing firm Houghton, Mifflin shifted its status from fiction to travelogue by adding photographs of Roman monuments such as the Coliseum and the Fountain of Trevi. In the Tauchnitz editions first sold in Rome in the 1860s, variable photographs were pasted in by the booksellers or by the customers themselves. The Houghton edition of 1889, with its standardized set of photogravures, marks an early experiment in "illustrating" fiction with photographs, anticipating Alvin Langdon Coburn's collaborations with Henry James and H. G. Wells in the first decade of the twentieth century. The Houghton *Marble Faun* also marks Anglo-Americans' transformation from travelers to tourists. Contextualizing his analysis with nineteenth-century assumptions about tourism and realism, Sweet shows how the book's photographic representation of Rome as a timeless, depopulated museum offers an inventory of aestheticized objects for Anglo-American tourists to consume.

Marja Warehime's "Photography, Time, and the Surrealist Sensibility" begins a cluster of three essays that addresses photo-textual transformations of autobiography and biography; the pressures between these texts' photographs and writing alter standard procedures for reading representations of historical persons and events. Warehime situates her assessment of André Breton's *Nadja* (1928) and Jacques-Henri Lartigue's *Diary of a Century* (1970) in the contexts of the Surrealist movement of the 1920s. Departing from Susan Sontag's conflation of surrealism and photography, Warehime shows how the photographs in Breton's and Lartigue's autobiographical books disrupt their respective written texts in opposing ways. Both sets of photographs present what Sontag calls mementos, yet they construct radically different senses of time. While the often banal photographs of Paris monuments anchor Breton's open-ended narrative in the logical-temporal world, Lartigue's more surrealistic photographs of family members escape the boundaries of his diary's social history by presenting a defamiliarized world of infinite possibilities. The intersection of photography and history is also addressed in other essays in this cluster.

In "Photographs in Biographies: Joyce, Voyeurism, and the 'Real' Nora Barnacle," Stephen Watt questions our "mimetic bias" of reading photographs for verification. Pointing to his paradoxical position as a reader informed by post-structuralist theories of representation yet desirous of accessing the elusive subject "Nora," Watt examines photographs of Barnacle in Richard Ellmann's and Brenda Maddox's literary biographies (published in 1982 and 1988, respectively). He engages with cultural contexts at several levels: nineteenth-century conventions of portraiture and theater, Joyce's writings, and contemporary uses of photography to verify historical reality (such as Ken Burns's PBS documentary *The Civil War.*) In addition, Watt brings gender issues to bear on interpretation, asserting that we view these images of Barnacle from an empowered "male" position, thus replicating Leopold Bloom's and James Joyce's scopophilia. Yet feminist film theories of "the gaze," he argues, offer insufficient explanation for our inability to "know" Barnacle through photographs. While acknowledging complications of gender, Watt proposes that we look for Barthes's *punctum* and Mieke Bal's "detail" to destabilize realist assumptions about photography.

The third essay in this cluster, and the final essay in part 1, explores the intersection of history and fiction in two postmodern novels. Instead of transforming a fictional literary text with a photographic accompaniment as did the Houghton *Marble Faun*, these books transform photographs of historical figures by inserting them into fictional contexts. In "Lost Objects: Photography, Fiction, and Mourning," Corey K. Creekmur takes a psychoanalytic approach to Michael Ondaatje's *Coming through Slaughter* (1977) and Richard Powers's *Three Farmers on Their Way to a Dance* (1985). Both novels are generated from photographic portraits: Ondaatje's begins with the only known photograph of jazz musician Buddy Bolden (who functions simultaneously as a novelistic protagonist and biographical subject), while Powers's opens with the famous photograph by August Sander that also provides the book's title (the farmers are each given fictional narratives). These recontextualized photographs in turn prompt us to reassess such literary conventions as Coleridge's "willing suspension of disbelief." For despite recent critiques of realism, Creekmur argues, our everyday *use* of photographs remains grounded in their bearing traces of their signifieds. His essay draws on Freud's theory of mourning and Barthes's *Camera Lucida* to investigate the negotiation of psychic loss in our camera-preserved culture.

Part 2, "Photo-Textual Interventions," interrogates representations of gender, sexual orientation, class, race, and nationality to assess the cultural work that photo-texts can perform. While four of the texts discussed here fall within the documentary category, a photo-textual genre long associated with political action, *Three Guineas* launches its political critique from outside traditional generic boundaries. Shloss's comment about one of the books she examines, *A Seventh Man*, applies to all of the photo-texts in this section: "They [Berger and Mohr] do not see their book—with photographs and texts—in opposition to life, but as a speech act within life." By foregrounding the political implications of the texts they discuss, the contributors in part 2 echo Duffy and Davis's claim that juxtapositions of photographs and words affect reading and representation as social acts. Their essays offer new ways of theorizing both photo-texts and interpretive strategies that subvert the dominant culture.

The first two essays in part 2 critique conventional documentary models of the 1930s, a decade that continues to shape documentary practice in America and Britain. In "The Alternative Vision: Lewis Hine's *Men at Work* and the Dominant Culture," Kevin G. Barnhurst investigates Hine's work portraits and the "iconography of masculinity" they present to assess the heterosexist vision shaping documentary photography and American culture. Published in 1932, the book's written texts (Hine's introduction and captions) occupy a marginal position with respect to the images. Barnhurst offers Hine's "purely male art" as a lesson in reading visual grammar, analyzing not only such formal properties as angle, framing, and tonality but also the depicted worker's postures, clothing, and tools. In several images of white male workers, he argues, Hine portrays the men as objects of desire through the positions of their bodies and their proximity to tools and machines. Bridging the visual contexts of Western painting and American documentary photography with a politics informed by feminism and gay liberation, Barnhurst proposes that Hine's images suggest possibilities for representing the sexuality of working-class males in nonexploitive ways.

My essay, "Auden and the 'Arctic Stare': Documentary as Public Collage in *Letters from Iceland,*" situates W. H. Auden's photo-textual intervention in the contexts of the British documentary film movement and high modernism. Coauthored with Louis MacNeice, *Letters from Iceland* (1937) marks Auden's first publication of his photographs, as well as his extended verbal impersonations of camera vision that rival Christopher Isherwood's. Reading Auden's texts as a response to his brief employment with the G.P.O. Film Unit, I show how the book's disruptive form appropriates and ultimately critiques the thirties documentary practice established by John Grierson. Auden fashions a photo-textual collage that simulates documentary's focus on workers and industry but erases its rigid line between observer and observed. At the same time, this radical disjunction subverts the authority of High Modernist collage by rejecting the academic canon for the mass media. Combining the populism of documentary with the fragmentation of High Modernist collage, *Letters from Iceland* constructs a less aggressive, more self-reflective gaze than either genre offers alone.

Julia Duffy and Lloyd Davis's essay, "Demythologizing Facts and Photographs in *Three Guineas,*" assesses a photo-text that critiques the dominant culture by revealing it to itself. The original Hogarth edition of Woolf's polemical text, published in 1938, contained five photographs of male authority figures—a general, a judge, heralds, professors, and an archbishop—never referred to directly in the written portion. Taken autonomously, Duffy and Davis argue, these images symbolize the vested power of the British patriarchy in ways similar to Victorian photographs' construction of empire. But read within Woolf's feminist text, which commands

us to look at an absent set of photographs depicting war victims, the actual photographs are reconfigured into a "verbal-pictorial discourse" that subverts both the British patriarchy and representation itself. Duffy and Davis show how Woolf's use of the actual photographs anticipates Julia Kristeva's semiotic level of discourse; the instability of image and text calls into question patriarchal discourse's reliance on denotation, facts, and evidence. Therefore, later editions of *Three Guineas* that omit the photographs enforce traditional reading practices by repressing the transgressive, unstable discourse that Woolf articulates.

The fourth essay in part 2 explores photo-textual means of constructing national identity, shifting our attention from America and England to Continental Europe and the Middle East. In "Double-Crossing Frontiers: Literature, Photography, and the Politics of Displacement," Carol Shloss examines photo-textual strategies for reassembling a nationality fragmented by modern capitalism. She explores two books that represent displaced people without reduplicating the supervisory authority which has forced them to cross frontiers; Jean Mohr took the photographs for each one. The first photo-text, John Berger and Mohr's *A Seventh Man* (1975), focuses on male migrant laborers from "underdeveloped" countries (such as Turkey) who find work in European industrial nations (such as Germany and Switzerland). In the second, *After the Last Sky* (1986), Mohr and Edward Said represent Palestinian refugees' dispersed sense of personal and cultural identity. Shloss draws on psychoanalysis to show how these combinations of image and text function similar to displacement in dreams: they make visible in art what social consciousness represses. By creating an artistic form that serves as a shelter, she argues, these photo-textual collaborations allow the migrant workers and Palestinians to "double-cross" the barriers that usually obscure them from our view.

Robert B. Ray's afterword reframes parts 1 and 2 by historicizing both photography's development and Western ways of thinking about photography and language. In "Snapshots: The Beginnings of Photography," Ray reveals striking connections among three cultural developments of the midnineteenth century: the invention of photography, the massmarketing of paperback *physiologies,* and the invention of the detective story. The convergence of these developments, one graphic and two literary, reflects the crisis of legibility signaling the onset of mass culture. Although the *physiologies'* cataloguing of urban types and the detective story's reliance on physical evidence seem to privilege photography, Ray shows that they actually work to suppress its proliferation of meanings. In their attempts to fix photographic meaning as empirical evidence, these literary forms anticipate cinematic conventions such as soundtracks and continuity editing—contemporary ways of policing photography. Ray proposes both Barthes's third meaning and surrealist viewing practices as ways to revalue the photograph's inherent instability. Rather than continue traditional practices of subordinating photographic image to linguistic text, Ray suggests that we find nonliterate ways of looking.

As this overview suggests, many essays form dialogues both within and across their respective sections. I do not intend the collection's two parts to be perceived as mutually exclusive categories; political relationships in society and properties of textuality are not so easily separated. All of the contributors address both cultural and formal implications of photo-textuality. For example, social class informs several essays' inquiries in Part 1—both directly and indirectly. While Barnhurst, Shloss, and I assess documentary's traditional exposure of the economically dispossessed, class operates more covertly in Watt's analysis of nineteenth-century photography's illusory, class-disguising conventions. Warehime also contributes to this dialogue by asserting that Lartigue's wealth granted him access to events he might not otherwise photograph. And class is certainly an issue for Sweet, who discusses bourgeois tourists' desire to remove from Rome all signs of the local underclasses. Inquiries about textual form also initiate dialogues across the anthology. Four contributors bring stylistic and formal concerns directly into their essays in productive, self-reflective ways. Taking on the spirit of Woolf's parodic text, Duffy and Davis energize their assessment of *Three Guineas* with a playfulness that punctuates the essay's theoretical discussions.

Likewise, Shloss's meditative style complements her exploration of "mise-en-page." In the afterword, Ray reconstructs the academic essay through formal experimentation—offering individual sections as a series of "snapshots," and thus extending the convention of describing photography and literature in terms of each other.[27] Indeed, this anthology as a whole brings form to bear directly on interpretation by *being* what it examines—a photo-text.

Moreover, the various critical approaches we bring to this anthology occasionally contend with one another. This productive debate is especially evident in the degree to which contributors reconcile post-structuralist theories of representation to feminism and to realism, respectively. For example, Watt, as well as Duffy and Davis, draws on feminist film theory's concept of the determining male gaze in visual representation. But while Watt finds this theoretical position irreconcilable with Barthes's and Bal's post-structuralist reading strategies, Duffy and Davis find it compatible with Kristeva's and Barthes's theories of *signifiance.* The contributors' assessments of realism are equally rich in critical departures. Ray asserts that while "the longing for strictly objective, and therefore *exact,* representation had motivated photography's invention," the inherent ambiguity in any photograph ultimately works against conventions for reading it as verification. Similarly, Watt contends that photographs "seldom deliver on their referential promises." On the other hand, Creekmur maintains that our culture's *use* of photographs—and Barthes's own *Camera Lucida*—shows a stubborn allegiance to the realist position. While some in photographic studies may consider this debate closed, *Photo-Textualities* shows that acknowledging photography's literary contexts reopens the issue of realism. Creekmur demonstrates that realist assumptions about photography remain important for two postmodern novelists. And as Sweet points out, the phenomenon of the photographically "illustrated" *Marble Faun* shifting critical attention from fictional to factual elements also attests to the ways photo-texts can reinvigorate our inquiries about representation.

We do not purport to offer a unitary, monolithic approach to photo-textualities or to larger issues in image/text relations. Instead, our dialogue offers imbrications, gaps, and even some contradictions. We investigate books in which a single photograph occupies the position of frontispiece, books in which words occupy the position of captions, and books at varying points along this continuum. Such plurality has been absent too long in critical assessments of photo-texts, especially in literary criticism. At the same time, we share common ground in finding that interactions with photography are crucial to our critical practice—they prompt us to read in new ways. By opening more sites for negotiating with photographs and words, this collection suggests possibilities for more markings on the map.

NOTES

1. The most famous of these essays, "The Daguerreotype," first appeared in *Alexander's Weekly Messenger* on 15 January 1840. More recently, the essay appears in Alan Trachtenberg, ed., *Classic Essays on Photography* (New Haven, Conn.: Leete's Island Books, 1980), 37–38; and in Jane M. Rabb, ed., *Literature and Photography: Interactions 1840–1990: A Critical Anthology* (Albuquerque: University of New Mexico Press, 1995). Poe's essays on photography initiate a dialogue of writers and photographers assessing each other's respective medium—an ongoing interaction that Rabb's anthology captures with its range from Poe and Nadar to Richard Howard and Robert Mapplethorpe.

2. See Ellen Goodman, "Read Books, Not Lips, This Summer," *Gainesville Sun*, 18 July 1990, A10; and Andy Grundberg, *Crisis of the Real: Writings on Photography, 1974–1989* (New York: Aperture, 1990), 15. Alan Trachtenberg has also discussed the "literariness" of Evans's *American Photographs*, asserting that the photographer renders his medium "inscriptive rather than mechanically transcriptive alone, or capable of converting transcript to writing." See *Reading American Photographs: Images as History, Mathew Brady to Walker Evans* (New York: Hill and Wang, 1989), 277.

3. See Judy Fiskin, "Borges, Stryker, Evans: The Sorrows of Representation," in *Multiple Views: Logan Grant Essays on Photography, 1983–89*, ed. Daniel P. Younger (Albuquerque: University of New Mexico Press, 1990), 247–69. The most recent and comprehensive Welty album is *Eudora Welty Photographs* (Jackson: University of Mississippi Press, 1989). For a critical assessment of Welty's earlier photograph album, see Louise Westling, "The Loving Observer of *One Time, One Place*," *Mississippi Quarterly* 39 (Fall 1986): 587–604.

4. See Jefferson Hunter, *Image and Word: The Interaction of Twentieth-Century Photographs and Texts* (Cambridge: Harvard University Press, 1987). In this essay I revise his term by bridging *photo* and *text* with a hyphen. While I share Hunter's concern with avoiding awkward labels such as texts-comprised-of-photographs-and-printed-language or Trachtenberg's "picture-and-word books" (*Reading* 252), I find the physical gap in *photo text* problematic. If Hunter's term designates the genre's two equal components, then it contains a hidden bias—aren't photographs also texts in

their own right? The double sense of *text* as written language and site of interpretation makes Hunter's term a slippery one; a similarly problematic term is *image/text relations*. These terms highlight the difficulty of assessing photo-texts in ways that do not privilege literature and language.

5. For examples of inter-art studies, see Mary Ann Caws, *The Art of Interference: Stressed Readings in Verbal and Visual Texts* (Princeton: Princeton University Press, 1989); Theo D'haen, ed., *Verbal/Visual Crossings 1880–1990* (Amsterdam: Rodopi, 1990); Claude Gandelman, *Reading Pictures, Viewing Texts* (Bloomington: Indiana University Press, 1991), and the journal *Word and Image*. For a discussion of illustrated novels within the larger context of word and image relations, see J. Hillis Miller, *Illustration* (London: Reaktion, 1992). See also Eric Lambrechts and Luc Salu, comps., *Photography and Literature: An International Bibliography of Monographs* (London: Mansell, 1992).

6. This direction of inquiry has been productive especially in American studies. For example, Walter Benn Michaels brings photography and material culture into his study of American literature in *The Gold Standard and the Logic of Naturalism: American Literature at the Turn of the Century* (Berkeley: University of California Press, 1987), as does Miles Orvell, to a greater extent, in *The Real Thing: Imitation and Authenticity in American Culture, 1880–1940* (Chapel Hill: University of North Carolina Press, 1989). Michaels's book does not address photo-texts, while Orvell's grants marginal attention to Jacob Riis's photo-text *How the Other Half Lives* and Henry James's collaboration with Alvin Langdon Coburn (*Let Us Now Praise Famous Men* receives fuller discussion). Two other comparative studies also address American culture. Carol Shloss examines American prose writers' interactions with photographers and photography in *In Visible Light: Photography and the American Writer, 1840–1940* (New York: Oxford University Press, 1987); see especially her chapters on Nathaniel Hawthorne and John Dos Passos. Shloss also considers some photo-texts, including *Let Us Now Praise Famous Men*. Timothy Sweet investigates poets' and photographers' constructions of the American Civil War in *Traces of War: Poetry, Photography, and the Crisis of the Union* (Baltimore: Johns Hopkins University Press, 1990). He shows how Walt Whitman's war poetry aligns itself artistically and politically with Alexander Gardner's and George Barnard's photographs, while Melville's work critiques these artists' naturalization of violence.

7. Kevin G. Barnhurst brings Western painting into his essay, while Robert B. Ray, Stephen Watt, and I consider film practices.

8. While their range of inquiry exceeds the novel and the documentary, Hunter's and Shloss's books engage most fully with these genres; each book discusses both James's New York Edition and *Let Us Now Praise Famous Men*. For a detailed assessment of the James-Coburn collaboration, see Ralph F. Bogardus's *Pictures and Texts: Henry James, A. L. Coburn, and New Ways of Seeing in Literary Culture* (Ann Arbor, Mich.: UMI Research Press, 1984). Scholarly accounts of *Let Us Now Praise Famous Men* are too numerous to cite here, but notable assessments since William Stott's (*Documentary Expression and Thirties America* [Chicago: University of Chicago Press, 1973]) that address both Agee's and Evans's texts include Margaret Olin, "'It Is Not Going to Be Easy to Look into Their Eyes': Privilege of Perception in *Let Us Now Praise Famous Men*," *Art History* 14 (March 1991): 92–115; W. J. T. Mitchell, "The Ethics of Form in

the Photographic Essay," *Afterimage* 16 (January 1989): 8–13; Miles Orvell's seventh chapter of *The Real Thing;* and T. V. Reed's essay "Unimagined Existence and the Fiction of the Real: Postmodernist Realism in *Let Us Now Praise Famous Men,*" *Representations* 24 (Fall 1988): 156–76.

9. John Rogers Puckett's *Five Photo-Textual Documentaries from the Great Depression* (Ann Arbor, Mich.: UMI Research Press, 1984) focuses on American photo-texts that have become standard examples. Besides the "classic" *Let Us Now Praise Famous Men,* Puckett addresses *You Have Seen Their Faces, Land of the Free, 12 Million Black Voices,* and *An American Exodus.* Hunter's study engages most fully with the American documentary book, especially with *Let Us Now Praise Famous Men.* American documentary photography has received much critical attention of late, including revisionist critiques of the Farm Security Administration (FSA) projects. See Maren Stange, *Symbols of Ideal Life: Social Documentary Photography in America 1890–1950* (Cambridge: Cambridge University Press, 1989); and John Tagg's chapter on documentary and the New Deal in his *The Burden of Representation: Essays on Photographies and Histories* (Amherst: University of Massachusetts Press, 1988). For a survey of American documentary photographers, see Carl Fleischhauer and Beverly W. Brannan, eds., *Documenting America* (Berkeley, University of California Press, 1988). Alan Trachtenberg's *Reading American Photographs* also devotes considerable attention to documentary.

10. Alan Trachtenberg, introduction to *Multiple Views,* ed. Daniel P. Younger, 6 (see note 3).

11. See Lawrence Grossberg, Cary Nelson, and Paula A. Treichler, eds., *Cultural Studies* (New York: Routledge, 1991), 2.

12. See Roland Barthes, "Rhetoric of the Image," *Image-Music-Text,* trans. Stephen Heath (New York: Noonday, 1977), 38. Of course, Barthes's later work is not so restrictive in theorizing photographic signification, as "The Third Meaning" (also in *Image-Music-Text*) and *Camera Lucida: Reflections on Photography,* trans. Richard Howard (New York: Hill and Wang, 1981) demonstrate.

13. Victoria Middleton assumes the photographs are simple illustrations in "*Three Guineas:* Subversion and Survival in the Professions," *Twentieth Century Literature* 28 (1982): 405–17. Yet she does offer an often convincing argument that Woolf's book provides strategies for reading culture.

14. This variation of the image/caption binarism can also marginalize a writer's career, as Helen Vendler notes in her discussion of American poet Marianne Moore: "One oddity of literary history is that Moore became known . . . as an animal poet, a writer of texts to go beside a *National Geographic* photograph of an ostrich or a pangolin." See *Part of Nature, Part of Us: Modern American Poets* (Cambridge: Harvard University Press, 1980), 70.

15. See Hunter, *Image and Word,* 78. MacLeish's words appear in his "Notes" at the end of *Land of the Free.* He stresses that his text "is the opposite of a book of poems illustrated by photographs." While MacLeish credits this approach to the photographs' power of "stubborn inward livingness," I suspect he is fighting against his poem being read as a caption. See *Land of the Free* (1938; reprint, with an introduction by A. D. Coleman, New York: Da Capo, 1977), 89. For a recent discussion of this photo-text in the context of MacLeish's career, see John Timberman Newcomb, "Archibald MacLeish and the Poetics of Public Speech: A Critique of High Modernism," *Journal of the Midwest Modern Language Association* 23 (Spring 1990): 9–26.

16. See William Stott, *Documentary Expression and Thirties America* (Chicago: University of Chicago Press, 1973), chap. 12.

17. Hunter, *Image and Word,* 44.

18. For a good discussion of the Cowboy series, see Rosetta Brooks, "Spiritual America: No Holds Barred," in *Richard Prince,* ed. Lisa Phillips (New York: Whitney Museum of American Art, 1992), 85–103.

19. See James Agee and Walker Evans, *Let Us Now Praise Famous Men* (1941; reprint, with an introduction by John Hersey, Boston: Houghton, 1988), eleventh photograph. I take the child to be Squinchy, who also appears in the eighth photograph. All further references to this book are cited in the text.

20. Orvell, *The Real Thing,* 245.

21. My reading is influenced by T. V. Reed, "Unimagined Existence," 166, who sees the white towel in the photograph immediately after this one as "a movie screen, a canvas, or photo paper."

22. Caws, *Art of Interference,* 4.

23. W. J. T. Mitchell, *Iconology: Image, Text, Ideology* (Chicago: University of Chicago Press, 1986), 43.

24. Hunter, *Image and Word,* 36. Hunter continues with a qualification of sorts, cautioning that successful photo-textual collaborations "do not insist on a perfect affinity." Yet the passage culminates by alluding to Henri Cartier-Bresson and Jean-Paul Sartre's *D'une Chine à l'autre,* the product of a canonized photographer and writer. The marriage-of-artists bias also shapes Lambrechts and Salu's bibliography, *Photography and Literature,* which limits its literary photo-texts to "books with texts in prose or verse by writers mentioned by name, and with photographs by photographers mentioned by name."

25. Thomas Jensen Hines, *Collaborative Form: Studies in the Relations of the Arts* (Kent, Ohio: Kent State University Press, 1991), 4.

26. Appropriately, Hawthorne's novel was entitled *Transformation* in British and Continental editions.

27. Ray's verbal snapshots also connect with Barnhurst's visual grammar.

Photo-Textualities

Part 1

Photo-Textual Transformations

1

Photography and the Museum of Rome in Hawthorne's The Marble Faun

Timothy Sweet

THE MOST POPULAR OF NATHANIEL HAWTHORNE'S four novel-length works in the nineteenth century, *The Marble Faun* (or *Transformation,* as it was entitled in British and Continental editions) was highly valued as travel literature.[1] Its extensive passages of "descriptive criticism" on the art, architecture, and scenery of Rome made it, in the eyes of a typical reviewer, "worth all the guidebooks we ever met with."[2] As such, the text invited substantial photographic illustration. Beginning in the 1860s, booksellers in Italy produced illustrated copies of the Tauchnitz edition of *Transformation* so popular among Anglophone tourists there, grangerizing them by pasting photographs of the objects and locations referred to in the text onto blank pages supplied by the publisher for this purpose. In 1889 an edition of *The Marble Faun* illustrated with photogravures, published by Houghton, Mifflin of Boston, supplanted the variability of the grangerized *Transformations* with a single set of images, appropriating and consolidating the process begun by Italian booksellers. Thus imbricated in the structure of tourism, these phototexts exemplified an attitude toward Rome proclaimed by William Dean Howells in 1872:

Rome really belongs to the Anglo-Saxon nations, and the Pope and the past seem to be carried on entirely for our diversion. Every thing is systematized as thoroughly as in a museum where all the objects are ticketed.[3]

Where the grangerized Tauchnitz *Transformations* bought by tourists functioned as guides to and souvenirs of the museum of Rome, the Houghton *Marble Faun* definitively "systematized" and "ticketed" this museum and permitted American readers at home also to consume its aesthetic value (as a sort of prepackaged package tour).[4]

By orienting the reader's attention so directly toward certain material objects, the photographs in *The Marble Faun* may seem to insist on a connection between text and world stronger than that required by Hawthorne's account of his literary intentions. Specifically, they may seem to ignore Hawthorne's claim that Rome, "as the site of his Romance, was chiefly valuable to him as affording a sort of poetic or fairy precinct, where actualities would not be so terribly insisted upon as they are, and must needs be, in America."[5] However, Hawthorne also remarked that in recopying the text for publication, he

was somewhat surprised to see the extent to which he had introduced descriptions of various Italian objects, antique, pictorial, and statuesque. Yet these things fill the mind everywhere in Italy, and especially in Rome, and cannot easily be kept from flowing out upon the page when one writes freely, and with self-enjoyment. (*MF* 1:15–16)

Thus he would not necessarily have been distressed by a photographic "insistence" on "actualities," so long as viewing the photographs would produce an experience consistent with the "self-enjoyment" he felt in recollecting his time in Italy.

Although Hawthorne was not significantly involved in the photographic illustration of his text, the photo-textual *Transformation* and *Marble Faun* were produced by, and registered the perceptual practices of, the culture of tourism in which Hawthorne participated.[6] In their solidification of the text's stance toward Rome as a repository of aesthetic value, these photo-texts worked to distance the reader from certain aspects of actual, quotidian Rome by offering an aesthetic experience that would satisfy the touristic desire for unproblematic "diversion" (Howells) and "self-enjoyment" (Hawthorne). The photographs had the power to confirm the idea that Rome consisted essentially of a museum because they were situated within the context of nineteenth-century assumptions about photography's capacity to provide unmediated representations.[7] By deferring the category of the aesthetic to the objects they depicted (unlike, for example, Alvin Langdon Coburn's photographs for Henry James's New York Edition), these photographs naturalized the museum of Rome.

TOURISM AND THE PHOTOGRAPHIC *TRANSFORMATION*

Many American tourists found *The Marble Faun* useful as a guide to Rome. Howells, whose post as consul at Venice afforded him the opportunity to travel Italy widely in the early 1860s, reports that he and his companions used it as an "aesthetic hand-book in Rome." They "devoutly

looked up all the places mentioned in it, which were important for being mentioned; though such places as the Tarpeian Rock, the Forum, the Capitoline Museum, and the Villa Borghese might secondarily have their historical or artistic interest."[8] With gentle self-mockery, Howells admits that *The Marble Faun* did influence his perceptions of Rome. He knows that Hawthorne described these places because they were generally regarded as important by all American travelers. Henry James, writing in the late 1870s, more directly identifies the book's utility as tourist's guide, souvenir, and advertisement: "It is part of the intellectual equipment of the Anglo-Saxon visitor to Rome, and is read by every English-speaking traveller who arrives there, who has been there, or who expects to go."[9]

The book that Howells and James praised had been available in photographically illustrated form since the 1860s, when booksellers in Rome began to offer copies of the pocket-sized Tauchnitz edition of *Transformation* grangerized with some fifty to one hundred pasted-in photographic prints. Such copies continued to be produced through the 1880s and possibly longer.[10] Customers could assemble their own collection of photographs from the catalogs of photographic dealers. Often, however, the bookseller selected the photographs. In some instances, the catalog numbers and identifying captions were not trimmed from the prints when they were pasted in the books; these marks remain as traces of the commercial origins of the representations.[11] One American critic of this practice remarked that "it is at once a cheapening of a pretty fancy when the trader steps in to do for the indolent or ignorant what the intelligent enthusiast does for himself."[12] This critic was not suggesting that tourists make their own photographs (for this was not practical until after the turn of the century, with the popularization of the Kodak and similar cameras designed for amateurs) but that they select, from photographic dealers' catalogs, images of objects that they had seen in person.

Tourists sometimes used the photographs in a grangerized *Transformation* as an itinerary, inscribing them with identifying captions and dates.[13] Thus recording their own presence before an important object, these tourists found that photographs gave a permanent, material form to the activity of tourism. A grangerized *Transformation* could thus come to embody the kind of experience that we see, for example, in the travel writing of Henry James. Attempting "to sum up for tribute and homage" his experience of Rome in 1873, James concludes: "What is simply clear is the sense of an acquired passion for the place and of an incalculable number of gathered impressions." These impressions "store themselves noiselessly away, I suppose, in the dim but safe places of memory and 'taste,' and we live in the quiet faith that they will emerge into vivid relief if life or art should demand them."[14] When photographs concretizing such impressions were gathered in a grangerized *Transformation*, the tourist's "quiet faith" in memory was transformed into certainty, because photographs were not merely mental impressions, but material tokens of the objects themselves.[15] As Susan Sontag has suggested, the appeal of such a collection lies in our feeling that "photography is acquisition. . . . In its simplest form, we have in a photograph a surrogate possession of a cherished person or thing, a possession which gives photographs some of the character of unique objects."[16]

Photography solidified the conception of tourism as the experience of viewing a set of discrete objects and then collecting representations of these objects as souvenirs, as an aid to recollection. But it did not in itself build the museum of Rome. Before the age of photography there was already a canon of important objects and places to be seen, as part of the grand tour.[17] Guidebooks such as Baedeker's and Murray's, first published in the 1840s, made the survey of this canon a matter of following a checklist. Although from the start they were illustrated with drawings, maps, and plans, such guidebooks did not contain photographs until well into the twentieth century, partly because it was relatively expensive prior to the advent of half-tone technology to publish a photographically illustrated book. Additionally, it seems that "literary" texts, such as *The Marble Faun* and George Eliot's *Romola*, were more attractive as souvenirs—more apt to be collected, cherished, and re-viewed—than were pure guidebooks, and thus were better suited to photographic illustration in the pre-

half-tone era.[18]

The guidebook to Italy most popular with Americans in the nineteenth century was *Six Months in Italy*, written by Hawthorne's friend George Stillman Hillard and first published in 1853.[19] Praised by Oliver Wendell Holmes Sr. for its "sound American thought," *Six Months in Italy* takes the form of a substantially annotated checklist of important objects and sights.[20] Over two-thirds of Hillard's text is devoted to Rome. He found a meticulously detailed organizational scheme necessary because "the first few days of residence [in Rome] will usually be passed in a sort of bewildering indecision, endeavoring to fix upon some plan by which [the traveler] may comprehend the mighty maze of interests that lies before him." There were various alternatives for organizing the tour. One might "follow the stream [sic] of chronology . . . studying each period in its monuments, binding the present to the past." Or one might "divide Rome into subjects, and take up painting, sculpture, architecture, separately, and resolutely exclude every thing but the matter in hand," or "cut it up territorially, and exhaust one section before he approaches another" (*SMI* 128).

This cutting up of Rome for ease of consumption indicates Hillard's appropriative, even imperialistic attitude (and anticipates Howells's proclamation that "Rome really belongs to the Anglo-Saxon nations"). He structures his experience according to a preconceived agenda motivated by a desire for easily consumed historical and aesthetic value. Similarly, grangerized Tauchnitz *Transformations* register this consumption of aesthetic value while at the same time preserving that value—in the form of a photo-textual simulacrum—for the pleasure of future consumption.

References in the *French and Italian Notebooks* indicate that during his tour of Rome, Hawthorne, like most of his American contemporaries, relied extensively on guidebooks, including the one written by his friend Hillard. Even if Hawthorne did not always concur with particular aesthetic judgments, his perceptual attitude could not help but be influenced by the guidebook approach to travel—as he remarked, "I am glad I have seen the Pope, because now he may be crossed out of my list of sights to be seen."[21] Such an influence is felt in *The Marble Faun,* specifically in several passages Hawthorne interpolated from the journals he wrote as a tourist, but also more generally in the overall experience of Americans in Rome represented in the text (such as visits to the Coliseum, St. Peter's, or the picture galleries). Grangerized *Transformations* called attention to this influence; a new edition of *The Marble Faun,* appearing in 1889, assumed it.

THE MUSEUM OF ROME

American tourists in Rome, expecting a repository of ancient and Renaissance aesthetic culture, were often surprised to find instead a city disturbingly similar to what they had left behind: "We can nowhere escape from the debasing associations of actual life," lamented Hillard (*SMI* 184). Hawthorne more vividly suggested that "all towns should be made capable of purification by fire, or of decay, within each half-century. Otherwise, they become the hereditary haunts of vermin and noisomeness. . . . In short, [they become] such habitations as one sees everywhere in Italy, be they hovels or palaces" (*MF* 2:346–47). The desire expressed by Hawthorne and Hillard to purify the sights of Rome gave rise to a perceptual process characterized by the construction of a set of discrete, idealized images (the guidebook approach) and the subsequent confirmation that such a set of images represented the true and essential Rome.[22]

Hawthorne's and Hillard's perceptual process is re-enacted by the edition of *The Marble Faun* published in 1889 by Houghton, Mifflin, which contained fifty photographic images, beautifully reproduced by means of photogravure, illustrating "the statues, paintings, and buildings referred to in the romance" (*MF* 1:i). This set of two octavo volumes—decoratively bound in red, white, and gold, "protected by slipcovers in the Italian style" (as one reviewer put it) and encased in a cloth-covered box—was perhaps better suited to the library or parlor than to the tourist's pocket.[23] Yet it was marketed to prospective and accomplished tourists as an improvement on the "well-established custom" of grangerizing copies of the book, since books with pasted-in prints were "apt to be displeasing to the fastidious collector" (*MF* 1:i). The publishers reported that because

every traveller knows that there is a wide difference between the best and the poorest of these photographs . . . no pains have been spared to obtain the best made directly from the objects themselves. . . . Some of the buildings illustrated have disappeared since Hawthorne saw them and wrote of them; others are likely to be altered or removed in the rapid change which is passing over Rome, and the work thus becomes a valuable record to the past as well as a pleasure to the eye. (*MF* 1:ii)

The nostalgic gaze is directed toward the objects as Hawthorne saw them, but also, beyond that, to the record of the Roman past now threatened by modernity: what was truly important about Rome to Americans, the publishers of the new edition recognized, was its pastness.

Hawthorne's friend Hillard had earlier focused on images of the Roman past in describing the importance of the city. But Hillard cautions that Roman ruins, for example, are often disappointing at first because the traveler will have come to Rome with certain preconceptions in mind derived

from engravings, and these are rarely true. . . . Not that the size, dimensions, and character of the object delineated are falsified; but liberties are taken with all that is in immediate proximity to it. Many of the Roman ruins are thrust into unsightly neighborhoods: they are shouldered and elbowed by commonplace structures, or start out, like excrescences, from mean and inexpressive walls. They are surrounded by decay which has no dignity, and by offensive objects which are like discordant notes in a strain of music. (*SMI* 129)

The discord in the traveler's experience results from a desire to separate quotidian Rome (full of distractions and so systematized for the tourist) from the Roman past (the idealized, nostalgic object of systematization). The ability to make this separation becomes a measure of aesthetic sensitivity, since "as a general rule," the traveler will experience an initial disappointment "in proportion to [his or her] susceptibility to all that is characteristic and peculiar in Rome" (*SMI* 128).

In order to aid the traveler in resolving this

perceptual discord, Hillard argues that beneath the quotidian, material textures of Rome as the traveler first perceives it there exists a Rome more essential and true, which engravings (even though they may be literally inaccurate representations of one's initial, unguided perceptions) capture more accurately than unmediated perceptions.[24] The "true" Rome as described by Hillard turns out to be identical with the aestheticized Rome that the traveler has been led to expect from the engravings that take "liberties" with the surroundings of important objects:

> Let him bide his time. *The Rome of the mind* is not built in a day. His hour will surely come. Not suddenly, not by stormy and vehement movements, but by gentle gradations and soft approaches, the spirit of the place will descend upon him. The unsightly and common-place appendages will disappear, and only the beautiful and the tragic will remain. And, when his heart and mind are in unison with the scene around him, a thousand happy accidents and cordial surprises lie in wait for him. (*SMI* 130, emphasis added)

Hillard's approach exemplifies Dean MacCannell's argument that tourism reflects the bourgeoisie's attempt "to overcome the discontinuity of modernity" by "coordinat[ing] the differentiations of the world into a single ideology" which "subordinate[s] other people to its values, industry, and future designs."[25] By systematizing Roman objects (the material traces of the city's cultural past) in order to reify their aesthetic value, Hillard overcomes the discontinuity of experience he feels when he confronts modern Rome. Jane Addams provides a roughly contemporary antidote to Hillard's approach when she criticizes those "who had crossed the sea in search of culture" for assuming that they "had nothing to do with the bitter poverty and social maladjustment that is all around, and which, after all, cannot be concealed, for it breaks through poetry and literature in a burning tide."[26] But Addams's social conscience was rare among the Americans who made the grand tour. More common were attitudes such as Hillard's, Howells's, and Hawthorne's, which either ignored the quotidian or employed various perceptual strategies (the systematized museum, the nostalgic gaze) in order to recuperate it.

Hawthorne invokes Hillard's perceptual model—the initial disappointment and subsequent validation of aestheticized preconceptions of Rome—at several points in *The Marble Faun*. In the very first chapter, for example, he invites us to "glance hastily" over "the edge of the desolate Forum where Roman washerwomen hang out their linen in the sun." This fleeting initial perception is effaced by invoking a nostalgic "perception of such weight and density in a bygone life, of which this spot was the centre, that the present moment is pressed down or crowded out" (*MF* 1:20). Yet Hawthorne is more willing than Hillard to engage with what he finds offensive about the place. His method of recuperation is at times less systematic, more mysterious. Consider the lengthy and problematic meditation that opens chapter 36:

> When once we have known Rome, and left her where she lies, like a long-decaying corpse, retaining a trace of the noble shape it was, but with an accumulation of dust and a fungous growth overspreading all its more admirable features . . .—left her, sick at heart of Italian trickery, which has uprooted whatever faith in man's integrity had endured til now, and sick at heart and stomach of sour bread, sour wine, rancid butter, and bad cookery needlessly bestowed on evil meats . . .—left her, crushed down in spirit with the desolation of her ruin, and the hopelessness of her future, — left her, in short, hating her with all our might. . . . (*MF* 2:372–73)

The hyperbolic disgust of this four-hundred-word passage indicates a more heightened sensibility than Hillard's and thus perhaps a greater need for recuperation:

> When we have left her in such a mood as this, we are astonished by the discovery, by and by, that our heart-strings have mysteriously attached themselves to the Eternal City, and are drawing us thitherward again, as if it were more familiar, more intimately our home, than even the spot where we were born. (*MF* 2:373)

The recuperation is possible only by means of the textual suppression of any material detail in the conclusion of the passage: we know what repels us, but we do not know what it is that, astonishingly, draws us back.

If Hawthorne's perceptual process is occluded here, it is clarified two chapters later, in a calmer moment, with the account of Hilda's visits to St. Peter's Cathedral. In this scene there are no potential objects of disgust to interfere with the American aestheticization of the object (except, possibly, the aura of Roman Catholicism, which Hawthorne recuperates by appealing to an ecumenical spirituality); thus the operations of the tourist's mind admit of a more systematic, rational description. In describing Hilda's impressions, Hawthorne follows the pattern outlined by Hillard, according to which initial perceptions are altered or ignored in order to construct an impression that fits with preconceived expectations. Hilda's "preconception" of St. Peter's as "a structure of no definite outline, misty in its architecture, dim and gray and huge, stretching into an interminable perspective, and overarched by a dome like the cloudy firmament" (*MF* 2:397) is perhaps more vague than we would expect, given Hillard's claim that engravings prepare the traveler with distinct (although often literally inaccurate) images. Yet Hilda's mental image does fulfill Hillard's model in its focus on the most "characteristic and peculiar" features of the object (*SMI* 128)—here, the cathedral's great size and characteristic dome. Hilda's first perceptions of the object disappoint her, as Hillard would predict: "Her childish vision seemed preferable to the cathedral which Michael Angelo, and all the great architects, had built; because, of the dream edifice, she had said, 'How vast it is!' while of the real St. Peter's she could only say, 'After all, it is not so immense!'" (*MF* 2:398). In constructing her final impression, Hilda substitutes the idealized, nostalgic preconception of her childhood image for her disappointing perceptions by claiming that her preconception has been validated by the authority of direct experience: "After looking many times, with long intervals in between, you discover that the cathedral has gradually extended itself over the whole compass of your idea; it covers the site of your visionary temple" (*MF* 2:398). Thus the preconception—the essential vastness of St. Peter's—becomes the lasting impression as well, as the image of the cathedral fills Hilda's mind completely.

The photographs in the 1889 Houghton *Marble Faun* foreground the text's engagement with the division of experience between actual and ideal Rome. By divorcing each object from its present surroundings—decontextualizing and depopulating the architectural views, sometimes removing even the frames from the paintings—these photographs help to construct the "Rome of the mind" that Hillard and Hawthorne both desire. The representation of the Pantheon is an exemplary case. According to Hillard, the Pantheon is "unhappily placed. [It] stands in a narrow and dirty piazza, and is shouldered and elbowed by a mob of vulgar houses. There is no breathing space around, which it might penetrate with the light of its serene beauty" (*SMI* 199). The Pantheon's surroundings are so unlikely (given the images of Roman sights disseminated in the engravings Hillard mentions) that, as Hawthorne remarks, it "often presents itself before the bewildered stranger, when he is in search of other objects" (*MF* 2:515). The Houghton photograph of the Pantheon is framed so as to minimize traces of the market in the piazza fronting the building, which Hillard had found to be offensively 'strewn with fishbones, decayed vegetables, and offal' (*SMI* 199). From its elevated perspective, the camera admits only the tops of two kiosks (which, at this early hour of the morning, are the only signs of the market)—attempting to efface the "vulgar," modern surroundings of this classical object. However, despite the photographer's apparent attempt to minimize the intrusion of the market into the image, we do see the tops of the kiosks. Their presence may suggest the sort of heightened aesthetic perception that Hawthorne remarks (with perhaps more sensitivity than Hillard) after describing the chaos of a market day in the town of Perugia:

> Through all this petty tumult, which kept beguiling one's eyes and upper strata of thought, it was delightful to catch glimpses of the grand old architecture that stood around the square. The life of the flitting moment, existing in the antique shell of an age gone by, has a fascination which we do not find in either the past or the present, taken by themselves. (*MF* 2:358)

The photographic medium itself inspires a similar "fascination" by means of its combination of presentness (our knowledge that the photograph

"The Pantheon." From The Marble Faun *(Boston: Houghton Mifflin, 1889).*

of the Pantheon was made, in a precise instant, with modern technology) and pastness (the venerable history evoked by the representation of this ancient building with a minimum of modern distractions).

According to Hillard, not all of the ruins in Rome require such overtly decontextualizing representation in order to fulfill aesthetic preconceptions. He finds the Coliseum, for example, to be a "perfect" ruin, matching all preconceived, picturesque criteria (*SMI* 193). Thus his account of the Coliseum concentrates on the picture it makes, which remains unmarred by the intrusions of modern Roman life. The travertine rock of the ruin has "a rich, dark, warm color, deepened and mellowed by time. There is nothing glaring, harsh, or abrupt in the harmony of tints. The blue sky above, and the green earth beneath, are in unison with a tone of coloring

not unlike the brown of one of our early winter landscapes" (*SMI* 194). The monochrome photograph of the Coliseum cannot help but supply (and even increase) the tonal harmony of the picture Hillard develops. This is one of only two architectural views in the Houghton edition to include a substantial foreground; the other shows the ruins of the Forum in a similar composition. The long foregrounds of these seamless images verify the picturesque effect that Hillard's description prepares us to expect and desire, without the appearance of isolating the Coliseum or the Forum from its surrounding material contexts.

In describing the Coliseum, Hawthorne complains that "Byron's celebrated description [in Canto 4 of *Childe Harold's Pilgrimage*] is better than the reality" because this Romantic representation is deserted, while in contrast, "as usual of

"The Coliseum." From The Marble Faun *(Boston: Houghton Mifflin, 1889).*

"Fountain of Trevi." From The Marble Faun *(Boston: Houghton Mifflin, 1889).*

a moonlit evening . . . the precincts and interior were anything but a solitude" (*MF* 1:182). Photographic illustration repairs this complaint by restoring the Coliseum to the solitude of Byron's famous musings.[27] Hawthorne himself (through the voice of his American artist, Kenyon) engages in a similar repair as he describes the Coliseum by moonlight: "The Coliseum was really built for us, and has not come into its best uses till almost two thousand years after it was finished" (*MF* 1:185). In locating the importance of the Coliseum only in terms of its value as an aesthetic object displayed for the traveler's consumption (ignoring even the social and architectural history of the edifice), Kenyon echoes Hillard's assessment that "the work of decay has stopped short at the exact point required by taste and sentiment," making it a "perfect" ruin (*SMI* 193).[28]

Ancient ruins are only one category of tourist attractions in Rome. Yet in the case of other famous objects, the photographs in the Houghton *Marble Faun* follow a decontextualizing, depopulating representational paradigm similar to that which structures the representation of ruins. Human life is completely absent, for example, from the Houghton photograph of the Fountain of Trevi. Hawthorne's characters happen on the fountain at night, when normally it is deserted. The depopulated photograph seems to have been darkened, and a cloudscape added, in order to simulate the moonlit atmosphere of the scene Hawthorne sets.[29] The photograph represents the fountain as pure architectural form, with no relation to its place in the social life it supports during the day.

Although Hawthorne begins with a description of the fountain by moonlight, he soon digresses from the initial image:

In the daytime, there is hardly a livelier scene in Rome than in the neighborhood of the Fountain of Trevi; for the piazza is then filled with the stalls of vegetable and fruit-dealers, chestnut-roasters, cigar-venders, and other people, whose petty and wandering traffic is transacted in the open air. It is likewise thronged with idlers, lounging over the iron railing, and with Forestieri, who came hither to see the famous fountain. Here, also, are seen men with buckets, urchins with cans, and maidens (a picture as old as patriarchal times) bearing their

pitchers upon their heads. (*MF* 1:173–74)

Hawthorne's special mention of a topic for a "picture" invites the illustration of this passage with the picturesque image of "A Roman Peasant." Isolated against the blurred, gray backdrop, this "maiden" is important in so far as her native typicality exemplifies a tourist's category. Since "A Roman Peasant" is the only photograph of the fifty in the Houghton edition that clearly depicts a person, it represents by default all native Romans. Text and image cooperate in encouraging us to view this woman as an abstraction, a "typical native" rather than an individual.[30] The photograph cannot record whether she resists this conceptualization; although we might read

"A Roman Peasant." From The Marble Faun *(Boston: Houghton Mifflin, 1889).*

resistance in her gaze and posture, it is doubtful that Hawthorne and his contemporaries would have done so. All we can definitely conclude is that both photograph and text exhibit her as part of the Roman museum. While Hawthorne's text assures us that this exhibit dates back to "patriarchal times" (that is, before the Roman empire), modern photographic technology gives it currency. Thus text and image collaborate to argue that this aspect of Rome, like the city itself, is eternal.

Prior to its inclusion in the Houghton edition, "A Roman Peasant" was included in some grangerized copies of *Transformation*.[31] In such photographs, persons were transformed into aesthetic objects according to the same logic that governed the photographic representation of architecture. According to a leading historian of Italian photography, most nineteenth-century Roman photographs made for the tourist trade removed inhabitants from their normal contexts and posed them, often in quaint festival costume, against artificial backdrops: "The more unreal they seemed, the more the tourists liked them."[32] Buildings and street scenes were usually photographed early in the morning so as to show architecture uncluttered by people, horses and carts, and the like. Thus while "the instantaneous photograph was possible. . . . Rome presented to us in photographs taken between 1850 and 1870 is deserted in a way it never was in reality."[33] Not all early photographs of Rome dissociate persons from their surroundings so completely.[34] But this was the dominant aesthetic because it suited the tourists' idea of the place.

The photographs in the Houghton *Marble Faun*, which epitomize this decontextualizing aesthetic, seem invulnerable to the charge of falsification that Hillard had leveled at engravings, because the photographic medium itself—with its conventional claims to truthful representation—seems to provide a guarantee of authenticity.[35] Evidently, none of the photographs has been significantly retouched or otherwise altered (possibly excepting the "Fountain of Trevi"). Yet they provide images of Rome that match the aestheticized "Rome of the mind" envisioned by the tourist. Hillard describes how the "offensive objects" surrounding important ruins are conventionally removed from view in engravings:

Everything is smoothed, rounded, and polished: holes are filled up, inequalities are removed, backgrounds and foregrounds are created, the crooked is made straight, and all deformity erased. Hence, though there is truth enough to suggest the resemblance, there is untruth enough to excite vexatious disappointment. (*SMI* 130)

The photographic medium silences any complaint about false representations while providing precisely the sort of picturesque image, purified of quotidian distractions, that Hillard desires. The photographers who made the illustrations for the Houghton *Marble Faun* have performed their equivalent of the engraver's technique of creating backgrounds and foregrounds (of smoothing, rounding, and polishing) by composing views so as to minimize or exclude any social or architectural context when these would distract from the viewer's preconceptions, or to emphasize context when it accords with preconceptions (as in the case of the Coliseum). The disappointment that Hillard notes is photographically countered not by altering the object—for this would have been inappropriate given nineteenth-century assumptions about photography—but by framing it in a way that urges the traveler who actually sees the object to refuse peripheral claims on his or her attention and to concentrate on the object's aesthetic value. As a result, the images provide authentications of idealizing preconceptions about picturesque ruins without the initial perceptual dissonance that Hillard's typical tourist often experiences before coming to perceive the "Rome of the mind." In this way the Eternal City, conceptually "cut up" (Hillard) and its aesthetic components "ticketed" (Howells) by photographs and texts, was made available for American consumption.

PHOTOGRAPHY AND "THE REAL"

The era of the half-tone, beginning around 1885 for magazines and about a decade later for books, saw the emergence of "categories of appropriateness" for relations between images and texts: fictional literature came to be illustrated with drawings, and factual literature, such as news and travel accounts, with photographs.[36]

The Marble Faun, since it was both fictional and factual, presented a borderline case; in some editions it was illustrated with engravings. In choosing to produce a new, photographically illustrated edition, the publishers argue that "they have given Hawthorne's classic a presentation more acceptable, not only to travellers but to all lovers of art and letters, than would have been possible had they resorted to the ordinary method of employing artists to illustrate the story" (*MF* 1:ii). Confirmation of this argument came in the fact that the edition was popular enough to encourage imitations by other American publishers.[37]

While the norms governing illustrative media were being established, there were various experiments with the photographic illustration of fiction, notably Alvin Langdon Coburn's frontispiece photographs for the New York Edition of James's works.[38] Many of the photographs in the Houghton *Marble Faun,* which anticipate the James-Coburn collaboration by nearly twenty years, fulfill two of the criteria that James would later specify for the interaction of photographs and fictional text. In describing their work on the New York Edition, James stated that Coburn's photographs were to be "small pictures of our 'set' stage with the actors left out"; additionally, they were to provide "optical symbols or echoes, expressions of no particular thing in the text, but only of the type or idea of this or that thing."[39]

The Piazza del Popolo, setting of a melodramatic confrontation between Miriam and the mysterious stranger, is empty in the Houghton photograph; the reader may populate it with the "motley crowd" mentioned in Hawthorne's text (*MF* 1:121). In addition to its function as a "stage," this photograph provides an "optical symbol or echo" in evoking Hilda's and Kenyon's perception of Miriam at this point in the narra-

"Piazza del Popolo." From The Marble Faun *(Boston: Houghton Mifflin, 1889).*

tive. To recall the plot: Miriam has been followed, since her party's visit to the catacombs early in the story, by an artist's model who holds some unknown power over her. As Miriam attempts to talk her way free of the stranger, Hilda and Kenyon watch her in the Piazza del Popolo, recognizing that

> the stream of Miriam's trouble kept its way through the flood of human life, and neither mingled with it nor was turned aside. With a sad kind of feminine ingenuity, she found a way to kneel before her tyrant undetected, though in full sight of all the people, still beseeching him for freedom, and in vain. (*MF* 1:121)

The emptiness of the photograph may suggest the way in which Hilda and Kenyon come to perceive Miriam's plight: they see her in effect disappear and thus conclude that apparently no

one can aid her in her struggle against the stranger so long as he remains alive.

The function of providing an "optical symbol or echo," although enacted by relatively few of the Houghton photographs, is especially interesting and disturbing in the case of the Jewish Ghetto. The Houghton photograph of "The Ghetto" shows a scene deserted except for a barely noticeable blur which may represent a person stepping out of the frame.[40] By contrast, in some grangerized Tauchnitz copies, the Jewish Ghetto was illustrated by crowded street scenes—the one instance in which the conventional, depopulating paradigm was regularly abandoned. Such a photograph of the Ghetto gestures toward Hawthorne-the-tourist's impression of life there—where "thousands of Jews are crowded within a narrow compass, and lead a close, unclean, and multitudinous life" (*MF* 2:441)—but at the same time ameliorates the

"The Ghetto." From The Marble Faun *(Boston: Houghton Mifflin, 1889).*

Jewish Ghetto in Rome. From Transformation *(Leipzig: Bernhard Tauchnitz, 1860). Courtesy of Special Collections, O. M. Wilson Library, University of Minnesota.*

harshness of Hawthorne's account (for it does not appear "unclean").

In contrast to the Tauchnitz photograph, the Houghton photograph, with its enigmatic blur, more closely matches the fictional aspect of the text. As with the photograph of the Piazza del Popolo, this image may be taken to suggest Hilda's subjective experience. We know that while delivering for Miriam a mysterious, sealed packet, Hilda "passed on the borders of [the Ghetto], but had no occasion to step within it" (*MF* 2:441). The photographic perspective replicates the narrative point of view: we peer into the Ghetto, but we do not enter. Like Hilda, we are protected from "whatever was evil, foul, and ugly, in this populous and corrupt city" by an "innocence [that] continues to make a paradise around itself." Hilda "trod as if invisible, and not only so, but blind" in this vicinity (*MF* 2:441). The manufactured innocence of photography similarly makes us invisible: we see without being seen. Yet, like Hilda, we are blind to the existence of the people who live in the Ghetto. The pho-

tograph tries to assure us that the people Hawthorne names will not impinge on our experience, since all we see is the blur that matches Hilda's tangential awareness of the Jews. If we detach ourselves from the fictional point of view, we can see that the blur signifies a person trying to remove him- or herself from representation. Perhaps this person was chased away by a photographer who was attempting to follow Hillard's program of expunging quotidian life from representations of Rome. It is equally likely that he or she left the scene intentionally, refusing to become an object of ethnography, like "A Roman Peasant," to be displayed in the Roman museum.

Coburn sometimes used photographs of fa-

"By St. Peter's," by Alvin Langdon Coburn. From The Novels and Tales of Henry James, *vol. 18 (New York: Charles Scribner's Sons, 1909). Courtesy of Clifton Waller Barrett Library of American Literature, Special Collections Department, University of Virginia Library.*

mous tourist sights to develop the symbolism James required, as for example in "By St. Peter's," which accompanies *Daisy Miller.*[41] Yet Coburn's photographs are usually less directly linked to the text than those in the Houghton *Marble Faun* or the grangerized *Transformations.* One scene in *Daisy Miller* does take place *inside* the cathedral (where Winterbourne's aunt, Mrs. Costello, perches on a camp stool and entertains Americans with gossip about Daisy's liaison with Giovanelli). But Coburn's photograph is taken, as the title indicates, "*By* St. Peter's," and depicts a part of the piazza in front of the cathedral. Thus subtly freed from textual specificity, the image invites free semiotic play. Ralph F. Bogardus, for example, argues that it "is the most purely poetic frontispiece in the entire series," reflecting James's conception of Daisy herself as "pure poetry"; like Daisy, the fountain's spray is fresh and evanescent but surrounded by solid and enduring structures.[42] The symbolic function of the Houghton photographs derives, to a greater extent than that of "By St. Peter's," from their match with the fictional point of view and their consequent ability to evoke sympathy between Hawthorne's characters (notably his heroines) and his readers.[43] Hilda's journey through the Ghetto is an especially sinister example, since the presumption of a shared anti-Semitism provides the channel of sympathy; yet this example is consistent with the photo-text's overall assumption of Anglo-American superiority to the inhabitants of modern Rome.

Although many of the Houghton photographs can be taken to function similarly to Coburn's, they differ in one important respect. James specified that each photograph should, "by a latent virtue in it, speak for its connection with something in the book, and yet at the same time speak enough for its odd or interesting self."[44] But unlike Coburn's pictorialist works, the Houghton photographs do not ask to be considered as works of art in themselves. Allan Sekula argues that it was *Camera Work* (first published in 1903) that first "outlined the terms on which photography could be considered as art."[45] Putting aside, for the moment, complications and exceptions to Sekula's useful generalization, we can see that *Camera Work* marks a division between the Houghton photographs

and Coburn's photographs—between an aesthetic in which the photograph is merely a technology for the elegant reproduction of objects and one in which the photograph is an aesthetic object in itself. Produced more than a decade prior to the first issue of *Camera Work,* the Houghton photographs defer the category of the aesthetic to the objects they depict. Presenting themselves as transparent representations, they aestheticize Rome while making the resulting aesthetic value seem to be a natural feature of the place, rather than the product of an artistic "genius" such as Coburn's.

The Houghton *Marble Faun* appeared in 1889 to a generation of readers accustomed to "realistic" novels but unfamiliar with the concept of photographically illustrated fiction. Critical reception varied with the extent to which reviewers approved of the generically mixed nature of Hawthorne's original, unillustrated text. One reviewer for the publishing trade praised it as "a noble conception, carried out with consummate skill and success."[46] But another objected that the original *Marble Faun* "was a work of the imagination" rather than of factual description and was therefore legitimately illustrated only with artist's drawings.[47] The most extensive and thoughtful review argued that in Hawthorne's text,

> mingled with what is strictly necessary to the scenic effect is a great deal of information which belongs to the guide-book rather than the work of art. . . . For this very reason, however, the illustration of "The Marble Faun" is withdrawn from the realm of the imagination. We would have no other Donatello than that of Praxiteles, desire no Hilda's tower but that of the Via Portoghese.[48]

This reviewer argues that while Hawthorne's descriptive commentary is at times "vital to the story," the extent to which such commentary is introduced is aesthetically problematic because its interpolation violates the "organic unity" of the fiction and "lessens its first effect as a work of art." Going far beyond the nonchalant placement of a few incidental details in order to establish "local color," Hawthorne self-consciously and unacceptably called attention to his use of description.[49] Thus the fiction did not meet the criteria of the realist aesthetic, and yet this critic praised its illustration with photographs. His logic was not inconsistent.

The inclusion of unmotivated detail is, in Roland Barthes's analysis, what produces the "reality effect" in fiction.[50] The very motivatedness of Hawthorne's descriptions—the characteristic that made them so useful to the tourist and encouraged the book's reception as travel literature—would seem to render them invalid as productive signs of "the real" in Barthes's sense. That is, the Houghton *Marble Faun* did *not* participate in the literary shift toward "realism" in the second half of the nineteenth century, if the constitutive characteristic of "realism" is understood to be an attention to incidental detail, significant only for its merely being registered, which produces a sense of "having-been-there" (the illusion of "denotation" or direct reference) as the most important value of the text's semiotic system.[51] A few of the photographs in grangerized Tauchnitz copies—those that appear full with quotidian detail, for example some photographs of the Jewish Ghetto—may evoke some sense of this "having-been-there"; however, photographs such as "A Roman Peasant," copies of artworks, and depopulated architectural views are the norm in Tauchnitz copies.

Rather than producing a Barthesian "reality effect," both the Houghton photographs and Hawthorne's text give us the materiality of the Roman settings primarily in order to propose the truth of the aestheticized representations that are the primary source of the city's value for tourists. The focus of the text urges us to transcend quotidian detail, rather than reveling in it as one caught up in the "reality effect" would do. For example, one of the broken columns of the Forum is to be valued not for its location or appearance in the present, but rather for its capacity to "mak[e] *old* Rome actually sensible to the touch and eye; and no study of history, no force of thought, nor magic of song, could so vitally assure us that *Rome once existed* [present Rome clearly not counting as 'Rome'], as this sturdy specimen of what its rulers and people wrought" (*MF* 1:179, emphases added). Standing in the Forum, we "seem to see the Roman epoch close at hand. We forget that a chasm extends between it and ourselves" (*MF* 1:194–95). Such textual representations gain their authority against Hawthorne's occasional mention of the actual, present-day Rome inhabited by ordinary Italians, by acknowledging and then discounting the importance of such modern distractions. The photographic representations of ideal Rome more directly efface these distractions.

Thus we find in the photo-textual *Marble Faun* an early example of what André Malraux would come to call a "museum without walls"—a published collection of photographic reproductions by means of which a painting, statue, monument, or building is decontextualized from its primary sociohistorical relations and recontextualized in terms of its aesthetic equivalence with other objects.[52] This recontextualization in turn produces a new social relation, here the verification of the Roman "museum" that Howells identified and others desired. The interplay of text, photographs, and the nineteenth-century Anglo-American attitude toward Rome defines a timeless cultural past, which has been embodied in a museum of aesthetic objects dissociated from whatever is mundane or distracting. In this way the objects become particularly amenable to aesthetic consumption as images. The fictional strands of the photo-text cooperate with the nonfictional in this production of aesthetic images. When the photographs resonate most strongly with the fiction, they often share the perspective of Hilda. And like Hilda—the American copyist who continues to prefer her preconceived view of St. Peter's to the actual building even after repeated and careful observation—the photographs "copy" Rome. Mimicking her artistic ability "to execute what the great master had conceived in his imagination, but had not so perfectly succeeded in putting upon canvas" (*MF* 1:77), the Houghton photo-text renders actual the idealized images preconceived by the American traveler. The apparently unmediated connection of the photographs with "the real" naturalizes the resulting perception, making it seem to contain more truth than did immediate, unguided perception.

NOTES

I wish to thank Michael Hancher, Kathleen Diffley, and Marsha Bryant for their helpful comments on this essay.

1. Nineteenth-century commentators were divided over

its merits as a novel, but were unanimous in their praise for its descriptions of Italy; see, e.g., Henry James, *Hawthorne* (1879; rpt., New York: Harper & Brothers, 1901), 160–64. For a summary of the book's reception as travel literature, see Bertha Faust, *Hawthorne's Contemporaneous Reputation* (New York: Octagon, 1968), 118–23. On its popularity, see James, *Hawthorne*, 160; and Claude M. Simpson, introduction to *The Marble Faun; or, The Romance of Monte Beni*, by Nathaniel Hawthorne (Columbus: Ohio State University Press, 1968), xxix. The edition published for the Continental trade by Tauchnitz (Hawthorne, *Transformation; Or, The Romance of Monte Beni*, 2 vols. [Leipzig: Bernhard Tauchnitz, 1860]) sold enough copies to require a fourth setting of plates—one of only two of the firm's five hundred English-language titles ever to do so; see William B. Todd and Ann Bowden, *Tauchnitz International Editions in English, 1841–1955* (New York: Bibliographical Society of America, 1988), 123–24.

2. In J. Donald Crowley, ed., *Hawthorne: The Critical Heritage* (London: Routledge and Kegan Paul, 1970), 330.

3. William Dean Howells, *Italian Journeys* (1872; rev. ed., Boston: Houghton, Mifflin, 1886), 158.

4. The idea of a photographic "tour" was not new in 1889. As early as 1861, Oliver Wendell Holmes, Sr., suggested that it was no longer necessary to go to Europe in order to see it. Inviting the readers of the *Atlantic* to embark with him on a vicarious "stereographic trip" while "sitting here by our own firesides," Holmes describes the Europe that was available to Americans in the form of stereographic prints; in Rome he pauses to point out the statue of "Hawthorne's Marble Faun (the one called of Praxiteles)" ("Sun-Painting and Sun-Sculpture; with a Stereoscopic Trip across the Atlantic," *Atlantic Monthly* 8 [1861]: 16, 28, 26).

5. Nathaniel Hawthorne, *The Marble Faun; or, The Romance of Monte Beni*, 2 vols. (Boston and New York: Houghton, Mifflin, 1889), 1:15; hereafter cited in the text as *MF*.

6. Henry Bright, one of Hawthorne's English acquaintances, asked Hawthorne for assistance in acquiring a photograph of the *Faun of Praxiteles*, evidently wanting it to accompany the autograph manuscript, which Hawthorne had given him; see Hawthorne, *The Letters, 1857–1864*, ed. Thomas Woodson et al. (Columbus: Ohio State University Press, 1987), 248, 276. Other than this, however, he was most probably not involved, since the grangerized Tauchnitz copies were prepared by individual booksellers or by tourists themselves; cf. Carol Shloss, *In Visible Light: Photography and the American Writer, 1840–1940* (Oxford and New York: Oxford University Press, 1987), 39. Except for "A Roman Peasant" (discussed later in this essay), I have not located the sources of the Houghton photogravures. The photographers are not identified by name, in contrast to a similarly produced 1897 edition of *The Alhambra*, illustrated with photogravures "from photographs taken by Mr. Richard H. Lawrence and others" (Washington Irving, *The Alhambra*, 2 vols. [New York: G. P. Putnam's Sons, 1897], 1:xii). Lawrence, who wrote a preface to this edition, was a photographer of some note; he had previously worked with Jacob Riis. Evidently none of the Houghton photographers had attained Lawrence's status, and were, simply, working photographers making conventional photographs.

7. Alan Sekula provides a useful framework for analyzing "realist" photography (as distinct from "art" photography) in his refusal "to separate the photograph from a notion of task" ("On the Invention of Photographic Mean-

ing," in *Thinking Photography*, ed. Victor Burgin [London: Macmillan, 1982], 87). The Houghton edition, which carries a preface emphasizing that the photographs have been "made directly from the objects themselves," assumes that the task of photographs is to provide unmediated copies of objects in the world (*MF* 1:ii).

8. Howells, *Roman Holidays and Others* (New York and London: Harper & Brothers, 1908), 226–27.

9. James, *Hawthorne*, 160.

10. Grangerized copies of *Transformation* containing as many as 102 and as few as 57 photographs have been documented, the earliest verified date being May 1868; see Lucien Goldschmit and Weston J. Naef, *The Truthful Lens: A Survey of the Photographically Illustrated Book, 1844–1914* (New York: Grolier Club, 1980), 204. A copy containing fifty-eight 4-x-5-inch photographs, now in the Special Collections of O. M. Wilson Library, University of Minnesota, is inscribed "Maude Cleveland, Rome, 1888."

11. For information on the practices of Italian booksellers, see Ann Wilsher, "The Tauchnitz 'Marble Faun,'" *History of Photography* 4 (1980): 61–66.

12. "Holiday Books," *Atlantic Monthly* 67 (1891): 122.

13. E.g., the "Maude Cleveland" copy (see note 10) contains several photographs with penciled captions—such as "Venus of the Capitol, Sunday, July 29, 1888."

14. James, *Italian Hours* (1909; rpt., New York: Horizon Press, 1968), 298–99.

15. Ralph F. Bogardus points out that James's frequent and consistent use of terms such as "image" and "impression" suggests that he shared the prevalent nineteenth-century sensitivity to "photographic vision," which may have influenced his thinking about memory and perception (*Pictures and Texts: Henry James, A. L. Coburn, and New Ways of Seeing in Literary Culture* [Ann Arbor, Mich.: UMI Research Press, 1984], 133). Although James seldom referred explicitly to photography in his travel writings, he did collect photographs during his travels—assembling a photographic album, for example, while preparing *A Little Tour in France*; see Adeline Tinter, *The Book World of Henry James* (Ann Arbor, Mich.: UMI Research Press, 1987), 277–78, 357–58. We do not know if he ever saw a grangerized copy of *Transformation*, but we can assume that he became generally familiar with the Tauchnitz "International Editions" series during his travels on the Continent; see William B. Todd, "Books in Series," in *Collectible Books: Some New Paths*, ed. Jean Peters (New York and London: R. R. Bowker, 1979), 90.

16. Susan Sontag, *On Photography* (New York: Farrar, Straus & Giroux, 1977), 137.

17. Emerson, for example, systematically organized his tour of the Continent in 1833 so that he could "admire by just degrees from the Maltese architecture up to St. Peter's"—the latter of course being one of the most venerated objects in the canon (*The Journals and Miscellaneous Notebooks of Ralph Waldo Emerson*, vol. 4, ed. Alfred R. Ferguson [Cambridge: Harvard University Press, 1964], 116).

18. The bibliography compiled by Todd and Bowden (*Tauchnitz International Editions*) shows that *Transformation* was one of four Tauchnitz "International Editions" in English to be grangerized with any frequency—the others being Bulwer Lytton's *Last Days of Pompeii* (1842), Macaulay's *Lays of Ancient Rome* (1851), and Eliot's *Romola* (1863). The nonfictional travel essays also published by Tauchnitz—e.g., Dickens's *Pictures from Italy* (1846), Thackeray's *Paris Sketch Book* (1873), James's *A Little Tour in France* (1885)—evidently

were not often grangerized. Bulwer's, Macaulay's, and Eliot's books are all directed toward the past, the primary locus of value for tourists in Italy, and thus were especially conducive to the production of a photo-textual museum.

19. George Stillman Hillard, *Six Months in Italy*, 9th ed. (Boston: Ticknor and Fields, 1866); hereafter cited in the text as *SMI*. In his exhaustive study of the impact of Rome on American writers and artists, William L. Vance frequently uses this book as a source of "standard received opinion," noting that it went through twenty-one editions in forty years (*America's Rome*, 2 vols. [New Haven and London: Yale University Press, 1989, 1990], 2:78).

20. Qtd. in Vance, ibid.

21. Hawthorne, *The French and Italian Notebooks*, ed. Thomas Woodson (Columbus: Ohio State University Press, 1980), 150.

22. For an excellent overview of this aestheticizing process, with special attention to its impact on Henry James's work, see James Buzard, "A Continent of Pictures: Reflections on the 'Europe' of Nineteenth-Century Tourists," *PMLA* 108 (1993): 30–44.

23. "Illustrated Books for the Holidays," *The American Bookseller* n.s. 26 (1889): 561.

24. Buzard links the sort of perceptual operation exemplified by Hillard—"making the original become what it (potentially) is"—with the persistence of the picturesque aesthetic in the nineteenth century ("A Continent of Pictures," 36).

25. Dean MacCannell, *The Tourist: A New Theory of the Leisure Class* (New York: Schocken, 1976), 13.

26. Jane Addams, "From *Twenty Years at Hull House*" (1910), in *The Norton Anthology of American Literature*, 3d ed., vol. 2, ed. Nina Baym et al. (New York: Norton, 1989), 666.

27. Jerome McGann identifies the importance of the trope of solitude, arguing that as an "emblem that a living culture has departed," the image of Rome as a city of ruins was crucial to the construction of the Romantic sense of self-consciousness ("Rome and Its Romantic Significance," in *Roman Images*, Selected Papers from the English Institute n.s. 8, ed. Annabel Patterson [Baltimore: Johns Hopkins University Press, 1984], 84).

28. Vance points out the similarity of Hillard's and Kenyon's views (*America's Rome*, 1:60).

29. According to Hillard, moonlight gives the most appropriate view of the fountain because "the mind's eye sees the shadows of the lovers" Corinne and Oswald, recalling a moonlit scene from Madame de Stael's novel *Corinne*. Hillard, true to form, "begin[s] with criticism," noting the "bad taste" with which the fountain's statue of Neptune is executed, but "end[s] with admiration" by making this famous literary reference order his perceptions (*SMI*, 261).

30. Bill Nichols argues that depictions of persons in ethnographic documentary films "focus attention upon a level of abstraction beyond the individual. . . . Individual social actors risk becoming no more than examples, illustrations of ethnographic principles, with their value assessed solely by the quality of exemplification" (*Ideology and the Image: Social Representation in the Cinema and Other Media* [Bloomington: Indiana University Press, 1981], 238). In still photography—a somewhat less densely coded medium than film—the risk that the person will function merely as an exemplar is compounded.

31. This photograph appears in the "Maude Cleveland" copy (see note 10). Grangerized *Transformation*s usually contain one or more photographs of Romans in picturesque

costume; see also Wilsher, "The Tauchnitz 'Marble Faun,'" 65.

32. Silvio Negro, "*I primi fotografi romani*," qtd. in Dyveke Helsted, "Rome in Early Photographs," *History of Photography* 2 (1978): 340.

33. Ibid., 340–41.

34. Cf. the photograph of the Jewish Ghetto from a Tauchnitz *Transformation* (discussed later in this essay) and Richard Pare, *Photography and Architecture, 1839–1939* (Montreal: Canadian Centre for Architecture, 1982), plates 37–39, 49.

35. For an early account of the representational power and fidelity of photography, including scientific and artistic applications, see Holmes, "The Stereoscope and the Stereograph," *Atlantic Monthly* 3 (1859): 738–48.

36. Neil Harris, "Iconography and Intellectual History: The Half-Tone Effect," in *New Directions in American Intellectual History*, ed. John Higham and Paul K. Conkin (Baltimore: Johns Hopkins University Press, 1979), 199. For a useful history of photographically illustrated fiction, see Bogardus, *Pictures and Texts*, 105–9.

37. Houghton issued a second printing in 1890. The same year, *Romola* appeared in two competing editions illustrated with photogravures: George Eliot, *Romola*, 2 vols. (Boston: Estes and Lauriat, 1890); Eliot, *Romola*, 2 vols. (Philadelphia: Porter & Coates, 1890). Like the Houghton *Marble Faun*, these standardized the tradition of grangerizing Tauchnitz copies. Works of travel literature and history also began to appear with photogravure illustrations—e.g., Hawthorne, *Our Old Home*, 2 vols. (Boston and New York: Houghton, Mifflin, 1891); Irving, *The Alhambra*, 2 vols. (New York and London: G. P. Putnam's Sons, 1897). As the half-tone replaced the photogravure, the publication of photographically illustrated travel literature increased— e.g., Howells, *Roman Holidays* (New York and London: Harper & Brothers, 1908). *Romola* and *The Marble Faun* were also illustrated with half-tones: Eliot, *Romola*, 2 vols. (Chicago and New York: Rand, McNally, 1898); Hawthorne, *The Marble Faun; or, The Romance of Monte Beni*, 2 vols. (New York: Thomas Y. Crowell, 1902). By 1902 a critic was complaining that "books of travel and description lend themselves too readily, perhaps, to illustration. We have had a surfeit of foreign photographs and 'views' of all sorts" ("Picture Books and Others," *Atlantic Monthly* 89 [1902]: 563).

38. Henry James, *The Novels and Tales of Henry James*, 24 vols. (New York: Charles Scribner's Sons, 1907–1909).

39. James, ibid., 23:xi.

40. The Houghton photograph may be quoting Albert Bierstadt's 1858 painting *The Arch of Octavia (Roman Fish-Market)*, but it omits Bierstadt's depiction of the crowded scene beneath the arch; Bierstadt's painting is reproduced in Vance, *America's Rome*, 2:plate 2. Vance points out that this arch demarcated one boundary of the Ghetto, to which all Jews were confined until the end of papal rule in 1870 (2:153). The Houghton editors seem uncharacteristically lax here in neglecting to supply the name of this important architectural feature of Rome.

41. James, *Novels and Tales*, vol. 18.

42. Bogardus, *Pictures and Texts*, 191.

43. Gordon Hutner argues that Hawthorne was highly successful in enlisting the "sympathy" of his readers—i.e., in inviting a privileged state of mutual understanding such that they "participate in the moral education that [*The Marble Faun*] observes" (*Secrets and Sympathy: Forms of Disclosure in Hawthorne's Novels* [Athens and London: University of

Georgia Press, 1988], 150). Hawthorne's success here may have derived from his use of a moral point of view familiar to his American readers, including a narrative voice that was, as James characterized it, "exquisitely and consistently provincial" (*Hawthorne*, 142).

44. James, *Novels and Tales*, 23:xi.

45. Sekula, "On the Invention of Photographic Meaning," 92. As in the Houghton *Marble Faun* and the New York Edition, the photographs in *Camera Work* were reproduced by means of photogravure.

46. "Illustrated Books for the Holidays," 561.

47. "Holiday Books," *Atlantic Monthly* 67 (1891): 124.

48. Arthur Sherburne Hardy, "Hawthorne's Italian Romance," *The Book Buyer* 6 (1889): 428.

49. Ibid.

50. Roland Barthes, "The Reality Effect," in *The Rustle of Language,* trans. Richard Howard (New York: Hill and Wang, 1986), 141–48.

51. Ibid., 147, 148.

52. André Malraux, *Museum Without Walls,* trans. Stuart Gilbert and Francis Price (Garden City: Doubleday, 1967). This idea culminated in an early twentieth-century edition containing twelve half-tone reproductions along with copious notes by "Annie Russell Marble, M.A." that provide general historical information and guidance for aesthetic appreciation—e.g., on the Coliseum: "Vast Flavian ampitheatre, . . . used as fortress in mediaeval age, partially destroyed by floods and invasions, but still grand in ruins; symbol of Rome's greatness; cf. Byron's 'Childe Harold' . . . [and] Mme. De Stael's 'Corinne'" (Hawthorne, *The Marble Faun; or, The Romance of Monte Beni,* intr. Annie Russell Marble [Boston, New York, and Chicago: Houghton, Mifflin, n.d.], 529).

2

Photography, Time, and the Surrealist Sensibility

Marja Warehime

"A photograph is only a fragment, and with the passage of time its moorings become unstuck. It drifts away into a soft abstract pastness, open to any kind of reading."

"Life is not about significant details, illuminated a flash, fixed forever. Photographs are."
— Susan Sontag, *On Photography*

ANDRÉ BRETON BELIEVED THAT THE INVENTION of photography "dealt a mortal blow" to old modes of expression, inspiring artists to "break with the imitation of appearances."[1] Yet the central figure of the Surrealist movement remained ambivalent about photography, which he saw as both a "blind instrument" and a source of images of unparalleled emotive power.[2] Surprisingly, however, despite his admiration for Max Ernst's photo-collages and Man Ray's experiments, Breton had relatively little to say about photography and, as Simon Watney indicates, "photography enjoyed but a tenuous place in the firmament of Surrealist practice."[3] Breton's remarks on the subject of photography, while frequently suggestive, remain incidental—like the parenthetical query in his famous 1925 essay *Surrealism and Painting* where he pauses to ask "and when will all the books that are worth any-

thing stop being illustrated with drawings and appear only with photographs?"[4]

Consequently, although he was Surrealism's foremost theoretician—so enamored of definitions that he created a pseudo dictionary entry for "Surrealism" in the first Surrealist manifesto—Breton's statements about photography do not add up to a coherent position on a medium that was intimately bound up with Surrealist textual production, most notably in Surrealist periodicals, where, as Dawn Ades points out, "the range and resources of photography within Surrealism are most fully realized."[5] Breton may have taken photography for granted, but Edouard Jaguer's *Les Mystères de la chambre noire: le Surréalisme et la photographie* makes it clear that the number of Surrealists who practiced photography, either briefly or seriously, was considerable.[6] In 1979 Nancy Hall-Duncan claimed that photographic surrealism represented "one of the most critically important but largely disregarded undercurrents in photographic history."[7] And beginning with "The Photographic Conditions of Surrealism," in 1981, Rosalind Krauss sought to reevaluate the role of photography in Surrealism. Her essays, including "Photography in the Service of Surrealism" and "Corpus Delicti," move photography from the margins of Surrealist activity to place it at the heart of a Surrealist aesthetics, discovering in the photographic image the "key to the dilemma of surrealist style."[8]

Less concerned with the questions that beset the art historian, Susan Sontag saw the problem differently. "Surrealism lies at the heart of the photographic enterprise," Sontag maintained in the series of essays that comprise her 1977 *On Photography*. Dismissing the medium's "unappealing reputation" as "the most realistic, therefore facile, of the mimetic arts," she insisted on its inherent surreality: its "creation of a duplicate world, a reality in the second degree, narrower but more dramatic than the one perceived by natural vision."[9] Yet if, as she claims, it is through photography that Surrealism has taken over the modern sensibility and "triumphantly" come into its own, the Surrealism that Sontag describes bears only a superficial resemblance to the movement launched by André Breton's first *Manifesto of Surrealism* in 1924. In fact, as if adding insult to injury, Sontag taxes Breton and company with completely misunderstanding the fundamental relationship between photography and Surrealism. In the final analysis, however, her assertion—that the Surrealists looked for photographic revelations of the surreal by disrupting photography's mimetic function—identifies their interest in photography too narrowly with Man Ray's experimental photographic activity.[10]

Nonetheless, happy accidents such as Man Ray's photograms, or the curious inversions of solarization (supposedly discovered when Lee Miller mistakenly turned on the light during a developing session in his studio),[11] or *brûlage* (the burning of the negative), when added to the suggestive evocations of montage, negative printing, double exposures, extreme close-ups, shadow effects and their various combinations, do become an impressive catalogue of the Surrealist techniques used to evoke the hidden dimensions of (sur)reality.[12] Unfortunately, as Sontag recognizes, these poetic visual experiments rapidly coalesced into a style that became fashionable, then dated. "Photographic Surrealism suffered a dramatic decline during the 1940's and 1950's," Nancy Hall-Duncan concurred, noting that, "ironically, one of the most enduring forms of

photographic surrealism was its adaptation in fashion and advertising photography."[13]

Where the Surrealists erred, Sontag contends, was in assuming that the surreal was universal, its source the timeless unconscious, when, she claims, "it turns out to be what is most concrete, local, ethnic, class-bound." "Moments of lost time, of vanished customs" she argues, are far more surreal than any of the Surrealists' abstract poetic images.[14] Sontag's argument derives a certain heuristic clarity from eliding a whole range of Surrealist "found image" practices, of which the recontextualization of old photographs was only one.[15] However, the rich complexity of her analysis—which turns on a provocative juxtaposition of the surreal of historical Surrealism, timeless and universal, with the ahistorical, yet time-bound surreal of the modern sensibility—underscores time's crucial role in the relationship between Surrealism and photography.[16]

Taking Sontag's analysis as a point of departure, this essay will explore the relationship between time and the surrealist sensibility in two autobiographical works where the fragmentary revelations of photography and the Surrealist rejection of history clash with the narrative elaboration of a life. The first, "historically" Surrealist, is André Breton's *Nadja*, originally published in 1928; the second is a work by a nonSurrealist contemporary of Breton's, the photographer Jacques-Henri Lartigue, who presents a collection of his photographs taken over a period of seventy years in *Diary of a Century*.[17]

Sontag's accusation that the Surrealists failed to comprehend the irrational mystery of time hardly does justice to their efforts to negate its rational form: history. They rejected the past as tainted, bound up with the horrors of the First World War and the bankruptcy of traditional values—family, country, and religion—that had served to justify it. However, they also attacked the present with all the intensity of their desire "to change life," to transform the nature of the human condition, and transcend the limitations of "the sole possibility of the things which 'are,'" denounced by Breton in the *Second Manifesto of Surrealism*. His argument links time with the "baseness" of Western logic and its refusal to give equal value to dream and waking realities. "We are not even sure that we will not do away *with time*, that sinister old farce . . . ," he declares, but the negative form of his assertion belies his bravado and underscores his uncertainty.[18] He expressed nothing but scorn for the normalizing function of logical categories that made the unknown classifiable, and consequently understandable, without acknowledging its irrational, radical difference from the known. Yet the power of convention may have dictated the "internalization" of his revolt against logic and time. In one of the most famous declarations of the *Second Manifesto*, he defines the aim of Surrealist activity as the attainment of a particular "point of the mind":

> Everything tends to make us believe that there exists a certain point of the mind at which life and death, the real and the imagined, past and future, the communicable and the incommunicable, high and low cease to be perceived as contradictions. Now search as one may one will never find any other motivating force in the activities of the Surrealists than the hope of finding and fixing this point.[19]

Breton's rejection of logical categories also informs *Nadja*, the first-person account of his relationship with an enigmatic woman in whom he saw the incarnation of a Surrealist ideal, that of living "without pragmatic considerations of any sort" and "dangerously—by thrusting one's head, and then an arm out of the jail—thus shattered—of logic" (142, 143). However, his account reveals not only his failure to understand Nadja and to save her from madness, but, in the final analysis, his own inability to escape the limitations of logic and time. Significantly, it is the photographs he included to illustrate his story that make this failure visible, even though the work itself ends on a positive note.

Nadja has eluded the logic of literary classification, and Renée Riese-Hubert notes that the book "has provoked debates concerning the literary genre, if any, to which it belongs, its reliability as autobiography, its psychological value and the nature of its narrative."[20] The second edition of *Nadja*, published in the sixties, contained a foreword by Breton (he subtitled it a "delayed dispatch") that claimed *Nadja* was not intended as a literary work, but a document *pris sur le vif*, "taken from life," an account of events that nei-

ther disguised nor fictionally transposed the real people it portrayed.[21] As evidence of his intentions, he adduced the "two anti-literary imperatives" that he claimed had governed its composition. One of these imperatives was the effort to model his account on the psychiatric case study, which included traces of the subjects' interaction transcribed without the slightest attention to style. The second imperative was his decision to eliminate useless literary descriptions and replace them with photographs—a decision foreshadowed by his aside in *Surrealism and Painting* on the necessity to illustrate books with photographs rather than drawings.

In insisting that *Nadja* be considered a document rather than a literary work, Breton reaffirmed the aversion to literary and artistic realism he had expressed in the first *Manifesto*, and he implicitly justified his inclusion of technically unmanipulated documentary photographs rather than "surreal" ones. He had attacked "the realist attitude" in the first *Manifesto* as the lowest common denominator of the mind and deplored its effect on literature: the creation of a "generous supply of novels" (6). Exasperated by what he called their "purely informational" style, he concentrated his ire on empty, "needlessly specific" descriptions that he considered no better than banal postcards. Deliberately making an example of a great writer, he took Dostoevsky to task for a passage in *Crime and Punishment* where the author undertook to describe "a room that held nothing in particular": old furniture, a sofa, a table and mirror, some worthless engravings. Expressing astonishment that Dostoevsky would bother to describe such an "empty moment," Breton concluded: "I have too unstable a notion of the continuity of life to equate or compare my moments of depression or weakness with my best moments" (8).

However, Breton's "unstable notion of the continuity of life" has other formal consequences in *Nadja*. It leads him to reject the traditional logic of a single continuous narrative with a clear beginning, middle, and end, in favor of a complicated arrangement of texts, beginning, not with Nadja's story, but an anecdotal prologue in which events were to be "related without preestablished order, and according to the mood of the moment" (23). "I intend to mention, in the margin of the narrative I have yet to relate," he declared, "only the most decisive episodes of my life *as I can conceive it apart from its organic plan,* and only insofar as it is at the mercy of chance . . ." (19).[22] Deliberately discarding the temporal logic of traditional autobiography, he also implicitly rejects the conceptions of causality and influence that led biographers and autobiographers to see the child as the father of the man.

Of course, *Nadja* is by no means Breton's attempt at writing traditional autobiography, although his insistence on "knowing the names" of characters in books, and "on being interested only in books left ajar, like doors," or transparent, like glass houses in which the occupant is always on view, makes the autobiographical dimension of his writing abundantly clear (18). The initial section of *Nadja* indicates how much he is aware of the difficulties of coming to terms with time in any effort to answer the fundamental question of autobiography: "Who am I?" with which he begins his story.[23] This initial section presents his account of the events that marked a crucial period in his life as an ongoing inquiry rather than an effort to present "a completed image of my mind that need not be reconciled with time" (12). Yet when we consider the work as a whole, it becomes clear that it is precisely Breton's inability to reconcile the photographic image with time that explains his dissatisfaction with the "illustrated part" of *Nadja.*

It is only in the concluding section of *Nadja* that Breton explains that he had begun the book "by going back to look at several of the places to which this narrative happens to lead; I wanted in fact—with some of the people and some of the objects—to provide a photographic image of them taken at the special angle from which I myself had looked at them." (151–52). Ultimately the photographs he included fell into a somewhat broader range of subjects: images of buildings, monuments, and storefronts, portraits, objects, as well as photographic reproductions of drawings, letters, and texts.

Breton did not take the photographs, contenting himself with whatever photographs were available or could be provided by friends and fellow Surrealists. Man Ray contributed portraits of Surrealists Paul Eluard, Benjamin Péret, and Robert Desnos, while Jacques-André Boiffard

and Henri Manuel took some other portraits and shots of Paris streets and monuments. None of the images has the "mannered" experimental qualities Sontag associates with the Surrealist legacy to photography. Man Ray's portraits of Eluard and Péret are surprisingly unremarkable—even boring—frontal views of his subjects, while his two photographs of Desnos, rubbing his eyes as he wakes from the hypnotic sleep during which he spoke and wrote with a Surrealist "voice," are sequential shots apparently snipped from the photographer's contact prints. The frequently puzzling, contradictory relationship of these photographs to Breton's story, their banal realism, and their striking similarity to the "postcards" he condemned make a curious impression on the reader and have drawn increasing critical attention. Breton himself deemed the *Nadja* photographs inadequate, mentioning in particular: "Becque surrounded by sinister palings, the management of the Théâtre Moderne on its guard, Po[u]rville dead and disillusioning as any French city" (152).

The inadequacy of the images would have been a serious blow to the realization of *Nadja* had they actually been substitutes for description. However, the photographs only rarely serve this function. In some cases the photographs actually repeat Breton's text, as in the passage that gives detailed notes on an unknown object found at the flea market: a "kind of irregular, white, shellacked half-cylinder covered with reliefs and depressions that are meaningless to me, streaked with horizontal and vertical reds and greens" (52). A black and white photograph of the same object follows some three pages later.[24] Nor do the photographs necessarily correspond to crucial elements of Breton's account. As Michel Beaujour points out, not even "the most obtuse reader" would require the photographs Breton provides of the *Librairie de l'Humanité* or the *Château Saint Germain,* both of which are mentioned only in passing.[25] Other photographs have only indirect connections to Breton's story and actually compete with it by reproducing tempting—just barely readable—fragments of other narratives: a page from an illustrated history text, a letter, a page taken from the scenario of the melodrama entitled *The Embrace of the Octopus.*

In fact, Breton's disappointment with the photographs of the statue of Henri Becque, the management of the *Théâtre Moderne*, and the city of Pourville led to their elimination from the first edition of the book. (The bust of Becque, minus the offending palings, appears in the second edition, but the others do not.) Consequently, it seems more likely that Breton counted on the photographs to authenticate or corroborate his account and, accordingly, most critics stress the photographs' value as documents. Nonetheless, Breton's dissatisfaction with them suggests that despite his visual sophistication, he let down his guard, "forgetting" that photography was not a simple mimetic technique for reproducing things as he saw them. A desire that photography be just such a medium seems to be the source of the somewhat melancholy ambivalence toward photography already apparent in his 1925 essay on *Surrealism and Painting:*

> The photographic print, considered in isolation, is certainly permeated with an emotive value that makes it a supremely precious article of exchange . . . ; nevertheless, despite the fact that it is endowed with a special power of suggestion, it is not in the final analysis the *faithful* image that we expect to keep of what will soon be gone forever.[26]

We would expect Breton to despise photography as the technical perfection of the realist attitude, and seen from this perspective the "faithful" image merely capitulates to the logic of things as they are. Nonetheless, Breton is also fully aware of the medium's inherent capacity for visual distortion: "It [photography] begins by requiring that [its subjects] assume favorable attitudes," he notes in *Surrealism and Painting* apropos of Man Ray's art, "or goes even further and takes them unaware at their most fugitive moments."[27] Missing from the image in either case, however, is the invisible network of subjective and imagined relations that links Breton to what he sees. Although this network is a product of experience and a function of time, it is the most crucial element in defining the "special angle" from which Breton hoped to obtain photographs. In this respect certainly, the fragmentary revelations afforded by the time-bound nature of photography conflict with discontinuous but ongoing nature of Breton's autobiographical project. As Sontag suggests, "Life is

not about significant details, illuminated a flash, fixed forever. Photographs are."[28] However, Breton's definition of photography as an ineluctably *unfaithful* image "of what will soon be gone forever" is by no means naive. In its juxtaposition of past and present, its anticipation of the future and of future loss, it suggests a temporal complexity that finds an echo in the textual complexity of *Nadja*.

Breton fragments his account by writing multiple beginnings, sometimes substituting them for conclusions. Clearly they provide opportunities to "start over," to change focus and direction, even if the reader might criticize them as "false starts" or delays. Without counting the "Foreword," separated from the original prologue by thirty-five years, there are still a number of beginnings in *Nadja:* Breton's account of "the most decisive events" of his life, begun ten pages into the story, concludes with another beginning as he announces "without further delay, Nadja's appearance on the scene" (60). In the closing section of the book Breton returns to the beginning to explain under what circumstances he started to write *Nadja* and concludes the book by evoking a new period, just opening before him, with the woman, so unlike Nadja, whose presence is to change his life "for all eternity" (158).

At the heart of *Nadja*, bracketed by these multiple beginnings, are fragments of a diary punctuated by ellipses ("the sudden intervals between words in even a printed sentence" [148]) that function both spatially and temporally, suggesting Breton's growing distance from the events he recounts and the passage of time that is responsible for it. The ellipses are echoed by footnotes that register the writer's changing perspective on the past events he recounts in the figurative present tense of the diary. While the text reflects Breton's experience by remaining open, "ajar," incomplete—allowing him to stage a series of new beginnings and to reinterpret past events as he comes to see them in a new light—the photographic image, which records only one moment in a temporal trajectory, injects an element of finality into his account. Breton's uneasiness about this finality, the sense of loss that he associates with it, emerges in an anecdote he appended as a footnote to the last section of *Nadja:*

I remarked, while idling on the quay of the Vieux-Port in Marseille, shortly before sunset, a curiously scrupulous painter struggling with skill and speed on his canvas against the fading light. The spot of color corresponding to the sun gradually descended with the sun. Finally, nothing remained. The painter suddenly discovered he was far behind: he obliterated the red from a wall, painted over one or two gleams lingering on the water. His painting, finished for himself, for me the most *unfinished* thing possible, looked very sad and very beautiful. (148)

What moves him about a painting whose "scrupulous" realism should have given him pause, is precisely the sense of loss he associates with his inability to recapture the places and people who figure in his account.

Despite his desire to capture his subjects from his own special angle, the photographs Breton chose are for the most part literal, frontal views

"Plate 26: The Sphinx Hotel, Boulevard Magenta." From André Breton, Nadja *(1928; reprint, New York: Grove Press, 1960).* ©1960. Courtesy of Grove Press, Inc.

"Plate 8: Porte Saint Denis." From André Breton, Nadja *(1928; reprint, New York: Grove Press, 1960).* ©1960. Courtesy of Grove Press, Inc.

that center their subjects. Evenly lit, they do not include shadows or play with visual patterns, nor do they fragment their subjects in extreme close-ups or distort them by adopting the unusual angles characteristic of much of the avant-garde European photography of the period. In fact, Boiffard's photograph of the *Porte Saint Denis* has more in common with Baldus's topographical views from early 1850s—photographs which were made as part of a survey of important monuments and buildings for the *Commission des monuments historiques*.[29] Even a more complicated photograph such as Boiffard's Paris street view, owes whatever enigmatic qualities it possesses to the curiously suggestive name "Sphinx Hotel" that can be read on the sign floating high above street-level in the upper center of the photograph. Boiffard eschews all formal effects in this photograph other than an evocation of deep space, which is in itself relatively unusual. Almost all of the photographs other than that of the *Porte Saint Denis* situate their objects in a shallow foreground, most frequently placing them parallel to the picture plane. Their relative "flatness" contributes to the viewer's feeling that they banalize their subjects. The reader tends to make sense of the "illustrated part" by seeing it as an adjunct or supplement to the text rather than as a mimetic extension of it.[30] As Judith Preckshot suggests, they might be compared to "mementos," visual equivalents for Breton of the matchbooks, ribbons, train tickets, concert programs, and postcards that get tucked in an album.[31] However, a traditional family album suggests a chronological progression, an "organic plan" that would have implicitly answered the question "Who am I?" with reference to a larger family group within which the unfolding of an individual history would parallel that of a generation and an era.

Breton's "album" attempts to exclude such a sense of history. Certainly this is in part because he refuses to impose the logic of chronological time on his experience, preferring instead to adopt "sudden parallels, petrifying coincidences" and "harmonies struck as on the piano" (19) as organizing principles for his story. However, it is also implied in the way he frames the nature of his autobiographical project. Given his hatred of family, Breton's effort to answer the question "Who am I?" would hardly have relied on family resemblances, but even when this frame of reference extends to a human family Breton deliberately seeks the nature of his *difference:* "I strive, in relation to other men, to discover the nature, if not the necessity, of my difference from them. Is it not precisely to the degree I become conscious of this difference that I shall recognize what I alone have been put on this earth to do, what unique message I alone may bear, so that I alone can answer for its fate?" (13).

Breton's effort to discern the grand design of his destiny deliberately focuses on what he refers to as the "petty events of daily life" where the personality "expresses itself quite freely and often in so distinctive a manner" (13). If the project suggests a fleeting resemblance to Freud's *Psychopathology of Everyday Life,* Breton does not acknowledge it. Rather, as an example of the sort of anecdotal evidence he is seeking, Breton cites a little ritual ascribed to the aged Victor Hugo, who, accompanied by Juliette Drouet, took the same carriage ride every day past a particular estate. According to Breton, Hugo never failed to point out the estate's carriage entrance to Drouet, who never failed to respond by pointing out the smaller pedestrian entryway. "How could the best possible study of Hugo's work give us a comparable awareness, the astonishing sense of what he was?" Breton asks (14). While not all readers of Breton's account will find this anecdote equally enlightening, Breton's conclusion is particularly revealing because it demonstrates his inability to draw conclusions about the meaning and relative significance of such anecdotes: "Those two gates are like the mirror of his [Hugo's] strength and his weakness," Breton asserts. "*We do not know which stands for his insignificance, which for his greatness*" (14, my emphasis). The reversibility of the signs is indicative of Breton's general uncertainty about how to weigh such evidence, and where to place it in the order of things. Consequently, he prefers the parataxis of juxtaposition to a chronological ordering that would require some judgment about the relative importance of events or require the subordination of one to another.

What Breton hopes to do, however, is to surprise the form of his unique sensibility in the pattern of its associations. In this sense, perhaps, the open, parataxic qualities of *Nadja* could be better compared to a collection than an album. The subjective order of the personal collection could then substitute for a chronological narrative. It would merely expand to accommodate new elements, reshuffling the order of things as different priorities dictated new arrangements. The ultimate referent of such a collection would not be the collector's life, but the collector's sensibility. Yet the particular qualities of Breton's sensibility, its perception of time and events, stand out more clearly when they are compared to the work of the photographer Jacques-Henri Lartigue in the album of photographs entitled *Diary of a Century*.

At first glance, nothing could appear farther from *Nadja* than *Diary of a Century*. While Lartigue was Breton's contemporary, his family belonged to an "aristocracy" of wealthy industrialists. His father, an avid amateur photographer, gave his son a camera when he was seven years old, in part, the reader gathers, because the younger Lartigue was obsessed with taking photographs of everything in sight. Lartigue grew up with the camera, and the innumerable photographs he took of his family suggest that they formed a warm, tightly-knit circle around him. In its focus on family activities, the album could hardly be more traditional, although as an amateur unhampered by convention Lartigue invented his own variety of candid shots and frequently opted for special effects: plunging perspectives, inclusion of shadows, backlighting, and (most characteristic of his work as a whole) stop-action shots, effects which anticipated the avant-garde photography of the twenties and thirties. Lartigue also kept a diary, jotting down notes on the weather, the events that filled the day, the games he played with his friends and older brother, what they had for lunch or dinner (all the descriptive minutiae Breton would dismiss from his account), and sketched little diagrams of the photographs he had taken that day in order to have a record of them if they did not turn out.[32]

Never a professional photographer, Lartigue worked as a painter before the First World War; his photographs were not "discovered" until much later and not exhibited until 1962. His work remains something of an enigma, its formal sophistication and sly humor suggesting an artist fully conscious of his powers and of the potential of his medium at an astonishingly early age. However, Lartigue has always insisted on his status as an amateur who paid little attention to the work of other photographers, even if he did enjoy looking at the photographs in *Vogue* and *Harper's Bazaar*.[33] The tension in his work between childlike naïf and conscious artist remains impossible to resolve, although Lartigue's insistence on his having kept the eyes of a child has gradually come to suggest a philosophical position.

Nonetheless, photography was an essential part of his experience of the world for seventy years. His diary and photographs represent an extremely valuable personal record of which *Diary of a Century* is only a selection. Not intended for publication, Lartigue's diary might be considered the perfect example of a family album, although the English title, *Diary of a Century*, asks the reader to view it, by extension, as social history.[34] The short, laudatory appraisal written by Anaïs Nin that serves as the epigraph to the English edition addresses both its value as a historical document and as the expression of a particular sensibility:

> The opening photograph, taken at the turn of the century, of Jacques-Henri Lartigue as an impish boy with his precious camera sets the tone of this book: one of human tenderness, humor and intimate charm. It is a family album illustrated by a keen, mischievous, and surrealist observer. Because of the wide range of the family's experience and Lartigue's curiosity, it becomes the history of a century. The first photograph of his father and mother also reveals the eye of the one who loves. He will not only photograph everything he loves but only at the moment of vivid life and motion, and incidentally give the portrait of an age. He has a sense of motion, change, elusiveness. No figure is posed.

It is Lartigue's sensibility, his role as "surrealist observer" that suggests a comparison of his work with that of Breton. Although only two years older than Breton, Lartigue was never a member of the Surrealist group or even in contact with them, so using the adjective *surrealist* to describe his work as a photographer does not have connotations of association or influence. Rather, Nin's choice of the term seems to reflect the intuitive perception of an unusual quality in many of the photographs that breaks the continuity of the narrative, creating a gap between these images and the story that accompanies and frames them.

Ostensibly consisting of excerpts from Lartigue's diaries, the text identifies the people and events represented in the photographs by giving some indication as to when, where, and in what circumstances they were taken. The narrative develops chronologically, according to an "organic plan," so the reader ages with Lartigue, watching his life unfold and moving with him in ever enlarging circles of persons and events. The photographs illustrate different periods of Lartigue's life, each marked by certain enthusiasms and key events: his acquisition of the camera, the games that led him to explore his world, his fascination with the workings of cars and planes that intensified his sense of movement and speed, his growing interest in women and fashion, his marriage, the birth of his first child, the death of his second child, his father-in-law's death, his divorce. While the photographs are intended to be the focal point of the diary, their association with the text frequently reduces them to illustrations of it, blunting the reader's perception of striking compositions, which viewed in isolation might alter the perception of seemingly traditional subjects.[35] The text focuses the reader's attention on the content of the photographs.

The chronological presentation of the photographs allows the reader to see the extraordinary changes in dress, lifestyle, and technology in the course of an individual lifetime. In fact, the success of *Diary* as incidental social history depends on the paradoxical relationship between ordinary and extraordinary in the events Lartigue portrays. Nin suggests one reason for considering Lartigue's experience extraordinary when she speaks of its range. In a truer sense, however, it is a very limited range, for Lartigue belonged to a privileged class and his vision of the world reflects this. Nonetheless, the fascinating photographs of early cars, balloons, and gliders that suggest the most dizzying and significant changes of the era would not have been possible had Lartigue's family not been wealthy enough to take a serious interest in them. Lartigue and his brother ("Zissou") play at realizing fantasies of flight by building and testing a wide variety of experimental vehicles ranging from hybrid contraptions—part bobsled, part kite, part airplane or bicycle—to full-fledged gliders. These and other fantastic inventions (including Zissou's "tire-boat," which its inventor confidently demonstrated by risking his suit, tie and—ultimate expression of faith—his wristwatch) attest to the entrepreneurship of an earlier industrial age. However, the Lartigues' neighbors and relatives are also representative, yet exceptional, person-

alities of the age: childhood playmate Suzanne Lenglen is the first woman tennis champion; Lartigue's father-in-law is the director of the Paris Opera. Through his family connections, Lartigue associates with famous actors and actresses, painters, and well-known socialites. His family is even among the first to travel to Saint-Moritz for the not-yet-popular "winter sports."

The slow, gradual progression of the diary softens the shock of the changes and conveys the comforting feeling that despite these incredible changes—a way of life that now seems natural will one day seem both odd and ridiculous; technology changes the form of our lives and our human possibilities; people we love will leave us and people we love will die—there is some continuity in life, in society, in history and we have our place in it. Every effort is made to present the photographs in the light of historical continuity. The first photograph of *Diary* shows Lartigue as a small boy with his first camera; in the last photograph Lartigue jauntily poses for the photographer Hiro while a friend snaps their picture. Although there is some variation in the chronological presentation where the reader is asked, by means of certain juxtapositions in the layout, to compare and to measure the "temporal" distance spanned by two photographs—Lartigue's parents as a young couple, with their portrait as aging grandparents; photographs contrasting fashion and manners then and now; a first photograph of Lartigue's cousin on the beach in 1904 with her birthday photograph "full of life sixty-five years later"—the reader is clearly intended to conclude that "plus ça change, plus ça reste la même chose."

However, the effort to place Lartigue's work in the category of social history normalizes and flattens the unusual qualities of the photographs that Nin intuitively ascribed to the "surrealist" observer. These "surreal" photographs surprise the reader and clash with the normalizing effect of the narrative. Unique images, they do not illustrate the narrative but disrupt its continuity, raising questions about the nature of experience and the meaning of individual events. It is the strangeness and singularity of the vision implied by certain of Lartigue's photographs that justify the use of the term "surrealist observer" in Anaïs Nin's appreciation of *Diary of a Century*.

"Zissou in his tire boat," by Jacques-Henri Lartigue.
From Diary of a Century *(New York: Penguin
Books, 1970).* ©*J. H. Lartigue/Photo Researchers.*

Long before the technology that would make such a choice commonplace, Lartigue stops time in his photographs, freezing his subjects in impossibly graceful and ridiculous gestures. He prefers his subjects when they are "out of their element," frequently portraying them as lighter than air. He practices his own version of the surrealist *dépaysement* or decontextualization of familiar objects, remaining outside the events he records by portraying them as though he were an observer from another time or another planet. That some of these photographs represent a kind of found surrealism is undeniable: a photograph of Lartigue's nanny "Dudu" watching a ball eternally suspended above her head by the click of the shutter is one such glimpse of a familiar world made strange by a new technology, but such images are far too frequent to admit the hypothesis that they are all happy accidents that befell a novice photographer. In the case of this particular photograph, the camera captures the event with a superreal precision in which every leaf on the trees behind Dudu seems to have an independent presence. The somewhat uneven exposure of the film gives the ball the eerie glow of an extra-terrestrial object about to descend. The photograph dilates time, transforming what must have been a simple game of toss and catch into a portentous event.

Other photographs memorialize events, but undercut their seriousness as memorials with a sly deflating suggestion of the ludicrous lurking in all (and particularly all "important") human events. Lartigue's photograph of his brother Zissou posing in front of the dirigible *Colonel Renard* is taken from so far away that Zissou seems to be lost in an empty landscape under the huge cigar-shaped cloud of the dirigible. Lartigue photographed his cousin Simone Roussel on the beach, yet he does not center the photograph on her, but on a large black dog (never mentioned in the narrative) who appears to gaze at her as though she were some wondrous or monstrous object emerged from the sea. Yet not all of the photographs are humorously surreal: a beautiful photograph of the "take off of the Gordon Bennet balloon race" shows two fragile fantastic figures in a balloon silhouetted against the sky, escapees from one of Odilon Redon's lithographs.

"Local, ethnic, classbound, dated," all of Lar-

tigue's photographs have the particularity Susan Sontag ascribed to the surreal but nothing of the surreal attractions she attached to lost images of the past adrift in the currents of modern sensibility, open to any interpretation. Sontag concluded that "what renders a photograph surreal is its irrefutable pathos as a message from time past and the concreteness of its intimations about social class."[36] However, in contrast, the surreal quality of many of Lartigue's images derives from the fact that they escape history and time by virtue of being frozen in the seemingly infinite potentialities of an incompleted gesture. Such photographs provide a way to overcome the sense of finality and loss that Breton associated with the photographs in *Nadja* (and with all "finished" works) because, like the artist's sunset, they embody only one possible representation of the subject, achieved by the exclusion of all other possibilities.

Yet the most powerful of Lartigue's surreal images are those that freeze time in moments of perception that displace normal or logical frames of reference. Like Lartigue's photograph of his cousin on the beach, certain of his images force the viewer to reconsider the nature of the obvious and consider the potential ridiculousness of reality seen from another point of view. Other photographs subvert the logic that determines the relative significance of events and consequently their place in the order of things. Lartigue frequently undercuts the seriousness of important events and raises the seemingly inconsequential to the level of the portentous. If this is a "child's logic," it is also a Surrealist "logic," because "the mind which plunges into Surrealism relives with glowing excitement the best part of its childhood," as Breton maintained in 1924, although he added more poignantly, "It is perhaps childhood that comes closest to one's 'real life'; childhood beyond which man has at his disposal, aside from his laissez-passer, only a few complimentary tickets; childhood where everything nevertheless conspires to bring about the effective, risk-free possession of oneself."[37]

Clearly, Breton felt his encounter with Nadja represented a significant moment in his life, perhaps even one of these "complimentary tickets." The writing of *Nadja* presented the opportunity, not only to fulfill Nadja's prophecy that he would

"My First photo of my cousin Simone Roussel" or "Simone Roussel on the Beach at Villerville," by Jacques-Henri Lartigue. From Diary of a Century *(New York: Penguin Books, 1970). ©J. H. Lartigue/Photo Researchers.*

write about her—about them—but to understand the significance of their relationship and, potentially, the enigma of his difference. His desire to avoid a logic that would reduce the unknown to the classifiable dictated his recourse to parallels, coincidences, and harmonies and explains his treatment of the events as "one of those chance arrangements, of more or less unfamiliar character, whose secret we feel might be learned merely by questioning ourselves closely enough" (17). However, he was not successful in eluding either the snares of logic or of history. Forced to concede Nadja's madness, or at least the desirability of restoring her to "an acceptable sense of reality" (142), he also reintroduced history at the center of *Nadja* where he related events as they happened, day by day, in order to insist on the factual nature of the account. Ultimately his own historian, he is forced to assign at least some provisional meaning to these events in order to conclude the book and be able to look toward the future.

The photographs in *Nadja,* unlike those in *Diary of a Century,* reinforce a sense of the "pastness" of these events. Time-bound, they reflect a particular moment of Breton's history and of the history of the city of Paris itself, and it is through these photographs, or the inability to take them, that Breton is forced to come to terms with the concrete effects of the passage of time. The city has changed: he can no longer recognize all of the strategic landmarks of his account. In this sense, the photographs remind the reader, as they must have reminded Breton, of the elusive character of "reality," the irreversible change in oneself and others over time and the irreparable loss of what escapes us even when we try to get some sense of who we are.

Yet Breton did not want to see the present in terms of the past. He concluded *Nadja* in the hope and the expectation that the unknown revelations of the future would reorder past events in accordance with what he would then recognize as his destiny. He left *Nadja* ajar, like a door, in order to leave an opening for "the event from which each of us is entitled to expect the revelation of his own life's meaning" (60). Lartigue's surrealist photographs, on the other hand, open doors in his narrative through which the viewer escapes, eluding the inexorable logic of time and the gravity of human events.

NOTES

1. Max Ernst, *Beyond Painting* (New York: Wittenborn, Schultz, 1948), 177.

2. Ibid.

3. Simon Watney, "Making Strange: The Shattered Mirror, in *Thinking Photography,* ed. Victor Burgin (London: Macmillan, 1982), 168.

4. André Breton, *Surrealism and Painting,* trans. Simon Watson Taylor (London: Macdonald and Co., 1965), 32.

5. Dawn Ades, "Photography and the Surrealist Text," in *L'Amour fou: Photography and Surrealism* (New York: Abbeville Press, 1985), 155.

6. Edouard Jaguer, *Les Mystères de la chambre noire: le Surréalisme et la photographie* (Paris: Flammarion, 1982).

7. Nancy Hall-Duncan, *Photographic Surrealism* (Akron, Ohio: Akron Arts Institute, 1979), 5.

8. Rosalind Krauss, "Photography in the Service of Surrealism," in *L'Amour fou: Photography and Surrealism* (New York: Abbeville Press, 1985), 24. See also Krauss's "The Photographic Conditions of Surrealism," *October* 19 (Fall 1981): 3–34; and "Corpus Delicti," in *L'Amour fou* (New York: Abbeville Press, 1985), 15–100.

9. Susan Sontag, *On Photography* (New York: Farrar, Straus & Giroux, 1977), 47, 48.

10. Of course other Surrealists, notably Tabard and Ubac, the latter having discovered and practiced *brûlage* and *petrification,* should be included here. The bulk of Brassaï's work for *Minotaure,* most of it documentary, does not really fit the critical framework Sontag establishes. More specific information on technique and particular photographers can be found in the individual biographies of Surrealist photographers included in *L'Amour fou.* See also Dawn Ades, *Photomontage* (London: Thames and Hudson, 1976), 132, and Edouard Jaguer's *Les Mystères de la chambre noire: le surréalisme et la photographie* (Paris: Flammarion, 1982).

11. Not that she was the first to discover the "Sabbatier effect."

12. See also Jaguer, *Les Mystères de la chambre noire.*

13. Nancy Hall-Duncan, *Photographic Surrealism* (Akron: Akron Arts Institute, 1979), 11.

14. Sontag, *On Photography,* 49.

15. The Surrealists discovered that the flea market was a more rapid-acting cultural solvent than time (and in some cases it accelerated the action of time) in separating objects and images from their historical contexts and utilitarian functions. They collected "found objects" as well as old and new photographs, postcards, and curious images of all kinds, some of which made their way into the pages of reviews such as *La Révolution Surréaliste,* along with photographs "borrowed" from scientific and anthropological disciplines. Such images were intended to disorient the reader by suggesting the mysterious nature of reality.

The importance of the flea market as a model for a kind of cultural refuse dump that dissolves the relationship between art, history, and junk by no means escapes Sontag. See *On Photography,* 69. Yet for the purposes of argument, one assumes she down-plays this aspect of Surrealist activity.

16. See also chapter 1 of "The Eye of Paris and the Surrealist Observer" in Marja Warehime, *Brassaï: Images of Culture and the Surrealist Observer,* (Baton Rouge: Louisiana State University Press, 1995).

17. André Breton, *Nadja,* trans. Richard Howard (New York: Grove Press, 1960). This is a reprint of the 1928 edition of *Nadja;* Jacques-André Lartigue, *Diary of a Century,* trans. Carla Van Splunteren (New York: Penguin Books, 1970), unpag.

18. André Breton, *Manifestoes of Surrealism,* trans. Richard Seaver and Helen R. Lane (Ann Arbor: University of Michigan Press), 128.

19. Ibid., 124.

20. Renée Riese Hubert, *Surrealism and the Book* (Berkeley: University of California Press), 256.

21. André Breton, *Nadja* (Paris: Gallimard, 1964). The Foreword appears in the second French edition of *Nadja* and is not included in the English translation of the novel, which is based on the 1928 Gallimard edition.

22. Critics have consistently emphasized the discontinuous nature of the narrative. In 1967 Michel Beaujour noted that "the book is presented as a series of notes hastily jotted down and assembled in an open dossier, always ready to include new material." Michel Beaujour, "Qu'est-ce que *Nadja?*" *La Nouvelle Revue Française* 170 (April 1967): 781. More recently, Dawn Ades referred to it as "a series of heterogeneous fragments and anecdotes with, at its center, the record of an encounter and subsequent relationship." Dawn Ades, "Photography and the Surrealist text," in *L'Amour fou* (New York: Abbeville Press), 161.

23. The problem of autobiography should also be linked

to the Surrealists' fascination with portraits and self-portraiture. As Martine Antle points out, "No other artistic and literary movement has put so much emphasis on the portrait as a medium" (46). See Martine Antle, "Breton, Portrait and Anti-Portrait: From the Figural to the Spectral," in *André Breton Today*, ed. Anna Balakian and Rudolf E. Kuenzli (New York: Willis, Locker and Owens, 1989), 46–58.

24. The use of the photograph is noted both by Beaujour in "Qu'est-ce que *Nadja*?" and Gerald Prince in "La fonction métanarrative dans *Nadja*," *French Review* (February 1976).

25. Beaujour, 786.

26. Breton, *Surrealism and Painting*, 32. The quote is taken with one modification from the English translation previously cited. However, I have altered the last line to make it reflect the French text more accurately. The Simon Watson Taylor English translation of *Surrealism and Painting* reads: ". . . that we aim to retain of something that will soon be gone forever."

27. Breton, *Surrealism and Painting*, 32.

28. Sontag, 73.

29. Dawn Ades suggests that this documentary look is intentional, in keeping with the desire to provide evidence, and defends Boiffard's work as a photographer from implicit charges of a lack of skill or talent. This seems quite probable, and it is one of the peculiar enigmas of *Nadja* that the photographs both satisfy and frustrate Breton's desire to illustrate his account of things.

30. Hubert, *Surrealism and the Book*, 256. Hubert con-tends that Surrealist illustrators "shunned mimesis."

31. Hubert calls attention (in a footnote to the chapter on "Displacement of Narrative") to an unpublished paper by Judith Preckshot: "Breton's *Nadja, a Family Album*," which suggests the book "resembles the unordered collection of mementos that characterizes a family album" (n.3, 257). The published version of Professor Preckshot's paper has a rather different focus, but contains very rich and valuable analyses of the photographic material in *Nadja*. See Judith Preckshot, "Le Nu et le texte," *Lendemains* 51 (1988):71–85.

32. See Avedon, the Afterword of *Diary of a Century*, unpag.

33. Paul Hill and Thomas Cooper, ed., *Dialogue with Photography* (New York: Farrar, Straus, Giroux, 1979), 35.

34. The French title, *Instants de ma vie*, emphasizes the fragmentary, autobiographical nature of the photographic records with no pretension toward representing a period.

35. Some of these formal effects are lost in reproductions where there was no attempt to preserve the integrity of the images. Some are enlarged to the point of becoming blurred and grainy, others, printed over two pages, are partly swallowed up in the spine of the book; still others are cropped, altering or dissipating the effect of the original composition. The volume devoted to Lartigue in the Aperture series provides a far better sense of the extraordinary qualities of Lartigue's photographs.

36. Sontag, *On Photography*, 49.

37. Breton, *Manifestoes*, 40.

3

Photographs in Biographies: Joyce, Voyeurism, and the "Real" Nora Barnacle

Stephen Watt

The camera, [one critic] explains, can give you only one version of a sitter: the painter can give you a hundred. Here the gentleman hits on the strongest point in photography, and the weakest point in draughtsmanship, under the impression that he is doing just the reverse. It is the draughtsman that can give you only one version of a sitter. . . . Even when the photographer aims at reproducing a favourite aspect of a favourite sitter, as all artist-photographers are apt to do, each photograph differs more subtly from the other than Velasquez's Philip in his prime differs from his Philip in his age.[1]

—Bernard Shaw

Writing in 1902 to adduce qualities of the camera's "un-mechanicalness" and refute suppositions of the photograph's "natural" relationship with its referent, Bernard Shaw with typical Shavian prescience anticipated the similar positions of later commentators on precisely these issues. The photograph (mis)construed as the "pictorial equivalent of vision" remains, as Joel Snyder has more recently asserted, the "source" of our "unshakable belief in the congruence of picture and world."[2] Photographs, moreover, "make a special claim upon our attention be-cause they are supposed not only to look realistic (although they do not all look realistic) but also to derive from or be caused by the objects they represent."[3] Citing Snyder's among other critiques of photography's referentiality, Walter Benn Michaels observes that these days the "question of photography's status as an art is more likely to be asked as a question about photography's 'essence.'"[4] In what follows, I shall scrutinize the even more powerful referential claims of photographs in biographical writing, using as examples pictures of Nora Barnacle Joyce in Richard Ellmann's revised *James Joyce* (1982) and Brenda Maddox's *Nora: The Real Life of Molly Bloom* (1988).[5] That some photographs verify spatial or historical facts is not at issue here, even though these same photographs may only "memorialize a moment that is over before it is reproduced"[6]; rather, I am concerned with the "reading" of biographical photographs in light of post-structuralist meditations both on representation and on the object or "reality" represented.[7] If at all sympathetic to these theorizations, readers of biography find themselves placed in a compromised, paradoxical position: all too aware of skeptical revaluations of technologies of representation and of the "reality" represented, yet also desirous of more intimate knowledge of the subject of the biography. Given this position, how are the photographs that often play a significant part in biographical discourse to be read?

Ironically, in the wake of numerous interrogations of the cultural construction of such "realities" as subjectivity and gender, photography continues to be employed to corroborate and, at times, constitute versions of historical reality. The latter was the case with the Public Broadcasting System's popular series *The Civil War*, the narrative of which along with some five hundred illustrations, most of them photographs, was published as *The Civil War: An Illustrated History* (1990). Both series and book intimate the primacy of the visual in contemporary culture by subordinating historical narration to montages of largely photographic images. Here language supplements the picture instead of the other way around, the conventional way around, in the scripting of history—and of biography as well.[8] More important, in *The Civil War* the camera, whose birth is nearly coterminous with the events that hastened America into war, is advanced as the purveyor of knowledge of the awful truths of this conflict. In this chronicle, scenes from Sharpsburg, Chancellorsville, and Antietam "speak" of a nightmarish chapter in American history, as the film's makers tacitly endorse the premise that photographs—and passages from the letters and diaries of such eyewitnesses as Mary Chestnut—seem, to borrow Susan Sontag's phrasing, "because they are taken to be pieces of reality, more authentic than extended literary narratives."[9] Historical narratives might be appended to this sentence; in such a context, the pictorial image furnishes evidence of a past reality and, with it, knowledge itself.

If this claim to truth underlies the historian's deployment of photography and inflects our reactions to such pictures—I almost said "historical" pictures, but then all pictures are historical—how much more seemingly "natural" is such a claim for those images complementing biographical accounts. Yet more than complementarity is at work here, for the analogy Sontag makes between the authenticity of photographs and that of quotations proves germane to the

biographer's method. In an interview given at the time his expanded edition of *James Joyce* was published, Ellmann was asked to outline his methodology in writing biographies. He responded that while he had "never been able to work out one," he had usually relied upon one principle:

> I always put in a fair number of letters of Joyce. I felt that even if my own construction of his situation at a given time might be valid, it was just as well to see how he was writing himself about it. . . . One could have some sort of check upon the biographer's interpretation.[10]

Like quotations, then, photographs in a biography serve *at the very least* as a standard against which one assesses the interpretive constructions of the biographer. Indeed, reviewers frequently turned metaphorically to the plastic arts in praising Maddox's *Nora*: Shari Benstock alluded to Maddox's ability to "paint a particularly chilling portrait of family life *chéz* Joyce," and Bonnie Kime Scott commended the "visual qualities" of Maddox's prose.[11] But appeals to the visual amount to more than a trope in reviews of literary biographies, because photographs and quotations constitute parameters for biographical writing, providing the "sort of check" on authorial interpretation Ellmann implies. Renderings of a subject's life, one might say, can go no further than the pictures will allow.

This circumscription seems especially ironic given Christian Caujolle's definition of photography, portraiture in particular, as a "struggle between the subject and the photographer's interpretation."[12] For if it is true that photographs in biographies delimit scholarly elaboration of the biographical subject, they may also convey the incompletely realized intentions of photographers (as Michaels explains in developing an analogy between writing and photography in *The Gold Standard and the Logic of Naturalism*). As significant as the photographer's unrealized intentions is the reader of biography's tendency to privilege accompanying illustrations as more genuine, more "real" or truthful than the writer's narrative. Such a reader may study photographs more intently than s/he does biographical prose, as W. J. T. Mitchell (echoing Nelson

Goodman) contends: "A picture is normally 'read' in something like the way we read an ungraduated thermometer. Every mark, every modification, every curve or swelling of a line, every modification of texture or color is loaded with semantic potential."[13] In the case of late Victorian photographic subjects—and this would include the young Joyce and Nora Barnacle— Miles Orvell offers a more historical understanding of this "semantic potential": the "nineteenth century's practice of photography was founded on an understanding of the medium as an illusion, and the realism of Victorian photography is properly understood as an 'artifical realism,' in which the image offers the viewer a representation of reality, a typification, a conscious simulacrum—though a simulacrum that elicited a willing suspension of disbelief."[14] Biography, therefore, frequently produces the interpretive dilemma of encouraging our attentiveness to putatively realistic photographs that, at the same time, are neither natural nor verificational of any unitary reality (even if they were selected, as Ellmann chose passages from Joyce's letters, for exactly this verificational purpose). This paradox will become even more apparent after considering, as I shall momentarily, the photographs of Nora Barnacle Joyce in both Ellmann's and Maddox's biographies.

Its use in criminal and other judicial proceedings notwithstanding, then, photography cannot ratify an objective or unitary "reality" for at least two reasons: the reason of the camera's "unmechanicalness" as Shaw and Snyder propound, and the fact that a person photographed may be little more than a *poseur,* transforming him- or herself "in advance into an image."[15] To take only one small aspect of such self-fashioning or image-making, consider Anne Hollander's observations that "clothes create at least half the look of any person at any moment" and that what clothing helps create is "not so much a good physical feeling but a satisfying self-image."[16] Then consider Maddox's emphasis of the Joyces' near obsession with fashionable clothing: Nora "basked in Joyce's interest in her wardrobe" (*Nora* 100), made a "triumphant return" to Ireland in 1911 wearing "fine clothes" (*Nora* 119), "liked to change [fashions] with the times" (*Nora* 138), and so on. It is therefore hardly surprising

that photographs of her project vastly different images, although much more than fashion is involved in imaging—and more than the image's content accounts for a viewer's perception of something *as an image,* for his or her "curious ability to say 'there' and 'not there' at the same time."[17]

While contemplating photographs of his mother and bemoaning his inability to locate her "being" in the pictures, for example, Roland Barthes laments being "compelled" to "perform a painful labor; straining toward the essence of her identity, I was struggling among images partially true, and therefore totally false."[18] It is not so much that photographs or other illustrations in biographies are prevarications (although doubtless some are), but that they so often reveal only radically contingent realities. The camera is not a human eye and the object viewed is, in various senses of the word, an image: an "absence as presence" in the ways that Mitchell adumbrates and Barthes's painful reaction to his mother's face implies. In portraiture especially, the photographic image might be conceived in Sontag's commonsensical observation that "People want an idealized image: a photograph of themselves looking their best"; or, more radically in Peggy Phelan's assertion of photography's "performative nature," that "portrait photography reflects the transference of image between the photographer and the model."[19] In sum, photographs in biographies provide partial authenticity at best midst their plays of presence and absence, within their typically seamless fabric of informal or spontaneous snapshots and more rehearsed "performances."

Having voiced my skepticism about the recuperation of realities from such photographs, I shall nevertheless endeavor to extricate from several pictures of the Joyces what truths I can. Clearly this project and the premises that subtend it beg questions both of interpretive strategy and of readerly motivation; that is, if the photographs in Ellmann's *James Joyce* and Maddox's *Nora* cannot be relied upon to reveal a "real" Nora—and here I should also mention photographs of Joyce himself in Gisèle Freund's photo-biography, *Three Days with Joyce* (1985)— what hermeneutic will make them speak with authority? This and similar questions underscore the necessity of our developing new strategies not only to read photographs in biographies, but to decode images in a wide variety of cultural forms. Such innovations might be slow in arriving, though, for as Herbert Lindenberger explains, Anglo-American readers and literary critics harbor a "need" for mimesis; they "demand" a "likeness to life" from the texts they consume and bring to the interpretive act a pronounced "mimetic bias."[20] The strength of this bias, according to Mieke Bal, is "enhanced by its complicity with other oppositions that pervade modern cultural behavior." In one such opposition—the unity/fracturedness of a work—the privileged left-hand term, the conception of organic unity, remains a "powerful ideological weapon because of the pressure it exerts on the reader to choose one interpretation over another rather than to read through the conflict of interpretations. . . ."[21] Instead of becoming implicated in this process of selection and consequent suppression, Bal proposes that, as exegetes, we no longer "take for granted the wholeness enhanced by the [iconic or textual] detail, but instead . . . open the detail of the subversion that makes it the dominant element rather than the whole."[22] In other words, we must "dediscipline," then re-discipline our eyes to seize upon those details of a photograph that, in our need to reconcile illustration with narrative, we might otherwise discount or ignore. This retraining entails an investigation of a photograph's pre-text and an increased awareness of how that pre-text shapes our response, and invariably leads us back to Barthes's *punctum:* an iconographic detail or partial object which opens the photograph to multiple readings.[23]

Finally, as the authors of *The Civil War* defined their intentions for the volume's illustrations (some 475 selected from over 16,000 possibilities), "the documents of the past must be allowed to speak for themselves, to convey meanings and emotions and stories on their own."[24] On the one hand, this statement seems both uncritical and disingenuous, as various principles of selection must surely have dictated what photographs appeared in the volume and television series. On the other hand, however, wresting these illustrations from the modeling effects of historical narrative—as, to some extent, the authors of *The*

Civil War attempt to do by supplying only a minimal narrative account—allows historical artifacts a kind of independence, enabling them to testify in a more authentic voice, however muted. Similarly, other "real" Noras, or rather traces of them, exist at those margins of the photographic image that most of us have heretofore neglected to look. My task is to lift these details from their contexts and narrative pre-texts, study them, and then reinsert them disruptively into the unitary constructions in which they once languished so inconspicuously.

PHOTOGRAPHS, ATOMIZATION, AND POSSESSION

The [literary] work continues and the world keeps fluently turning, . . . never fixed in a definitive formulation. The critic cannot by any means get outside the text, escape from the blind alleys of language he finds in the work. He can only rephrase them in other, allotropic terms.[25]
—J. Hillis Miller

Like the fluid world Hillis Miller invokes, the protean world of *Ulysses* is always in flux, forever changing. In a motif Joyce appropriates from the W. V. Wallace-Edward Fitzball operetta *Maritana* (1845), life resembles a stream constantly flowing. So, in the "Lestrygonians" episode, Leopold Bloom, contemplating water, thinks, "It's always flowing in a stream, never the same, which in the stream of life we trace" (8: 94–95).[26] No one can own water, Bloom concludes; its fluidity protects it from possession. Miller suggests that the literary text's "literariness" imbues it with similar fluidity; as a result, literary criticism merely reforms or reinscribes it, constructing an allotrope of the original. Can photography, like Miller's criticism, continue "the activity" of the literary text, be regarded as a "continuation" of the reality it apparently replicates? Probably not. Photographs, as the evidence of *Ulysses* makes clear, in no way function in allotropic ways. Instead, photographs atomize or fragment reality, enabling it to be possessed more readily; they do not "continue" the stream of life, nor are they isotopes of their referents.[27] To borrow for the moment Orvell's more materialistic language, photography in the late nineteenth century promoted a kind of "surrogate ownership": "what could not be owned outright" could by means of photographic images be brought "into the eye of the parlor" and thereby increasingly whet the consumer's appetite for "vicarious experience."[28]

The desire to possess intimate knowledge of another through privileged spectation is, curiously enough, both a Joycean and a Bloomean one, as Joyce's protagonist in *Ulysses* unsuccessfully attempts to maneuver himself into a position of advantage in viewing the women (or artistic renderings of women) with whom he comes in contact.[29] To what extent do readers of biographies share the motives of various Joycean characters like Bloom who, even after they realize that "woman, in essence and in particular, has eluded" them, still possess her "by holding her image" in their eyes, thus fixing her "into a single position adapted" to their purposes?[30] In "Calypso," for example, Bloom spies a neighbor's slavey walking out of a butcher shop and plans, after concluding his business there, to follow her: "To catch up and walk behind her if she went slowly, behind her moving hams. Pleasant to see first thing in the morning" (4: 171–73). His plot is foiled, however; as he exits the shop, he scans the street to no avail: "No sign. Gone" (4: 190). In the next chapter, he "gazed across the street" to see a stylishly dressed woman board an "outsider" or coach: "Watch! Watch! Silk flash rich stockings white. Watch!" (5: 130). His view is quickly ruined by a passing tramcar, about which he concludes, "Always happening like that. The very moment. Girl in Eustace Street hallway Monday was it settling her garter" (5: 132–34). In "Circe," Bloom is accused of trafficking in "obscene photographs," and in "Ithaca" we learn of his possession of two sexually explicit "photocards." Such artifacts might be regarded as compensation for Bloom's inability to take specular possession of the women who move too quickly past his view. Something always impedes it, much as the biographer stands between us and Nora, slightly obstructing ours. The comparatively less mediated, more immediate photographs promise something more.

Photographs, unfortunately, seldom deliver on their referential promises, both in *Ulysses* and in biographies. Stated alternatively, of what or whom does one gain possession in a photo-

graph? In the "Nausicaa" episode, Gerty MacDowell, alluring until her movement reveals her heretofore undisclosed lameness, provides one possible answer: "See her as she is spoil all," Bloom opines. "Must have the stage setting, the rouge, costume, position, music" (11: 855–56).[31] Similarly flawed, yet for the diametrically opposite reason that the representation fails to match the reality instead of the reality not meeting the fantasized qualities of the representation, is the wrinkled picture of Molly that Bloom displays to Stephen Dedalus in "Eumaeus." Bloom's proffering of the photograph follows close on the heels of his dissertation on "female form" and the classical aesthetic: ". . . I was just looking at those antique statues there. The splendid proportions of hips, bosom. You simply don't knock against those kind of women here" (16: 891–93). Even though Molly's picture was taken by Lafayette of Westmoreland Street, "Dublin's premiere photographic artist," Bloom concludes that "no photo" could attain the beauty of classical statuary because photography "simply wasn't art in a word" (16: 1435–36; 1454–55). Moreover, even though the photograph was "very much like" Molly, it failed, Bloom decides, to "do justice" to her figure which "did not come out to best advantage in that getup" (16: 1445–46). Nor could the camera "do justice" to her "stage presence" (16: 1459–60). Hence, photographic representation either falls short of reality or, alternatively, reality falls short of representation (theatrical or photographic, and the performative aspect of both should not be overlooked); the camera cannot capture Molly's beauty adequately, and Dublin women cannot always match the anatomical splendor or sexual ardor of their counterparts on the stage, pedestal, or photocard. And men may not always want them to, as Bloom's admission in "Nausicaa" would seem to indicate.

Still, Joyce's male characters typically want to "fix" fleeting women in a single position—to impede the receding feminine and finally contain it.[32] And so do we in viewing photographs in a biography, unless one is prepared to argue, which I am not here, that gender differences obtain in the reception of these images. Following the theoretical articulations of such film scholars as Laura Mulvey, E. Ann Kaplan, and Mary Ann

Doane, my point is premised on the notion that in the viewer's position, the male or empowered position, all readers of biographical photographs "fix" or construct the identities of the photographed in whatever ways satisfy them. Until the publication of Maddox's biography, most Joyceans were apparently contented with Ellmann's representation (photographic and narrative) in *James Joyce* of the attractive, albeit intellectually inferior, Galway maid who became a loyal companion of the artist and a caring mother to his children.[33] The issue of Nora's "reality," however, finally involves more than identity politics or the dynamics of reading, although both topics present sufficient complications all by themselves. Watching his shadow fall over the rocks along Sandymount strand in "Proteus," Stephen Dedalus thinks, "I throw this ended shadow from me, manshape ineluctable, call it back. Endless would it not be mine, form of my form?" (3: 412–14). He decides probably not. It must be bounded, framed in some way: "Falls back suddenly, frozen in stereoscope. Click does the trick" (3: 419–20). "Trick" here retains a productive ambiguity: "does the trick" in the popular idiom implies resolution or answer, a finality demolished by the denotations of "trick." The click of the camera does both, producing a frame or container that seduces us into a presumption of intimate knowledge ("brief exposure?"), yet collapsing the potential for knowledge through its capacity for deception. Click does all sorts of tricks.

THE NORA WE DON'T KNOW, THE JOYCE WE DO

"She, she, she. What she?" Stephen wonders in "Proteus" only seconds after "Click does the trick." Some photographs of Nora are so dissimilar from others that we might find ourselves mumbling Stephen's question, or wondering if archivists and biographers are guilty of perpetrating their own perverse tricks. Surely all of these photographs cannot be of the same person. Or, perhaps this plurality of images is as it should be—or is exactly what Bernard Shaw meant some ninety years ago when debunking the notion of photography's mechanical limitations. Those reviewers of Maddox's biography, for ex-

ample, who could not find a "real" Nora by the volume's last pages (Mary O'Toole in the *James Joyce Quarterly*) or who felt that Maddox's Nora remained the same "shadowy figure" Ellmann had sketched earlier (Pat Carr in *Modern Fiction Studies*) might, in my view, have taken their theses from the photographs in both Maddox's and Ellmann's biographies.[34] For, based only on the photographic evidence in them, I am reduced to repeating Stephen's question: "She, she, she. What she?" All of them, of course. And the photographs present several more Noras than the pair most of us have known all these years: the vivacious and unschooled peasant girl with whom Joyce became infatuated in 1904 and the faithful companion whom he finally married nearly twenty-seven years and two children later. But *what* she could have so decisively conquered the young artist? And, what other shes might we locate?

Those photographs that foreground Nora's past in Galway, for instance, a past braided into both Gretta Conroy's revelation of a girlhood romance in "The Dead" and Molly Bloom's monologue in "Penelope," strike me as especially tricky business to decipher. I am thinking in particular of the first picture in Maddox's book of a very young Nora, taken by the Galway photographer R. W. Simmons some time between 1895 and 1900; Simmons's slightly later and more formal portrait of Nora used as the frontispiece of Padraic O Laoi's *Nora Barnacle Joyce: A Portrait* (1982); and the widely-viewed photograph of Nora in the role of Cathleen from a 1918 production of J. M. Synge's *Riders to the Sea* (reproduced by both Ellmann and Maddox).[35] As Bonnie Kime Scott remarks, *Nora* "makes a rich addition to the published photograph collection of the Joyce family," a collection embellished by Maddox's "detailed description of the apparel, as if that is Nora's contribution to the art of the family."[36] Based on Bloom's (and Joyce's) numerous observations and appraisals of women's appearances, it seems clear that Nora was *not* the only member of the family with a refined sense of fashion. More important, it is indeed matters of fashion and hairstyle that complicate these three photographs of Nora, in the process presenting us with three drastically different representations of her life in Galway. (Oddly, and by

*Nora Barnacle and most likely her grandmother, Cath-
erine Healy (ca. 1895–1900), by R. W. Simmons.
Courtesy of the Division of Rare and Manuscript Collections, Cornell University Library.*

*Nora Barnacle in Galway, by R. W. Simmons. Cour-
tesy of the Division of Rare and Manuscript Collections, Cornell University Library.*

Nora as Synge's Cathleen in Riders to the Sea
(1918). Reproduced in Richard Ellmann's James
Joyce *(Oxford: Oxford University Press, 1982, rev.
ed.) and Brenda Maddox's* Nora: The Real Life of
Molly Bloom *(Boston: Houghton Mifflin, 1988).*

contrast, whereas there are several distinct Noras to be discovered in these photographs, the vast majority of photographs of Joyce himself after he and Nora left Dublin in 1904 replicate his self-invention as a literary man—the bookish, at times dandyish, figure in suit or jacket living the contemplative life. John Berger's comment—"The suit was the first ruling class costume to idealise purely *sedentary* power"—seems especially apposite in this regard.[37] Sedentary power is virtually synonymous with literary power, as most photographs of Joyce confirm. The Joyce we know wears a coat and tie.)

The three "Galway Noras," as I shall term them, present three very different women, an assertion consistent with Maddox's aim to counter the prevalent stereotype of Nora as a "barefoot peasant from the moorland like J. M. Synge's Pegeen Mike." Among other things, Maddox insists, she was also "irretrievably urban . . . a city girl street-smart, with a ribbon in her hair, a sharp tongue in her head, and an uncle in the civil service" (*Nora* 11). Derived largely from O Laoi's account, Maddox's rendering of Nora's early years rebuts the myth that she was "ignorant and untutored"; in fact, she earned "good grades" in spelling and writing until she left school at age twelve (12–13). Maddox underscores Nora's "facility with fabric, ribbons, and starched ruffles" (20), a skill demonstrated to advantage in her portraits by Simmons, Galway's most "fashionable" photographer at the turn of the century. As I have mentioned before, Maddox returns again and again to Nora's good taste, even sophistication and cosmopolitanism (her cultivated taste for opera, for instance), an emphasis intended to refute Ellmann's portrayal of her. Ellmann's Nora, regardless of the several virtues he finds in her, has "no understanding of literature, and no power of or interest in introspection" (*JJ* 157); she is "handsome, jaunty, daring" yet woefully "untutored" (159). More or less following Ellmann's lead, save in the matter of Nora's social class, O Laoi, whose study, with the sole exception of the frontispiece, contains photographs only of Galway (as if it were really the subject of his book), pays tribute to Nora's physical beauty and spirited personality. In O Laoi's words, she was a "vivacious girl full of fun and devilment. She was very good looking, rather

tallish, blessed with beautiful auburn hair and sparkling eyes" (*NBJ* 23); and he quotes Henrietta Mulvagh, sister of a young man Nora knew in Galway, who remembers her as a "handsome, beautiful girl, with lovely auburn hair . . . a charming girl. She was the daughter of very respectable and highly respected parents" (37–38). According to O Laoi, she arrived in Dublin in 1904 a "tall, striking woman with a beautiful head of auburn hair and many is the man who met her and turned his head in amorous pursuit" (44).

One man captivated by this beauty was the young Joyce, who in his letters in the summer of 1904 reserves special praise for Nora's hair. "I looked for a long time at a head of reddish-brown hair and decided it was not yours," wrote a dejected Joyce after waiting for her on 15 June 1904; "Adieu, dear little brown head," he closed a letter to her on 8 July (*Letters* 2:42–43).[38] He was also quite obviously struck by Nora's statuesque carriage and vivacity, assets Michelene Wandor still finds lacking in the photographs in *Nora*, although such an indictment could be more justifiably brought against the illustrations in Ellmann's biography.[39] But, more to the point and to my quandary, does the Nora of the second photograph boast the same head of reddish-brown hair (or aura of "devilment" for that matter) which so enchanted Joyce in June 1904? How might we reconcile this self-consciously contemplative Nora with Ellmann's suggestion of her lack of introspection—or with the Nora described in Joyce's letter to his brother Stanislaus on 3 December 1904: a young woman who "admits the gentle art of self-satisfaction" and who has had "many lovers" (*Letters* 2: 72)? The very young Nora in the first photograph, tall with shoulder-length hair adorned with a ribbon, might very well be viewed as consonant with the young woman Joyce woos in his letters and O Laoi recounts in his book. But what are we to make of the second "Galway Nora"?

To begin, we might recognize that all three Galway Noras have in common their direct gaze toward the camera, an assertiveness indicative of confidence, strength, and independence. Nora returns our gaze with her own, never deferring to the viewer—or even to her own grandmother. Her own sense of empowerment distinguishes these and other pictures of Nora, and one might say that her own self-confidence as a woman also helped "make Joyce a man," his now famous characterization of her sexual aggressiveness in the early stages of their intimacy. Beyond this, we might also return to Orvell's privileging of illusion in Victorian photography and examine more carefully the conventional theatricalization of Simmons's photographs. That is, Simmons employed almost identical panoramas and properties for the backgrounds of both Galway photographs, creating a setting resembling Victorian productions of *Twelfth Night* or *A Midsummer Night's Dream*: a heavy stone terrace carved in classical fashion, a stone balcony complete with urn upon which one might rest a hand or arm, a backdrop painted with an appealing botanical vista. Such scenes were conventional not only in late-Victorian theatrical productions, but in highly illusory photographs as well. This was the case, for instance, with numerous photographs of late-nineteenth-century actresses as realized by America's preeminent theatrical photographer, Napoleon Sarony. He captures the international star Adelaide Neilson as Shakespeare's Juliet (1872) in the familiar surroundings of stone balcony and nearby garden. For Sarony, the camera was never "an instrument for recording a slice of life, for discovering the poetry and beauty in the real or commonplace world"; rather, Sarony's "business" was "illusion."[40] So, too, apparently, was Simmons's. Anyone who doubts this might compare these two pictures of Nora with any taken by Synge of Aran Islanders and collected in *My Wallet of Photographs* (published in 1971, although most of the book's fifty-three plates were shot between 1900 and 1905).[41] "The spinning-wheel," taken on Inishmaan and first published in 1901, shows two women in peasant dress standing in front of the crude stone walls so frequently found in Synge's photographs. The fashion, hairstyles, and setting all strongly distinguish Synge's Aran peasants from the "Galway Noras"—and his unvarnished realism from Simmons's more theatrical style.

The crucial difference between the two Simmons photographs, neither of them approximating the "slice of life" perspective of Synge's pictures of peasant life, resides in the features of the women themselves: in the image each pre-

Adelaide Neilson as Juliet (1872), by Napoleon Sarony. By permission of George Eastman House.

sents to the camera. The second Nora, in addition to looking quite different from the first "Galway Nora," hardly strikes one as "untutored" or "full" of "devilment"—and both portraits scarcely intimate a peasant upbringing. Just the opposite image seems strategically created in the second Nora through clothing, gesture, and hairstyle: a high-collared, rather formal-looking blouse complete with bow; the thoughtful posture of her head resting gently on her right hand; and, most conspicuously, the tightly drawn hair. Can it be said that *this* Nora "had no power of or interest in introspection"— or that she was unusually "jaunty" or "daring"? Can social class or specific information about family wealth be inferred from either photograph? Perhaps this absence reflects one aspira-

"The spinning-wheel," by J. M. Synge (ca. 1901). By permission of The Board of Trinity College Dublin and the J M Synge trustees.

tion of the late-Victorian illusory style practiced by such artists as Simmons and Sarony: precisely to erase class distinctions by resituating their subjects in an ahistorical and idyllic world more like the Forest of Arden than the harsh shores of Inishmaan or ghettoes of New York. Unlike the photograph from Synge's collection in which the spinning wheel predominates—or the numerous other images in *My Wallet of Photographs* of Aran Islanders boarding their fishing boats (*currachs*), minding their horses, or threshing grain—Simmons's contain no indication of the distribution of labor in western villages. In brief, no peasant or coquette appears in Simmons's portraits; instead, we see two remarkably different, highly

idealized, evocations of Nora's youth in Galway.

Of the three representations of Nora and her Galway heritage, perhaps the most compelling—and in some ways most misleading—is in actuality another sort of theatricalized simulation, again a highly stereotypical one: the photo from the 1918 production of Synge's *Riders to the Sea* by the English Players, a company founded by Joyce in Zurich to produce English-language plays (one of which was his own *Exiles*). As the *only* photograph in Ellmann's biography that conveys any connection between Nora and her past in western Ireland—indeed, as one of the few photographs of Nora of the over one hundred in *James Joyce*—this third "Galway Nora" has fascinated Joyceans for years. The third Nora is, in fact, not "really" Nora at all, but Nora playing Cathleen, the Aran Islander in Synge's tragic play. I find myself, on the one hand, in broad agreement with Maddox's reading of the picture:

> When photographs were taken of the production, Nora posed in character. Her picture was one of the best ever taken of her. In Aran costume and bare feet, with a hand on her hip and a saucy smile on her face, she is the embodiment of confident sensuality and of amused awareness of the absurdity of acting. (157)

Maddox's implication that from this time on Nora enjoyed conversation about the theater—and such other allusions to her cultural growth as her increasing fondness for Wagner's operas over Joyce's objection to them—more than counterbalances the pejorative connotations of Ellmann's adjective "untutored." Maddox, on the other hand, fails to recognize that all the sauciness and independence she finds in this photograph have very little to do with Synge's Cathleen. That is, whereas Nora is clearly *in costume*, she is *not* "in character" as Maddox claims; the differences between the two are enormous.

These differences render problematic Maddox's assertion that this is one of the "best" photographs ever taken of Nora and recall Maddox's similarly difficult characterization of Pegeen Mike in Synge's *Playboy of the Western World* as a "barefoot peasant," when in fact she is the daughter of a shebeen keeper and quite unlike the peasant girls who descend upon the tavern to meet Christy Mahon, the "playboy." The elder and more domestic of Maurya's two daughters in *Riders to the Sea*, Cathleen is kneading cake dough as the opening curtain rises and, after placing it in a pot-oven by the fire, begins to spin on a wheel. This, the most tragic of Synge's plays, thus begins with an elaboration of the same economy of labor that his photographs depict. Later, Cathleen breaks bread to give to her brother and frets over various superstitions associated with the perils of traveling from the Aran Islands to Galway, as her brother Bartley finally attempts, never to return. All the men in her family have taken this trip to death, leaving the women at home to occupy their days with "crying and keening." The gendered economy of Aran Island labor is hence rendered not only clearly but poignantly: the men travel to the outside world as often as the sea will allow them, while the women are tied to the home and to lives of baking, spinning, and, inevitably, mourning. The pre-text of the picture, therefore, totally opposes Maddox's reading of Nora's independence and confidence.

Other than its obvious overstatement of features associated with the Irish peasantry—the "saucy" smile on Nora's face and the right arm cocked confidently at her hip, aspects certainly of interest for any number of reasons, among the catalogue of these stereotypes—the photograph also presents a kind of fracture or *punctum* I find intriguing: namely, Nora's raised right heel. In the two Simmons portraits, Nora is immobile, poised in a meticulously composed frame, whereas in this picture she has been caught on the move. The arm on her hip signals her perturbed toleration of the photographer's interruption. Yet her body is canted slightly in the frame, leaning ever so slightly to the right. Once the shutter opens and closes, she will be on her way. This slight indication of movement, canted body and raised heel, makes all the difference, as the subject of the photograph has relented momentarily, "suffered" our "gaze" as the narrator of *A Portrait of the Artist as a Young Man* might phrase it, and cannot be posed or draped as a statue might. We get in this picture, therefore, a reiteration of the constantly moving woman in *Ulysses* conflated with a stereotypical exaggeration of the sensuality of the primitive (or of the colonial subject for that matter). The women in *Riders to the Sea* and *My Wallet of Photographs* never attain such mobility; their subservience to men in the play and their rootedness to the land make such inklings of "saucy" self-assertion unthinkable.

Stated alternatively, the *punctum* or fracture in both the stereotype and pre-text reveals the "sauntering" Nora whom Joyce found so attractive. As both Maddox and Ellmann agree, this term, suggestive of both confidence and mobility, accrues meaning in Joyce's correspondence with Nora at a crucial, anxiety-filled time in their relationship: the summer of 1909 when, having returned to Ireland, Joyce is led to suspect that Nora had been "seeing" another man when they first met in 1904. This crisis in their relationship, as has been much discussed, instigated a series of "dirty" letters between the two illuminating an extremely lurid side of their sexual life. But it also prompted, on Joyce's part, reveries of their early meetings in 1904 when the girl he loved "sauntered over" to him and assertively "took" him in her arms (*Letters* 3:233)—when his soul became a "pearl" after she came "sauntering" to him in "those sweet summer evenings" (*Letters* 3:237). The third Galway Nora, in no way Synge's Cathleen, might very well move purposefully after something or someone she wants. By contrast, the first Nora is constrained by her grandmother's hands on her left arm and shoulder; the second Nora, by the image of refinement she has fashioned for the portrait. The raised heel of the third Nora, the self-confident actress, might augur welcoming arms as well *and* the absence of any sense of embarrassment at initiating the embrace—or walking away from unwanted attention.

Maddox also presents other images of Nora, images selected for their potential to upset Ellmann's construction of a unitary Nora (mother and companion). The plates in Ellmann's volume are arranged into two groups, organized more or less chronologically, each of which would appear to advance a thesis insofar as Nora is concerned. The first grouping contains some sixty-eight photographs from roughly the first two-thirds of Joyce's life. The initial picture in the section is one of Joyce at age two taken in 1884, the last one of Joyce in Zurich in 1919. Nora appears in only four of these illustrations: the same photograph discussed above from *Riders to the Sea,* two with her family (one by Ottocaro Weiss with Joyce and the children at a restaurant, the other a lovely formal portrait from 1918 with her children Giorgio and Lucia which Maddox also reproduces), and a plate of Tullio Silvestri's impressionistic portrait of Nora painted in 1914. My point here is that outside of depictions of Nora as wife-companion and attentive mother—and excluding only the picture from the production of Synge's play—Ellmann's photographs in no way reproduce the Nora that O Laoi portrays. Instead, these photographs advance the notion of Nora as a dutiful wife and mother, fixing her to this single, extremely predictable identity. The second group of photographs in *James Joyce* covering the years 1920–1941 is more varied

in its representation of a middle-aged Nora, expanding her repertory of domestic selves (wife, mother) in a clear social direction. Of the nine photographs in which Nora appears, two reiterate her motherhood while several emphasize her friendships outside the home: with Galway residents on her 1922 homecoming trip, with Moune and Stuart Gilbert, with the John Sullivans, and so on. The famous photo of Joyce and Nora walking briskly on their wedding day with their solicitor also appears in this section, as does another painting. Ellmann's thesis for this latter set of images? An older Nora continues her duties as wife and mother, albeit within an expanded ambit of friends, critics, and literati.

One exception to this limited iconographic depiction of Nora in *James Joyce*—and to me the most complex after the "Third Galway Nora"—is a snapshot capturing a playful, slightly mysterious, and certainly informal side of the woman who took great care in attiring herself for more formal portraits. This picture, along with the two I have selected from Maddox's book, form another triptych of what I shall call mature "European Noras." The middle panel of this triad, the somewhat conservative 1928 portrait by Berenice Abbott, seems totally alien flanked by a playful Nora on one side and what Maddox terms a "Hollywood-style" Nora on the other. Besides her curious smile and the uneven lighting that adds a sense of mystery to the first of these— Nora is crossed horizontally by two lines of shadow, one across her breast and one near her forehead that denies us a clear view of her hair— two other details interest me. First, her right hand supporting her head virtually replicates the pose of the earlier Simmons portrait—what *could* she be thinking?—and second, unlike the blouses with the high or rounded necklines of the earlier portraits, the blouse here and in the other "European Nora" pictures has an open, slightly plunging neckline. The "Hollywood-style" Nora, of course, wears a dress with the most revealing neckline, but nonetheless all these pictures share this single quality. In the Abbott portrait, this may be a minor detail, and part of the portrait's conservatism is produced by the loose-fitting chemise Nora is wearing that prevents even the faintest sketching of the contours of her figure. The closed position of her hands

Nora in the late 1920s. From Ellmann's James Joyce *(Oxford: Oxford University Press, 1982, rev. ed.). By permission of the British Library.*

in her lap creates much the same effect—formal stiffness—whereas the elegant "Hollywood" Nora presents a totally different image of formality. For me, anyway, the first and third photographs in this triptych, so dissimilar in terms of costume, posture, and countenance, are very much alike in their production of a powerful sensuality. The former image promotes a playful, warm Nora; the latter, the statuesque beauty so many commentators remembered. And it is because this latter Nora is *too* perfect—too composed, too much like the Hollywood star Maddox sees—that one inevitably wonders to what extent this Nora, like the barefooted peasant of Synge's *Riders to the Sea,* is merely playing a role.

As this brief catalogue of photographic images and my readings of them are meant to

Portrait of Nora, by Berenice Abbott (1928). From Maddox's Nora *(Boston: Houghton Mifflin, 1988). By permission of Berenice Abbott/Commerce Graphics Ltd., Inc.*

Nora in the 1930s. From Maddox's Nora *(Boston: Houghton Mifflin, 1988).*

imply, there are more Noras in Maddox's biography than one can classify or conflate into a unitary figure. And details like a raised heel, folded hands, or theatrical backdrop—or a pretext—can help us gain access to these multiple personae, disrupting and subverting any fixed identity that an author or reader might ascribe to (impose on) the biographical subject. Barthes's *punctum* or Bal's fracturing iconic detail, if moved from the margins of our attention or transposed from what appears to be the background to the foreground, reconfirms the critique of essentiality both writers make. More important, it serves to help us check our own mimetic bias, our own desire for narrative unity in biographical writing.

Most photographs of Joyce, by contrast, pose a serious challenge to this method of interpretation, for in them he seems to perform the same role over and over again: the self-representation of a modern artist. Whether he is relaxing with his son Giorgio and grandson Stephen, consulting with Sylvia Beach or Eugene Jolas, or quietly reading at home, he is the well-known author: somewhat frail in the European pictures, nattily dressed in almost *fin de siècle* dandyish style, and almost always thoughtful in pose and gesture. All forty photographs in Freund's *Three Days with Joyce*—taken in Paris in 1937 and 1938, several of which appeared in *Gisèle Freund—Photographer* (1985)—tell this same story through similar conventions. Photographs of Paul Valéry, T. S. Eliot, Stephen Spender, Hermann Hesse, and others in the latter volume bear strong resemblances to those Freund took of Joyce, thus confirming conventions of self-representation for the modern writer visiting or living in Paris in the 30s and 40s. Invariably, the writer is sitting, shot in a close-up or medium close-up that just allows for a glimpse of well-stocked bookshelves in the background, and is reading intently or deep in contemplation, supporting his or her head with a hand. In this latter instance, a book typically lies sprawled in a lap or on a table; eyeglasses and smoking cigarette, frequent accoutrements of the artist, are optional but important and frequently utilized props. Moreover, Freund's several shots of Joyce, Sylvia Beach, and Adrienne Monnier at the Shakespeare and Company bookstore verify the close relationship between literature and photography in the Parisian art world in which Joyce moved. The walls of Beach's shop are adorned with nearly one hundred photographs (Monnier's shop La Maison des Amis des Livres was similarly decorated) and, in one of Freund's photographs of Shakespeare and Company, Joyce's portrait is prominently displayed under pictures of Shakespeare and Chaucer. Photography and the great tradition of British literature are thus closely related, as one of the color photographs Freund took of Joyce intimates: Joyce, neatly attired in tie and vest, seated in front of shelves of books, quietly studying a poem with the aid of his magnifying glass.

Freund's sessions with Joyce, in short, although productive of quite brilliant portraits of the artist as an older man, seem nonetheless constituted, as I have mentioned, of the predictable conventions of representing well-known modern writers. These portraits, therefore, depict and then reiterate the sedentary, contemplative life of a man in a suit with failing eyesight and a lively mind. And the same man reappears in earlier and later photographs alike, regardless of the setting or occasion.

Coda: Just about the time I actually began to believe in my thesis about photographs of Nora and Joyce—that there exist several Galway and European Noras, yet only one Joyce—I noticed Joyce's left hand in the shot of him holding the magnifying glass. Joyce apparently liked wearing large, even garish, rings, two of which are plainly visible on his third and fourth fingers in this picture taken in 1939. A year earlier, however, because she was attracted to Joyce's "extremely fine" hands, Freund took a close-up of him fingering his cane as if he were "playing a musical instrument."[42] The ever-present rings are still there, only this time on the index and middle fingers. Why the change? A hand ailment? A riposte of unconventionality to those who found his domestic arrangements too bourgeois? We shall probably never know—and we probably do not need to. But such fractures and *puncta* lurk in most iconic representations awaiting our recognition and valorization—and the provocative rereadings they might stimulate.

NOTES

I wish to express my gratitude to James Naremore for his insights into "Proteus" and to Laura Walls, Marsha Bryant, and several anonymous reviewers for their helpful criticism of this essay.

1. Bernard Shaw, "The Unmechanicalness of Photography—An Introduction to the London Photographic Exhibitions, 1902," in *Bernard Shaw on Photography*, ed. Bill Jay and Margaret Moore (Salt Lake City, Utah: Peregrine Smith, 1989), 77.

2. Joel Snyder, "Picturing Vision," *Critical Inquiry* 6 (1980): 514.

3. Snyder, 504.

4. Walter Benn Michaels, *The Gold Standard and the Logic of Naturalism: American Literature at the Turn of the Century* (Berkeley: University of California Press, 1987), 217.

5. Maddox's biography was in fact published with two different subtitles: in England, by Hamish Hamilton, as *Nora: A Biography of Nora Joyce;* in America, by Houghton Mifflin, as *Nora: The Real Life of Molly Bloom.* Throughout this essay I shall be quoting from the latter volume: *Nora: The Real Life of Molly Bloom* (Boston: Houghton Mifflin, 1988), hereafter cited in the text. I shall also cite in the text two other biographies: Richard Ellmann, *James Joyce*, rev. ed. (Oxford: Oxford University Press, 1982); and Padraic

O Laoi, *Nora Barnacle Joyce: A Portrait* (Galway: Kennys Bookshops, 1982). All quotations from these texts will be followed by abbreviated titles and page numbers.

6. Cathy N. Davidson, "Photographs of the Dead: Sherman, Daguerre, Hawthorne," *South Atlantic Quarterly* 89:4 (Fall 1990): 672.

7. One such critique of the thing represented is offered by W. J. T. Mitchell in *Iconology: Image, Text, Ideology* (Chicago: University of Chicago Press, 1986). For Mitchell, "There is no neutral, univocal, 'visible world' there to match things against, no unmediated 'facts.' . . . What we are matching against pictorial representations is not any sort of naked reality but a world already clothed in our systems of representation" (38).

8. The sole exception to this rule is Gisèle Freund's *Three Days with Joyce* (New York: Persea, 1985), composed of some forty photographs and little explanatory commentary, and orginally published in France in 1982 in celebration of the centenary of Joyce's birth.

9. Susan Sontag, *On Photography* (New York: Farrar, Straus & Giroux, 1977), 67.

10. Ellmann, as quoted in William K. Robertson, "A Portrait of James Joyce's Biographer," in *Essays for Richard Ellmann: Omnium Gatherum*, ed. Susan Dick, Declan Kiberd, Dougald McMillan, and Joseph Ronsley (Montreal: McGill-Queen's University Press, 1989), 43.

11. Shari Benstock, "Portrait of the Artist's Wife," *Times Literary Supplement*, 30 September–6 October 1988: 1065; Bonnie Kime Scott, "Review," *Journal of Irish Literature* 18 (1989): 58. Other reviewers of Maddox's biography rely upon similar visual metaphors. Michelene Wandor in "The Silent Partner," *The Listener* 30 June 1988, refers to the book as a "portrait of a pretty extraordinary woman" (32); and Edna O'Brien ("She Was the Other Ireland," *New York Times Book Review* 19 June 1988) endorses Maddox's biography as a "new and fascinating portrait" of Nora that successfully redresses the pejorative implications of such biographies as Ellmann's (3).

12. Christian Caujolle, "Foreword," *Gisèle Freund—Photographer* (New York: Harry N. Abrams, 1985), 9.

13. Mitchell, *Iconology*, 67.

14. Miles Orvell, *The Real Thing: Imitation and Authenticity in American Culture, 1880–1940* (Chapel Hill: University of North Carolina Press, 1989), 77.

15. Roland Barthes, *Camera Lucida: Reflections on Photography*, trans. Richard Howard (New York: Hill and Wang, 1981) 10.

16. Anne Hollander, *Seeing Through Clothes* (New York: Avon, 1975), 314–15.

17. Mitchell, *Iconology*, 17.

18. Barthes, *Camera Lucida*, 60.

19. Sontag, *On Photography*, 77; Peggy Phelan, *Unmarked: The Politics of Performance* (New York: Routledge, 1993), 36.

20. Herbert Lindenberger, "The Mimetic Bias in Anglo-American Criticism," in *Mimesis in Contemporary Theory: An Inter-Disciplinary Approach*, ed. Mihai Spariosu (Philadelphia: John Benjamins, 1984), 5.

21. Mieke Bal, "De-disciplining the Eye," *Critical Inquiry* 16 (1990): 506, 507.

22. Bal's point resembles Mary Ann Caws's enunciation of the so-called "elliptical effect," the paradox that what often "activates the fullest imagination may be itself as fragmentary as a torso, as empty as an empty shoe" in *The Art of Interference: Stressed Readings in Verbal and Visual Texts* (Princeton: Princeton University Press, 1989), 48.

23. For further discussion of the *punctum*, see Barthes, *Camera Lucida*, 40–60.

24. Geoffrey C. Ward, with Ric Burns and Ken Burns, *The Civil War: An Illustrated History* (London: Bodley Head, 1990), xvii.

25. J. Hillis Miller, "Stevens's Rock and Criticism as Cure, II," *Georgia Review* 30 (1976): 331.

26. All quotations from *Ulysses* come from *Ulysses: The Corrected Text*, ed. Hans Walter Gabler (New York: Random House, 1986), and are followed by chapter and line numbers. Thus, a passage from the first three lines of the "Penelope" episode would be followed by (18:1–3).

27. In addition to Maddox's chapter on Nora as a model for Molly Bloom, like Ellmann she develops analogies between Bloom and Joyce. See, for example, Maddox, *Nora*, 205–6.

28. Orvell, *The Real Thing*, 73.

29. Joyce shared Bloom's scopophilia, although Maddox and Ellmann disagree about Joyce's claim to have watched out his window in Zurich as Marthe Fleischmann, a woman with whom he shared a minor flirtation, pulled the chain of her toilet in an apartment in a nearby building. Ellmann relates the episode as truthful (448), while Maddox contends that Joyce's failing eyesight and the location of the two buildings would have made this act of voyeurism impossible (159–60). In either case, the episode suggests the voyeuristic impulses shared by Joyce and Bloom.

30. Blanche Gelfant, "'A Frame of Her Own': Joyce's Women in *Dubliners* Re-Viewed," in *James Joyce: The Augmented Ninth*, ed. Bernard Benstock (Syracuse: Syracuse University Press, 1988), 263–64.

31. In *Joyce, O'Casey, and the Irish Popular Theatre* (Syracuse, N.Y.: Syracuse University Press, 1991), I read Gerty's movement and the revelation of her infirmity differently: namely, within the context of the romantic staging conventions that structure "Nausicaa" (130–42). This theatrical context is related, I think, to the posings and containments of photographic subjects. In describing Ellen Terry's practical education as an actress on the late Victorian stage, for example, Nina Auerbach emphasizes that as a young girl Terry was compelled to cultivate "motionlessness" on stage. See her *Ellen Terry: Player in Her Time* (New York: Norton, 1987), 133; 223–37.

32. For further discussion, see Garry M. Leonard, "The Question and the Quest: The Story of Mangan's Sister," *Modern Fiction Studies* 35.3 (1989): 459–77.

33. After reading Maddox's biography, some reviewers still found Nora "fixed" into the nearly invisible, insignificant roles of wife and mother. In her review (*James Joyce Quarterly* 26 [1988]: 160–65), Mary O'Toole complained that in Maddox's book we "still do not find Nora . . . (nor am I convinced that we need to)" (161).

34. See O'Toole, ibid. See also Pat Carr, "Review," *Modern Fiction Studies* 34 (Winter 1988): 690–91.

35. I wish to express my gratitude to Ms. Lynne Farrington of the Cornell University Library Department of Rare Books for her assistance with the two early photographs of Nora.

36. Scott "Review," 57 (see note 11).

37. John Berger, *About Looking* (New York: Pantheon, 1980), 34.

38. All quotations from Joyce's letters come from *The Letters of James Joyce, Volumes Two and Three*, ed. Richard Ellmann (New York: Viking, 1966). Quotations will be followed by volume and page numbers in the text.

39. Wandor "The Silent Partner," 32 (see note 11).

40. Ben L. Bassham, *The Theatrical Photographs of Napoleon Sarony* (Kent, Ohio: Kent State University Press, 1978), 20.

41. John M. Synge, *My Wallet of Photographs* (Dublin: Dolmen Editions, 1971).

42. Freund, *Three Days with Joyce*, 52.

4

Lost Objects: Photography, Fiction, and Mourning

Corey K. Creekmur

Du schnell vergehendes Daguerreotyp
in meinen langsamer vergehanden Handen.
[Oh quickly disappearing photograph
in my more slowly disappearing hand.]
——Rainer Maria Rilke[1]

VOLUME 21 OF THE *INTERNATIONAL JOURNAL OF Psycho-analysis*, published in 1940, contains three subtly interrelated "texts." Two are essays: an obituary by Ernest Jones that begins with the Nietzschian declaration that "Freud is dead," and a now well-known article by Melanie Klein entitled "Mourning and its Relation to Manic-Depressive States." Klein's essay advances earlier work by Freud (1917) and Karl Abraham (1924) on mourning and melancholia by in part "working through" her own reactions to the loss of a son in 1934; Klein argues that even "normal mourning" reactivates infantile "anxieties, guilt and feelings of loss and grief derived from the breast situation, the Oedipus situation and all other such sources."[2] In an essay which pays tribute to yet "advances" the work of Freud, Klein claims, "In my experience, feelings of triumph are inevitably bound up even with normal mourning, and have the effect of retarding the work of mourning, or rather they contribute much to the difficulties and pain which the

mourner experiences."[3] However, in the immediate institutional context of a professional journal eulogizing the father of psychoanalysis, the essay serves as theory to Jones's practice, analyzing for Freud's "triumphant" professional offspring the very activity they have officially, publicly undertaken. The third "text" is the first photograph to ever appear in the journal, a portrait of the elderly Freud over the caption "Born Freiburg, Moravia May 6, 1856, Died London September 23, 1939." What interests me is the unstated yet overdetermined relation among these texts: an expression of mourning, a theory of mourning, and the mechanically reproduced image of a lost loved object.[4] If the first two can be read as theory and practice (though each in itself, with Freud's own writing as a model, conflates these functions), what exactly is the role of this photograph in the process being performed officially through language? How, broadly, might a photograph participate in the reorganization of human memory and, more specifically, the psychic activity—or what Freud called "the work"—of mourning, the regular form of remembrance or memorialization performed in response to the loss of a loved object?

Commentary on photography frequently asserts the medium's uncanny relation to or connotation of death; André Bazin begins his famous essay "The Ontology of the Photographic Image" by suggesting that a "mummy complex," a continual concern with "the practice of embalming the dead," underlies the plastic arts from the Egyptian tombs to photography and cinema.[5] In fact, for much of its early history, commercial photography depended upon the now surreptitious (because "tasteless") genre of "postmortem" or "memorial" photography in which the stillness of its corpse-subjects allowed for unusually clear exposures; from the context of our own snapshot-saturated experience, it is jarring to realize how many people were photographed for the first time "in their lives" in their coffins.[6] But the association of photography and death is hardly limited to the now questionable practice of photographing corpses; John Berger notes that "photography, because it stops the flow of life, is always flirting with death"[7]; Roland Barthes recognizes "that rather terrible thing which is there in every photograph: the return of the dead"[8]; and Susan Sontag succinctly declares that "all photographs are *memento mori*."[9] What we sometimes call "stills" of animate beings anticipate their and our eventual stasis through a visual figuration of *rigor mortis;* countering common assumptions that photographs either "capture the present" or "preserve the past," Barthes shudders at the anterior future enacted by every photograph, a vertigo summarized in his uncanny recognition that the human subject of a photographic portrait "is dead and . . . going to die."[10] Most commonly, photographs of lost loved ones, displayed on a headstone or mantlepiece or entombed in a wallet or locket, function as memorabilia for survivors, visual *aides-memoire* supporting fading mental images. So if photographs continually signify death (Barthes claims "every photograph is this catastrophe"[11]), they nevertheless play an extremely ambivalent role in the work of mourning as that process is commonly undertaken and as it has been defined by classical and contemporary psychoanalysis.[12]

Mourning, which Freud notes "does not seem to us pathological . . . only because we know so well how to explain it" is presented in "Mourning and Melancholia" (written in 1915, published in 1917, and so with the losses of the Great War as

its backdrop) as a struggle between reality, which insists "the loved object no longer exists," and libidinal opposition to this painful recognition, an opposition that "can be so intense that a turning away from reality ensues, the object being clung to through the medium of hallucinatory wish-psychosis."[13] Until "respect for reality gains the day . . . the existence of the lost object is psychically prolonged."[14] Melancholia is defined by Freud as failed mourning, the result of the inability to acknowledge the object's loss; the object has been introjected and placed in an ambivalent relation to the ego, which finds itself both impoverished by and, since it survives, contemptuous of the lost object. For Abraham, Klein, and various contemporary analysts, this internal struggle characterizes *all* mourning, as any loss in the external world threatens and tests the original internal objects with which later objects ("loved ones") are identified.

What happens, however, if the lost object, or a part or trace of it (like a footprint, or a death-mask, as Andre Bazin suggests), is prolonged, not psychically, as a wish or a hallucination, but in the family album, or (as John Berger describes) behind glass on the headstones in a Moscow cemetery? What if the lost object is preserved in a photograph? Might the medium of photography be more effective in the insistence on absence, in providing evidence of the "that-has-been" (Barthes) of lost objects, than a painfully besieged libidinal position? Or, on the other hand, would a photograph preserve at least an element of the lost object's presence, like a lock of hair, and so delay the mourner's recognition that the object is fully gone? Kathleen Woodward has argued that "the difference between mourning and melancholia (in Freud's essay) is cast in clear-cut binary terms, and this false opposition has paralyzed discussions of mourning ever since."[15] Recent analysts like John Bowlby have in fact obscured Freud's hard distinction by suggesting the possibility of prolonged (even interminable) mourning, the duration or recurrence of which questions Freud's emphasis on mourning as a process that ends.[16] Photographs, as traces of the dead and so reminders of our loss, may then delay, sustain, and even encourage mourning when our psyche seems otherwise ready to "let go" of the lost loved object. Memorial photographs perhaps went out of fashion as photographs of the living simply became more common, but our contemporary resistance to this practice also suggests that their testifying to the death of their subjects was too brutally convincing; despite the tendency to position corpses in "life-like" poses, the subjects of memorial photographs begin to share affinities with the murder victims in the crime photographs of Weegee. Photographs of the living, preserved and viewed after their deaths by survivors, are more easily accepted as evidence of animate life (through their recognizable gestures or expressions), and therefore potential hedges against reality's continual demonstration of the lost loved one's absence.

What I am suggesting here depends upon an understanding of, or more correctly *a belief in* and *use of* photography technically and theoretically insupportable: that, to put it briefly, photographs have a direct, analogical or indexical relation to their referents, affirming or serving as evidence of the existence of what they depict; in short, that photographic portraits are in some ontological sense *of* the people "captured" in them. Something like this view is behind Barthes's famous (and much debated) description of photography as a "message without a code" and his declaration in *Camera Lucida* that "the referent adheres."[17] This is also the position that leads photography critics like John Tagg to express dismay at Barthes's ultimate and apparently regressive, "poignant reassertion of the realist position" in his final work.[18] Since, Tagg asserts, "there cannot be found any ontological or semiological basis for the privileging of photography as a means of representation which renders a direct transcription of the real," he accounts for "the real force which photography exerts in modern social life" in "the absolute continuity of the photograph's ideological existence . . . with its existence as a material object whose 'currency' and 'value' arise in certain distinct and historically specific social practices."[19]

Although such arguments are important and persuasive on their own terms, I am troubled by their implicit demand that those who respond to photographs as evidence of the actuality of the objects they represent can only, finally, be characterized as (ideological) dupes. Might the realist

belief in photographic truth be at times a conscious, even if desperate, fantasy of the sort acknowledged by disavowal: "I know [a photograph doesn't guarantee a pre-photographic referent], but . . .?" Whether or not photographs have a unique, direct (indexical) relationship to their subjects or represent them through conventionalized (iconic) signs, I would like to consider (as I think Barthes intends) the psychopathology of the everyday *use* of photographs, specifically as a medium (here allowing the term's mystical connotations and recalling the short history of "spirit photography") bridging reality and fantasy, the living and the dead, and history and fiction. Although it's only sentimental evidence for any claim about the nature of photography, I believe a photograph of a lost loved one might have the affective power to make even a semiotician, who knows better, weep. Freud and Abraham locate the roots of melancholia in the late-oral, literally introjective, stage of libidinal development; setting aside here the question of whether or not they're (psychologically or ideologically) good for you, I am concerned with *how* photographs are emotionally consumed, though not necessarily internalized.

I want to draw on one of the oppositions just mentioned, between history and fiction, by discussing two extraordinary postmodern novels of the sort Linda Hutcheon terms "historiographic metafictions," those "novels which are both intensely self-reflexive and paradoxically also lay claim to historical events and personages": Michael Ondaatje's *Coming through Slaughter* (1977) and Richard Powers's *Three Farmers on Their Way to a Dance* (1985).[20] Aside from their generic similarities (a weave of historical and fictional materials, multiple narrators, and an emphasis, through sudden temporal leaps, on the enunciative situation of the work being written and read) both works are largely generated out of single photographs: Ondaatje's novel is prefaced by the only known photograph of its protagonist, legendary jazz pioneer Buddy Bolden, actual photographer unknown, while Powers's book begins with the famous photograph that provides the novel's title, made in 1914 by August Sander, as its matrix.[21] Bolden and the three farmers (whose names weren't recorded but who are given names and histories by Powers) are central *characters* in these novels; that is to say, they are fictional constructs that, through the mute insistence of the photographs, are continually claimed by the "real" world, by history. Like all fictional characters they don't "really exist" except as textual signs; but like all photographed subjects, we may believe (but not necessarily *know*), as Barthes says, *"they were there."*[22] Although both Ondaatje and Powers take advantage of the novelist's freedom to create narrative circumstances as well as psychologies for these characters, the photographs establish constraints in regard to physical description and setting; each photograph provides readers with a means to check, ironically, an imaginative writer's accuracy. Although, again, both novels are apparently generated out of their prefatory photographs, these pictures are demanding muses. They require, on a formal level, description that can be judged accurate, which becomes, on another

level, a moral responsibility to honor the memories of the dead.

This tension between attachment to a referent and pure symbolic signification exceeds the specific narratives of these novels so that each raises questions not only about the meaning of "fiction" (a general concern of postmodern writing), or the relation between narrative and history (a general concern of postmodern theory) but, I think, each asks how the psychic negotiation of *loss* is conducted in a century that has been, more or less, recorded, preserved, even visually embalmed, on film; these novels concern, to allude to the Walter Benjamin essay which Powers's novel explicitly narrativizes, "the work of *mourning* in the age of mechanical reproduction."

In addition to making the subjects of these photographs into characters, both novels dramatize the making of the photographs themselves. Sander, along with the farmers, is a character in

Frontispiece to Coming through Slaughter *(New York: Norton, 1976).*

Young farmers, 1914, by August Sander. ©August Sander Archiv/Stiftung City-Treff, Cologne; VG Bild-Kunst, Bonn 1994. Frontispiece to Three Farmers on Their Way to a Dance *(New York: Beech Tree Books/William Morrow, 1985).*

as well as the "origin" of *Three Farmers*. He is introduced bicycling through the Rhineland province of Prussia in early May 1914, when he comes across three young men walking along in their Sunday clothes, and is then identified, in one of the "essays" that punctuate the book, as the man who "hit upon the idea of an epic photographic collection to be called *Man of the Twentieth Century*," an impossible project that "it took a man of the nineteenth century to conceive of (39). In his imaginary description of the taking of the photograph, Powers has the sun setting and the three young men anxious to get to their dance: "They had best shoot the picture now or lose the chance forever. . . . The first plate is

spoiled because Hubert drops the cigarette out of his mouth and bends down to pick it up just as the photographer opens the lens. The second has got to do because he has no more plates and cannot make his customary backup image" (27). When the lens is covered, the three farmers begin to walk towards another demonstration of recent technology, the First World War. As readers, we are allowed to participate imaginatively in the simple, curious production of a photograph that we otherwise know only as product, finished, catalogued and, in this case, well-established in the now-institutionalized history of the medium. The description of a ruined and presumably "lost" first plate restores radical contingency to this often reproduced image: this particular composition was not available for capture in the moments before and after its exposure. In fact, unlike so many of Sander's other subjects, the farmers do not plant themselves firmly for the photographer, but only turn their heads and hold still for a moment, unwilling to even shift their bodies from the direction of the dance. As Powers writes late in the book, "We have died away from the conditions of the photographer's moment. Every mechanical landscape, interior, or portrait comes to the viewer over time, a memory posted forward from the instant of the shutter waiting to come into conjunction with the instant of viewing" (257). But the novelist's ability to narrate the past as present, to narrativize the historical content and context of Sander's photograph, returns "a memory posted forward" to sender; our "instant of viewing" is not only a reception, but the cue for a fantasized perception of the "pre-history" of the "instant of the shutter," the circumstances that the details of the photograph indicate preceded its recording. The desire to reanimate what has been stilled not only characterizes mourning, but may be an interpretive impulse common to all but the most formal attention to a photograph. As I will suggest shortly, this recursive procedure, where a photograph anticipates our future present while its fictional contextualization returns us to its past present, neatly describes the multimedia reading activity that both books establish.

Ondaatje takes an imaginative leap by making the photographer of the Bolden picture a historical figure as mysterious as Bolden himself (and as curious in his "project" as Sander), the New Orleans photographer E. J. Bellocq, known for his haunting photographs of Storyville prostitutes taken around 1912 and first exhibited after their rediscovery in 1970.[23] Bellocq's purpose in making and hiding these photographs is obscure; they seem as much motivated by the documentary spirit as by fetishism. A detective in Ondaatje's novel who sees the photographs finds them "sad stuff," and the narrator notes that for this observer "the only difference between these and morgue files was the others were dead" (50). Ondaatje does not actually depict the taking of the photograph of Bolden, but rather gives us the making of the *print* which survives:

> Ten minutes later he [the detective] bent over the sink with Bellocq, watching the paper weave in the acid tray. As if the search for his friend was finally ending. In the third red light the man tapped the paper with his delicate fingers so it would be uniformly printed, and while waiting cleaned the soakboard in a fussy clinical way. The two of them watching the pink rectangle as it slowly began to grow black shapes, coming fast now. Then the sudden vertical lines which rose out of the pregnant white paper which were the outlines of the six men and their formally held instruments. The dark clothes coming first, leaving the space that was the shirt. Then the faces. Frank Lewis looking slightly to the left. All serious except for the smile on Bolden. (52)

Here and throughout the novel, Ondaatje draws our attention to the small details of the photograph; he directs us to Bolden's "bright shirts that have no collars" (51), the odd position of his instrument held flat in his hand, and most frequently to Bolden's "smile which may not have been a smile at all" (53), which Bolden's internal voice calls "my grin which is my loudest scream ever" (69). As I've noted, Ondaatje's description of the making of an object we first encounter as finished, as a historical artifact, is imaginatively dramatized (produced here, again, by a photographer who probably didn't make it) but responds to the details of the photography with what might be called a responsibility for accuracy. The writer is a skilled perceiver who draws our attention to details our careless glances may have overlooked, but which we nonetheless ac-

knowledge to be indeed contained by the image. With Ondaatje, however, we also scan this single surviving photograph desperately as retrospective evidence or explanation for Bolden's genius and madness.

More obviously, but most fundamentally, we attend to the photograph as proof of Bolden's existence and so as a counterweight to the descriptions and monologues of Ondaatje's writing, which can only provide an imagined history and subjectivity for his main character. This tension is registered by *Coming through Slaughter*'s collage construction, which shifts from dramatized action and subjective description to meta-discourse: between the fictive conjunction of Bellocq, the detective, and Bolden (whose popularity with New Orleans prostitutes allows the misshapen Bellocq's entrance to the brothels), Ondaatje summarizes what little we—from our historical distance and perhaps our sanity— know and can *reasonably* imagine about the circumstances and purposes of Bellocq's work. The book's fragmentary arrangement continually figures the "border tensions" between the fact of Bolden's and Bellocq's existence (which includes the slim evidence of one photo taken of the former and the surviving eighty-nine made by the latter), and the fiction of Ondaatje's writing. Our notorious "willing suspension of disbelief" is not seriously taxed when a photograph offers us apparently objective proof and so reason to believe.

Like Ondaatje, Powers provides and thus encourages a rigorous examination of the photograph which precedes his narrative: his second chapter fills the three farmers with personalities as well as political and national identities, and surrounds them with their historical and social context. After the taking of their photograph is quietly dramatized, the chapter ends with a detailed description of the frozen image that, ironically, generated the animated fictional portrait we've just read. This scene will return, formally balanced, in the book's penultimate chapter, but now with the accumulated significance surrounding this photograph and our awareness of its profound effect on subsequent viewers. This final description of the photograph's making now can acknowledge the weight of this moment, which bisects the farmers' personal futures and our historical past:

They [the farmers] become aware of the open lens, of light streaming from them into the box, drawing with it all memory of the moment and of their own outwardness. All three see it for the briefest interval hovering above and just beyond the photographer's shoulders: the third party, a vision of billions. They see a movie, played out instantly on an infinitesimal screen, of machine-inflicted suffering on a scale incomprehensible to these three rustics. Then, without any time passing, the lens opens a clear portal, and they look past the photographer on countless people who, museumgoing, file by clinically, uncomprehending, curious.

This is the vision the lens arrests; it explains the quality in the subjects' eyes that so haunts and transcends. Their look fixes on the numbers and suffering of future viewers. They look forward—and back. (340–41)

Three Farmers unfolds through three interwoven stories and narrative levels; one line follows the young farmers through their created histories, while the other two, set in the present, have characters intersect with those histories when they encounter Sander's photograph, becoming the future viewers the young men anticipated. Photographs, which by freezing a moment in time only emphasize the temporality of the moments just before and after the shutter's opening, model any section of Powers's novel, where past and present, or cause and effect, are reversible and shuttle between memory and perception. *Three Farmers,* like *Coming through Slaughter,* moves among speakers and historical perspectives, but where Ondaatje's novel is focused and reduced to fragmentary phrases and images, Powers's book is expansive and indulges in a rich accumulation of information, ideas, and anecdotes. Its subject is our experience and comprehension of this century (Ondaatje's novel seems to visit a lost world), with particular attention to the intersection of human perception and the technologies of reproduction. (While the novel draws upon "world-historical figures" as seemingly diverse as Sander, Henry Ford, and Sarah Bernhardt, Walter Benjamin remains its intellectual tutor.)

Although it takes its inspiration from an image of frozen time, *Three Farmers,* through this structure, situates its readers in a temporal gap that returns us to the work of mourning, which, as we say, "takes time." We are jostled between the imaginary presence of the three farmers (they "live" as characters) and the recognized absence of these same figures (never real as we meet them here and surely dead as the historical beings in the photograph). We begin each book with its generative photograph, but only come to the moment of that photograph's creation as we move into the narratives; I cannot imagine a reader of either book resisting returning frequently (if not obsessively), as another facet of the image is illuminated, to scan each photograph again and again. One of Powers's contemporary protagonists, for example, notices the curious position of the central farmer's left hand: "The hand did not form a ring of negative space, but instead closed around something actual. Yet the photo lacked definition precise enough to reveal whether the new way of seeing the area corresponded with the reality of that day" (291). The odd hand is highlighted for us, and thereafter remains an unavoidable element—a Barthesian *punctum*—of our experience of the photograph. The novelist's observation seems "correct": there is surely something there. But our return to the image to check this description only widens the gap between our "new way of seeing" (which seems painfully inadequate, far from improved) and the irrecoverable "reality of that day." We begin each book with its inaugural photograph, but find it difficult, as we seem to proceed in our reading, to really ever get past them; each return trip only underlines the distance of the journey. A quick and curious museum-like glance is disallowed by both books; descriptions that move us forward in the narrative send us back to the photographs, which come to haunt us even as they become more fully known.

Because both *Coming through Slaughter* and *Three Farmers on Their Way to a Dance* are preceded by photographs, but construct plots that precede the making of those same pictures, we witness "an anterior future of which death is the stake."[24] The photographs, which remain prefaces outside the *bodies* of the texts, and of course as artifacts historically precede these novels, are nevertheless narratively *incorporated* or internalized by each work so that the figures in them can become what they were originally not for most readers: lost loved objects capable of being mourned. These two public images (neither a family snapshot, one image serving as publicity, the other part of a "scientific" project) are thus made personal or identificatory, stunningly realizing Barthes's recognition that "the reading of public photographs is always, at bottom, a private reading."[25]

In addition to the internalization of these (newly) loved, (long) lost objects, both works encourage our recognition of the potential loss of other, more immediate objects: the photographs themselves. In *Coming through Slaughter*, Bolden and Bellocq are doubles, artists whose work barely sublimates their growing insanity; a great deal of the mystery surrounding Bolden is due to the fact that, as the book emphasizes, "he was never recorded . . . while others moved into wax history, electronic history" (37). The only "record" of Bolden's musical career is, indeed, the photograph of him "holding his cornet an unusual way, flat in his open palm."[26] (The other "records" of Bolden's life are from the asylum where he spent the last thirty years of his life.) Eighty-nine of Bellocq's glass plates of prostitutes, found in his desk after his death, have survived by accident, and many of them are slashed and scarred by a knife: "You can see that the care he took defiling the beauty he had forced in them was as precise and clean as his good hands which at night had developed the negatives, floating the sheets in the correct acids and watching the faces and breasts and pubic triangles and sofas emerge" (55). The photograph of Bolden "is not good or precise, partly because the print was found after the fire [Bellocq set to kill himself]. The picture, waterlogged by climbing hoses, stayed in the possession of Willy Cornish [Bolden's trombone player, on Bolden's left in the picture] for several years" (66). Ondaatje writes that after Bellocq made this print, he "dropped the negative into the acid tray and watched it bleach out to grey. Goodbye" (53). Although Powers's novel, after Benjamin, recognizes that "a print was by nature only a print, entirely interchangeable with any other print, antique or contemporary" (291), it also recognizes that not all images are disseminated through reproduction. Sander's work, as Powers reports, "crossed the view of the German people the Nazis were trying to foster" and his lab became "subject to periodic searches and seizures

of negatives" (42–43). The picture of the three farmers is made as its illumination is fading and without backup; the picture of Bolden is almost ruined by fire and water, and its negative has been destroyed. This emphasis on the fragility of photographs, despite their reproducibility, reminds us that *they* might be, as objects, literally lost. The objects of these photographs, now lost (dead), are preserved through a medium that is itself—as glass, paper, chemical—fragile.

These works, finally, ask their reader-spectators to prolong the existence of lost objects with the aid of external objects that are nonetheless themselves perishable.[27] Once again, the practice of memorial photography seems unnecessary in a world saturated by photographs, but in an earlier time one can perhaps understand why parents might cherish a single photograph of a dead child's body if no other photographs of the child had ever been made. That photograph and its negative (if the photographic procedure included one) become themselves precious objects also subject to loss and destruction. Even today, those with the easy means to reproduce photographs still find it difficult to destroy or discard photographs—especially, of course, of lost loved ones. The historical accidents, emphasized by these novelists, through which these particular photographs have been preserved remind us that mourning—one of our most personal acts—can have a public dimension. Between fiction and history, as between private and public experience (and, importantly, in the context of the avoidance and repression of mourning rituals, in a culture that finds death "pornographic"),[28] affective attention to the photograph of the lost loved object is perhaps the most important means by which a fundamental psychic experience is undertaken in our time.

In late 1913, when Sander's photo-anthropological project was under way and the threat of war grew, Sigmund Freud began a regular exchange of letters with Lou Andreas-Salomé. After completing a walking tour with her close friend Rilke, Andreas-Salomé wrote from Berlin to Freud in Vienna, requesting a copy of a "large and extremely good photograph" of the professor she had seen in Dr. Max Eitington's office. Freud agreed to send her a picture (though not the one requested, which he felt "today makes a very anachronistic impression") "if I can do a deal on it, i.e., if I get a picture of you in return for my likeness." Accepting Freud's "deal," the resourceful Frau Andreas also located the Zurich source for the "anachronistic" photograph and wrote Freud that "in this way I shall have you twice over." She also argued that "what makes so 'anachronistic' an impression on you in the Zurich photo seems to me completely contemporary. But your remark is so much more true of the only photos of me that exist that I can scarcely recognize myself in them: they are over a dozen years old!" By early 1914 the deal was done; Andreas-Salomé wrote that "as enclosure there comes to you a young lady about whom I said in my letter from Berlin in November that my connection with her was very remote. But since you wish it, I am sending her—even if with mixed feelings." In acknowledgement, Freud recognized that "the young lady who has now accepted my invitation is clearly a close relative of yours, even if she is perhaps not you yourself. In any case this connection assures her a place of honour."[29]

If the role photographs play in this little flirtation appears unrelated to the public function encouraged by the memorial photograph of Freud with which I began, we have forgotten Freud's willingness to take play—verbal, aesthetic, or erotic—seriously. Like Ondaatje and Powers, Freud and his creative disciple (herself a novelist) generate fiction out of photographs, creating a historical romance between characters whose contemporary descendents are "anachronistic" narrators literally looking back in time and "scarcely recognizing" themselves in their thinly autobiographical narrative. Freud continues Andreas-Salomé's fiction of "the young lady," overlooking the photograph's evidence of who she "really" is. Moreover, the game the letter-writers play is conducted in obvious defense against not the unconscious, but the apparent end of the world; on 19 November 1914, Andreas-Salomé, admitting that "states cannot be psychoanalyzed," allows that "I don't really believe that after this we shall ever be able to be really happy again." Freud, in the year "Mourning and Melancholia" is composed, writes back with the news that his talented "son has been invited to design the memorial for his troop; this

will no doubt have been his first job as an architect."[30] While his son accepts the task of constructing a conventional public memorial, Freud is attempting to distinguish between forms of remembrance and psychic pain that are already being renegotiated in response to the presence of photographs in our lives, which despite their simplicity seem far more capable of reflecting the depth and irreducibility of our own losses than noble civic monuments. Exchanging old photographs and constructing little fictions out of them—mingling adolescent fantasy and adult memory in not only the painful experience, but also the dreaded anticipation of loss—Freud's "wartime romance" tangles together threads of art, technology, and psychic trauma even more deeply knotted for us by Ondaatje and Powers in their remarkable works.

NOTES

1. Rainer Maria Rilke, "Portrait of My Father as a Young Man," trans. Stephen Mitchell, in Mitchell, ed., *The Selected Poetry of Rainer Maria Rilke* (New York: Random House, 1980), 39.

2. Melanie Klein, "Mourning and Its Relation to Manic-Depressive States," in Juliet Mitchell, ed., *The Selected Melanie Klein* (New York: Free Press, 1986), 156. Klein's essay follows, as noted: Sigmund Freud, "Mourning and Melancholia," in *The Standard Edition of the Complete Psychological Works of Sigmund Freud*, vol. 14 (New York: Norton, 1953–74), 239–58; Karl Abraham, "A Short Study of the Development of the Libido, Viewed in the Light of Mental Disorders," in *Selected Papers on Psycho-Analysis* (London: Hogarth Press, 1927), 418–501.

3. Klein, "Mourning and Its Relation to Manic-Depressive States," 157.

4. According to Stanley B. Burns, M. D., "The first book published with a photograph is an English memorial book, *Record of the Death-Bed of C. M. W.*," an 1844 volume which included a Calotype paper print "life portrait of the deceased." See Burns, *Sleeping Beauty: Memorial Photography in America*. (Altadena, California: Twelvetrees Press, 1990), n.p.

5. André Bazin, "The Ontology of the Photographic Image," *What is Cinema?*, vol. 1 (Berkeley: University of California Press, 1967), 9.

6. For examples of American memorial photography and discussions of its cultural context, see Burns, *Sleeping Beauty: Memorial Photography in America* (see note 4); Karen Halttunen, *Confidence Men and Painted Women: A Study of Middle-Class Culture in America, 1830–1870* (New Haven: Yale University Press, 1982): 124–52; Michael Lesy, *Wisconsin Death Trip* (New York: Pantheon, 1973); and Cathy N. Davidson, "Photographs of the Dead: Sherman, Daguerre, Hawthorne," *South Atlantic Quarterly* 89 (Fall 1990): 667–701.

7. John Berger, *The Sense of Sight* (New York: Pantheon, 1985), 122.

8. Roland Barthes, *Camera Lucida: Reflections on Photography*, trans. Richard Howard (New York: Hill and Wang, 1981), 9.

9. Susan Sontag, *On Photography*. (New York: Farrar, Straus, & Giroux, 1977), 14.

10. Barthes, *Camera Lucida*, 95.

11. Barthes, *Camera Lucida*, 96.

12. Helpful overviews of the psychoanalytic theory of mourning include: Lorraine D. Siggins, "Mourning: A Critical Survey of the Literature," *International Journal of Psycho-Analysis* 47 (1966): 14–25; Kathleen Woodward *Aging and Its Discontents: Freud and Other Fictions*. (Bloomington: Indiana University Press, 1991); and Woodward, "Grief-Work in Contemporary American Cultural Criticism," *Discourse* 15 (Winter 1992–93): 94–112. Woodward's illuminating analysis of Barthes's *Camera Lucida* in *Aging and Its Discontents* oddly underestimates the role photography plays in that book's dramatization of the work of mourning.

13. Freud, "Mourning and Melancholia," 244.

14. Freud, "Mourning and Melancholia," 244–45.

15. Woodward, *Aging and Its Discontents*, 115.

16. See John Bowlby, *Loss: Sadness and Depression*, vol. 3 of *Attachment and Loss*. (New York: Basic Books, 1980).

17. Barthes, *Camera Lucida*, 6.

18. John Tagg, *The Burden of Representation: Essays on Photographies and Histories* (Amherst: University of Massachusetts Press, 1988), 1.

19. Tagg, *The Burden of Representation*, 188.

20. Linda Hutcheon, *A Poetics of Postmodernism* (London: Routledge, 1988), 5. References to Michael Ondaatje, *Coming through Slaughter* (New York: Penguin, 1977) and Richard Powers, *Three Farmers on Their Way to a Dance* (New York: William Morrow, 1985) will be cited in the text.

21. Ondaatje's earlier *The Collected Works of Billy the Kid* (New York: Penguin, 1974) is also prefaced by the only known photograph of William Bonney, and his autobiographical memoir *Running in the Family* (New York: Penguin, 1982) includes and discusses the sole photograph which the author knows to picture both of his parents. These books and those under discussion remind us that *not* being photographed, or even being photographed only once, now seems highly improbable.

22. Barthes, *Camera Lucida*, 82.

23. See *E. J. Bellocq: Storyville Portraits: Photographs from the New Orleans Red-Light District, Circa 1912*, ed. John Szarkowski (New York: Museum of Modern Art, 1970). Louis Malle's 1978 film *Pretty Baby* provides another fictional version of Bellocq's enigmatic life.

24. Barthes, *Camera Lucida*, 96.

25. Barthes, *Camera Lucida*, 97.

26. Donald M. Marquis, *In Search of Buddy Bolden* (New York: Da Capo Press, 1978), 77.

27. On the fragility of photographs, and the suggestion that their destruction eliminates the final traces of the lost (photographed) object, see in addition to Rilke's "Portrait of My Father as a Young Man" (see note 1), Thomas Hardy's "The Photograph," in *The Complete Poems of Thomas Hardy*, ed. James Gibson (New York: Macmillan, 1976), 469; thanks to Teresa Mangum for alerting me to Hardy's haunting poem. I also discuss the burning of photographs in "The Cinematic Photograph and the Possibility of Mourning," *Wide Angle* 9 (Winter 1986): 41–49.

28. This characterization is most commonly associated with the work of Geoffrer Gorer; see his famous essay "The Pornography of Death" in Gorer, *Death, Grief, and Mourning: A Study of Contemporary Society* (New York: Doubleday, 1965).

29. Sigmund Freud and Lou Andreas-Salomé, *Letters*, ed. Ernst Pfeiffer (New York: Norton, 1972), 14–16.

30. Freud and Andreas-Salome, *Letters*, 20, 36.

Part 2

Photo-Textual Interventions

5

The Alternative Vision: Lewis Hine's Men at Work and the Dominant Culture

Kevin G. Barnhurst

LEWIS W. HINE'S REPUTATION AS A FIGURE IN American documentary photography rests largely on his child labor pictures, which appeared in the magazines and research reports of the progressive movement. By 1932, when that earlier glory had all but passed, he published his only book.[1] *Men at Work* is a strange and puzzling volume of the portraits Hine made of men working in a variety of industries and the construction shots he took of the Empire State Building. Although the portraits lacked the obvious political drive of his earlier work, Hine considered them the best he'd ever done. His ostensible purpose was education—a recurrent theme in his career. Issued as an adolescent picture book, *Men at Work* received an award from the Child Study Association, but within a year Hine had become unfashionable.[2]

Neither progressive politics nor pedagogy can make much sense of *Men at Work*. The pictures and text do not clearly explain what the men were doing or how their work fit into industrial processes. Even the construction shots—almost half the book—hardly make all the digging, hoisting, and riveting seem related. Other picture books have described construction much more coherently without many workers.[3] But for Hine, the *men* were the point. His portraits went beyond the political tinkering of progressivism. By focusing on the men, he fixed the image of the American industrial worker and began to explore the icon of the American male. The dress, tools, and mechanical settings of the portraits, unimportant for their industrial information, constitute an iconography of masculinity, not unlike the symbols used in painting to characterize the landed gentry or to depict Christian saints.

Critical opinion has usually looked unfavorably on *Men at Work*.[4] The work portraits, especially, appear limpid and didactic compared to Hine's child labor pictures, and critics consider his shift from criticizing society to glorifying workers unfortunate. Judith Guttman says, "The photographs for the most part are stilted, formalized, and lacking in feeling."[5] Alan Trachtenberg calls the work portraits "the most troubling, the most problematic of Hine's pictures"[6] and joined a movement to reevaluate them.[7] He considers *Men at Work* "tepid and accommodating."[8]

Like popular fictions, Hine's work portraits repeat the same formulations again and again: that work is honorable, that workers are intelligent, and that men—not machines—deserve the credit for making things. Don Gifford suggests that didactic and idealistic American literature at any given period reveals the structures of desire and of dreams.[9] Our own view of those structures also reveals the present American dream. Hine's pictures of American workers play a similar role. At a time when jobs were scarce and workers undervalued, the images expressed a dream of work glorified. And the reappraisal of *Men at Work* reflects contemporary desires—after the movement toward feminism and gay liberation, the discovery of the male body in advertising, and the rise of visual culture.

Men at Work is significant not only because it anticipated these movements but because it now opens a crack in the wall of the dominant culture. The dominant view rests on the ideology of objectivity, which defines reality geometrically and justifies appropriating its image to subdue the natural world. This mode of vision has so engulfed American life that, until recently, any other perspective was unimaginable. *Men at Work* survived, not on its own reputation, but on the strength of Hine's documentary reputation. A rare example of purely male art, it exposes a vista on masculinity and on culture that depicts men not as gods or animals, but as fully sexual, individual, and particular humanity.

THE PERFIDIOUS CANDID CAMERA

The first tenet of objectivity is naturalism. The history of the camera in the twentieth century reveals an undeviating search for the technology of the candid shot. Cameras got smaller, easier to operate, and more versatile, conquering action, distance, and color. Photojournalism moved from posed to action shots. In documentary work, the posed picture came to convey artificiality, while the candid shot approximated truth. The more enterprising the photographer and the more unobtainable the image, the greater the picture. The ideology of objectivity makes candid photography seem natural. Objects have no consciousness, and to appear natural, a photograph must catch a person unaware. The dominant view turns individuals into objects with no con-

trol over their own depiction. Of course, the ethical photographer may appropriate pictures to serve the greater good—a good defined by the dominant culture—but must never falsify or invent them. Falsehood is defined narrowly as any depiction intentionally at odds with what the photographer believes to be true.

Lewis Hine was a man of duty, who presented the truth of what he saw.[10] When taking pictures of child laborers, he often lied to managers, posed as a salesman, or claimed to be interested in the machines, not the children. But he never faked an image. His rationale was utilitarian—a subterfuge to combat the evil of exploitation. But a girl placed before an industrial machine (to set the scale) perceives herself as a prop, perhaps in the way, certainly of little value. That same girl, told she is herself the important image, may be equally ill-used, but her demeanor, stance, and gesture will change. The great power of Hine's child labor pictures lies not only in his masterful aesthetic but also in the look of insignificance in the children's eyes and postures.

These children were neither wealthy patrons, who could reject work or withhold payment, nor models who sold their likenesses for a fee. Their images were simply appropriated. The dominant view justified the theft by defining them as the *other*, representatives of another class, and by identifying their difference as a problem. The progressive movement called for an improvement—"let them be like us"—based on a paternalistic rationalization—"it's for their own good." But the individual children weren't necessarily better off (they may have actually had less opportunity). Instead, their abstract class designation became reified—assigned a fixed and material position in society—and then banished or obliterated for the sake of the grand principle that child labor must end. The dominant perspective gave them a visual representation, only to demand that they change (into its own reflection) or be expunged. Either way they would inevitably vanish. In the child labor pictures, the photographer was doing the dirty work.

The construction shots in *Men at Work* are likewise troubling. Hine used the camera to appropriate images with the connivance of management. The men are objects, props in the fantastic geometry of the construction of the

Untitled construction shot, by Lewis Hine ("This derrick gang is moving a heavy load of planks while men in the foreground extend the bull-stick of the derrick for greater leverage"). From Men at Work *(1932; reprint, New York: Dover, 1977). By permission of the International Museum of Photography at George Eastman House.*

world's then-largest building. The dominant viewer (a male voyeur) positions himself with the photographer, imagining the risks and measuring his own courage against Hine's. Predictably, critical opinion has favored these candid shots.

The worker portraits of the twenties spring from another vision. The workers posed, participating in their own representation. Hine saw himself as a man at work and identified closely with his fellows. The portraits convey the unity

between photographer and sitter. But to the dominant eye, they lack the crackle and edge of Hine's documentary work. Both ways of shooting pictures produced aesthetic images, and both, in hindsight, show working conditions equally dreary and dirty. But the documentary view put the photographer above his subject. History has judged Hine well, crediting him with being factual, enterprising, and even daring. But that judgment reveals the perversity of the dominant view. In the dominant perspective, all creatures are objects and all moments are scenes, waiting to be exploited.

THE HETEROSEXIST POSE

The candid view objectifies by assuming sexual difference. John Berger says that, in Western representation, "Men act and women appear. Men look at women. Women watch themselves."[11] The dominant view defines the female body as either a symbolic ideal of nature or a voyeuristic object of sexual desire.[12] To make the woman stand for nature, her individuality must be obliterated. Her face is played down, cropped from the frame, covered up, or shown with limited detail. Her eyes are closed or hidden by shadow or a draped arm. The woman who stares out at the spectator, as does Manet's *Olympia* (1863), is the exception, considered wanton. Languorously, the figure reclines, sits or stoops, or closes in on itself, with the limbs crossing. And the flesh is exposed as a flowing unity of curves, unmarred by blemishes, marks, or individual details. The breasts may defy gravity to avoid distracting creases. To make the woman into the object of sexual fantasy, she must be isolated and unconscious. Her genitals are emphasized, either shown in detail or draped suggestively. Her body is set off by a bland or blurry background. And she is taken unawares, while sleeping, looking off, or turning her back to the spectator. This effect is heightened by showing the male spectator fully clothed, each sex in its natural state.[13]

These conventions, which seem "natural" for women, prove utterly artificial for men. In Joseph Wright of Derby's portrait of *Sir Brooke Boothby* (1789), the English nobleman's pose, reclining in the woods, appears fay and feminine.

A more striking example is Botticelli's *Venus and Mars*. The male nude reclines before the appraising glance of the clothed woman, his limbs crossed, his eyes closed, and his face turned away from the woman and the spectator, as drapery both conceals and reveals his genitals. Explicitly homoerotic art generally shows men either in feminine postures or as "aggressively over-muscled"[14] and emphasizes the buttocks or genitals. The male body becomes an object of muscle or penis.[15]

The "natural" male figure follows different conventions.[16] His pose is seated or upright, in a stance of absolute control or of careless ease, reclining only in death. He directs his gaze at the viewer or at a woman. He appears fully clothed, his face and hands shown in detail. Instead of being a flowing unity, any exposed flesh is divided into panels or sections like armor. His genitals, frequently covered or hidden in darkness, are evoked by phallic objects or forms. And the surrounding ground presents other tokens of wealth, learning, or power.

Most authors of text and image books have adopted an exclusively dominant view that rests on sexual difference. Men are more frequently depicted than women. When at the center of attention, men look authoritative, strong, and noble. But usually they assume the spectator's pose. In Walker Evans's *American Photographs*, men stare indifferently at the camera or turn their gaze on women. The pattern is just as pronounced in the work of female photographers.[17] William Saroyan and Arthur Rothstein in the sixties, Chauncey Hare in the seventies, and even Andy Warhol in the eighties showed men in a greater variety of attitudes. But their women were ideals or objects. The pattern has few exceptions. *Let Us Now Praise Famous Men* depicts both men and women with direct gazes and uniform poses. Men turn their backs to the camera and embrace their children as often as women do. These pictures reflect Evans's and James Agee's empathy with their subjects. But even so, men may occupy authoritative spaces and stand, hands on hips, in a pose of power in the fields. At those moments, Evans shares the dominant vision. Although it springs from the same culture and shares in its prejudice, *Men at Work* is significant because it also stands outside the tradition. Only in *Men at Work* do men cross over the dominant sexual dichotomy—becoming the explicit subject, the object of the gaze.

THE DOCUMENTARY PARADOX

Hine also defies classification within the traditional periods and schools of photographic style. Like the pictorialists, he assumed the privileged position of the artist. But pictorialism served only itself, turning the human subject into texture, shape, and value—in essence collapsing the eye, camera, subject, and perhaps even spectator into a unitary vision. In contrast, Hine's photography served utilitarian interests.

Like the documentarist, Hine recorded history, political actions, and social conditions.[18] His child labor pictures, his war coverage for the Red Cross later in his career, and many of the construction shots from *Men at Work* fit neatly into the documentary style category. His work portraits do not. Yet he became an exemplar of the style.

Like other style classifications, documentary ultimately breaks down because it draws overly sharp distinctions, encourages an institutional division that is ultimately sterile, and fails when applied to complex artists whose work evolves. Documentary pictures express an aesthetic, just as pictorialism reveals a certain politics and history. Both styles serve the dominant culture, the documentary more so because it enshrines naturalism.

But the work portraits are not naturalistic. Nor are they crossover works, an experiment in pictorialism. Although they transform men into aesthetic style, they seem to reflect the workers' own misty view of themselves. The portraits document a political reality, but the agenda is the workers' own. They call for a change, not in working men but in the spectator. The dominant viewer is invited to participate, to learn appreciation and respect.

But the viewers could not join in. Documentary photography appeals to the government official who can change things, art photography to the class with taste. As Hine said of his documentary photography, "I wanted to show the things that had to be corrected. I wanted to show the things that had to be appreciated."[19] To viewers with power and the leisure to enjoy art, the aspirations of the worker would seem presumptuous and romantic. Viewers see what they believe, ignoring images that contradict their expectations. Dirty manual labor is not the desirable occupation in America as portrayed by pictures.[20] The work portraits exist as a contradiction. They repel critics because they hold up the other, not out of scorn or pity, but as the object of desire. Their position as homoerotic icons makes them difficult, perhaps impossible to see.[21] So the link between photographer, sitter, and spectator is incomplete. The rapport between Hine and the workers repels the spectator. The worker portraits breach the wall segregating the homoerotic from the popular, as they violate the barrier dividing the documentary from the artistic.

THE CYBORG EYE

Hine not only defies customary categories, he also explodes our comfortable conflations. When we think of Hine the photographer, we fuse a man with a machine. But their two eyes at work, one mechanical, one human, have little in common. C. L. Hardin lists several differences between camera vision and human eyesight: The resolution of the retina is limited, so that we cannot see the minute differences in alignment that a camera can record. The photographic image has the same grain throughout, whereas the eye sees at different grains, producing a cone of vision with more detail at the center. And Hardin cites other differences. The eye contains a blind spot twelve full moons in diameter; the scattering of light onto the retina blurs the image; the image is unstable from the eye's constant motion; and the eye responds continuously to light.[22] Finally, the eyes also see in stereo. By any standard, the camera makes a poor analog for human vision.

Although we commonly conflate the two, "the metaphor is apt to deceive, for it represents the eye as a passive conveyer of images."[23] William Stott, in his extended treatment of documentary, asserts the common wisdom that "machines communicate facts passively, transparently, with an almost pure impersonality."[24] This objective record is the ideal of the dominant view.[25]

The visual literacy movement works to deconstruct the camera eye of the photographer.[26] Simple practice with a viewfinder reveals how choosing a specific moment to release the shutter wrenches the image from its context and imposes a point of view—a position that projects a relationship, making objects closer or more distant, higher or lower, enlarged or shrunken. Roland Barthes called these decisions "the photographers' contortions to produce effects that are 'lifelike.'"[27]

Instead of the flow of human vision, the viewer of photographs has no choice in the moment, position, frame, or arrangement. Rather than being an objective document, a photograph is a statement out of context—poor evidence at best. But the viewer is captive to the view. One response—perhaps the most common in America—to this lack of freedom is to extinguish the photographer, joining his male eye with the camera mechanism and the chemistry of the film. In the place of agency, ours or his, we construct the ideology of photographic objectivity, arguing that camera vision is superior because it is fixed, uniform, framed—the very things that distinguish it from human sight. Without the author, we lose any insight that might be gained by empathy. And we surrender our own vision to the camera—the all-seeing eye of Masonic iconography.

But Hine, the author, cannot be banished easily. Throughout his career, he was identified as difficult—either negatively as an unsuitable employee (Roy Stryker refused to hire him for Farm Security Administration work during the Depression) or positively as an artist in pursuit of his vision (he was the only notable photographer of the period who never sought the approval of Alfred Stieglitz). Hine strongly advocated a separation between camera and eye. He warned that "liars may photograph," and he urged his hearers in the progressive movement "to see to it that the camera we depend upon contracts no bad habits." He characterized himself as a social interpreter, and he placed greater value on the posture of the shooter than on technical skills: "Better little technique and much sympathy than the reverse," he said. He treated the camera as a tool and called it a "light writer," invoking the imagination of the man.[28]

THE CYCLOPS IN A BOX

Pictures made with a camera resemble not eyesight but paintings. The history of painting in the Western tradition is an evolution of technique toward an ever more objective approximation of the real.[29] The development of linear perspective took a giant step toward naturalistic representation. But the progress of the craft was supposedly derailed by the machine. By simply recording nature, the camera took over the task of representing reality. But this rendering of history is misleading.

Rather than approaching human vision, paintings substitute a thoroughly contrived and artificial analog. Western painting records a version of things seen by a Cyclops, whose eye remains immobile, recording uniformly the details before it as it peers from a box that sharply and geometrically demarcates the edges of its field of vision. Alberti made this mode of sight seem natural by describing it as seeing through a window.[30] As Joel Snyder has shown, the subsequent development of optical instruments aimed to make pictures that conformed to the Renaissance construct.[31] The verticals and horizontals, the frame, the straight diagonals and elliptical foreshortening of curves, and the uniform detail of linear perspective ruled the development of lenses.[32] The definition of the picture itself predicted a mechanism, and the Cyclops in a box became, of course, the camera. The syntax and symbol system of painting were carried intact into the new technology. Photographs may *seem* more factual, because, unlike paintings, they have acquired the imprimatur of nature. Our error is conceptual—we see a discontinuity where none exists. Rather than being a break in the tradition of Western representation, the camera is in fact its culmination.

Photographs are the icons of a culture that places the machine above the male and the corporate entity above them both. The measures of greatness are competition and hierarchy. The dominant culture is made manifest by a faith in technique—a belief that once invented, a machine takes on an objective existence, natural in itself. The autonomous machine then drives history and supplies neutral evidence. In this scheme, photographs are a proof more reliable than any human witness. The evidence establishes a hierarchy. By competing, each man rises above another, and for the others to accept their losses, the measure of defeat must be objective, brooking no dissent. To appear impartial, the camera must, paradoxically, be partial, favoring one way of seeing above all others by slicing away from the complex experience of vision all other contexts, dimensions, foci, and perspectives. The freeze-frame and the photo-finish typify the culture of competition. Each day the race begins anew. To perpetuate the race, the dominant culture has granted immortality to corporate entities. Man, measured by technique, is the expression of these larger constructs. Technology, social class, and America itself are corporate—personifications that absorb the individual and collapse the author into technical, objective oblivion.

Both Trachtenberg and Maren Stange see the triumph of documentary photography as a triumph of capitalism—the accommodation of the camera artist to the style and order of corporate America.[33] But Lewis Hine's relationship with industry changed only superficially during his career. Even when he needed work, sometimes desperately, he did not betray himself. His own writing suggests a man driven by principle and artistic vision. When he turned to making work portraits, he changed his relationship—not to his patrons, but to his subjects. His work portraits seem to stand outside the market. No money was exchanged between artist and model. Although he shared the models' dependence on industrial corporations, his consideration appears to have been human and personal, identifying with the sitter. Like many workers, he lacked a steady job and a regular income (eventually he lost his home, and friends arranged for him to stay on as a renter). His message about workers paralleled his own need for work and his inability to support himself with photography. After a decade of trying to get industry to underwrite the portrayal of workers, he was left "isolated and essentially bitter."[34]

Hine's portraits are works of art, extending the tradition of portraiture to the worker. Only Gisèle Freund among historians of photography identified the portrait as a pivotal image in culture and also recognized in the camera the mechanization of portrait making.[35] As exceptions to the mass of documentary representations, the worker portraits express not the dominant values and relations in society as Berger suggests,[36] but an alternative vision.

THE INFINITE TITLE

The ancients defined painting linguistically, with the phrase, *ut pictura poesis*. Photography, being of a lower order, is defined as a "language."[37] Words describe scenes from the experience of vision. Pictures supposedly give the same description directly, the painting poetically, the photograph prosaically. Michel Foucault says that pictures and language have an "infinite relation":

> Neither can be reduced to the other's terms. . . . But if one wishes to keep the relation of language to vision open, if one wishes to treat their incompatibility as a starting-point for speech instead of an obstacle to be avoided, so as to stay as close as possible to both, then one must . . . preserve the infinity of the task.[38]

Language conventions help to perpetuate the cultural distinction between paintings and photographs. Ulrich Keller exaggerates when he says, "A painting usually is more or less complete in itself."[39] Conventional presentations of paintings, in museums as well as in reproduction, identify the artist, the date, the medium, the donor or owner, and, of course, the title—five clues to the spectator about the work's position in specific discourses: authorship, contemporary history, artistic genre, patronage, and subject matter or content.

The titles of history paintings refer the viewer to the historic discourse, religious paintings to religious narratives. Portrait titles relate the patron or sitter to society or politics. When painting shifted to everyday subject matter in the mid nineteenth century, the language applied to the works revealed how narrow a purpose was served. Common *themes* were elevated, not common people. Men working as stonecutters, for example, became a type. The sower was another type, but the man himself had no narrative. An untitled work pointed to the self-referential

form or subject. In all these narratives, the viewer was cast as an active participant, who brought a store of personal experience and knowledge to the interpretive task.

Walter Benjamin says that the captions of photographs "have an altogether different character [from] the title of a painting."[40] On every point the captions contrast. The photographer as author is invisible or credited in fine print, often set on its side as a legal notice of ownership. Photographs rarely have a title or name. The size and genre are absent. The caption eliminates all the potential narrative frames but one, the depicted content. According to Stuart Hall, "the caption selects and prefers one of the possible readings, then amplifies it."[41] Benjamin says that "captions have become obligatory"[42]; they free the viewer from the terror of indeterminacy.[43] By claiming to restate the event or scene as a natural fact, captions reveal the ideology of objectivity.

Lewis Hine used captions variably throughout his career. His 1934 pictures for the Tennessee Valley Authority appeared without captions in a report that grounded them in fact. His child labor pictures were captioned. He collected meticulous details: the place, the date, the machinery, the age of the children, their heights, and so on, but he didn't name the children. The documentation reflected the progressive survey method, in which anonymity served scholarly objectivity. The language sometimes worked at cross-purposes with the picture or the sponsor, illuminating the individual,[44] but usually the caption situated the person as a type. Stange says the text confirms the "fixed assumptions" about working people and about the viewer.[45] Documentary captions discourage interpretation by offering a stereotype.

In *Men at Work*, language is a minor element. The photographs occupy three-quarters of the forty-eight unnumbered pages. Most of the remaining quarter is white space framing the pictures and typography. In the quarto book (roughly letter size), the typical two-page spread displays two pictures, one filling one page and the other framed by white space that also holds a single caption. Half of the spreads include a two-word title, a generic identifying phrase, such as "Foundation Men" or "Tire Makers." The captions are short—averaging about thirty words—but, because most captions serve more than one picture, on average only twenty words describe each picture. Like the titles, the captions are generic. No individual in the book is identified by name. Instead, the men are labeled by job: engineer, welder, mechanic, miner. The captions describe the work generally, sometimes without mentioning the workers.

The language in *Men at Work* positions Hine prominently as author. In his introduction, he acknowledges the system of patronage, or corporate "cooperation," and identifies his medium as "photographic studies." The pattern of captioning differentiates the pictures. Work portraits have fewer than half the words used for construction shots. And construction workers are labeled more specifically, often with invented names—"plumber-up," "bell man," "bucker-up"—describing their work. Captions for the work portraits have fewer than half the job titles and avoid neologisms in favor of generic terms.

The language throughout conveys an upbeat tone and reveals several recurrent motifs. Men are described as physical bodies, engaged in hard work to express strength. They are also given mental attributes: skill, care, and pride in their work. In the construction pictures they are called team players, cooperating with each other for the general good, ambitious and indifferent to personal risk. This quality is absent in the work portrait captions, where men are described as spiritual and engaged in work larger than life, majestic to the point of dwarfing their bodies. These motifs also reflect a larger theme. The introduction calls the workers "real men," and the captions allude to manhood. One worker is called a "modern Thor," invoking the Norse god of thunder, war, and strength. Although no cowboys appear, the American mythical figure is invoked by a railroad brakeman "who has galloped over America." The language in *Men at Work* resembles the titles of paintings, referring the viewer to the discourse of manhood.

THE CIRCUMSCRIBED BODY

Barthes calls photography not a language but a noncoded iconic message.[46] His analysis sharply contrasts photographs to paintings, which transform their references to objects seen. He wrote that "there is no drawing, no matter how exact, whose very exactitude is not turned into style (the style of 'verism'); no filmed scene whose objectivity is not finally read as the very sign of objectivity."[47] The imitative arts, according to Barthes, turn the denotation of external things into style through a second order of connoted meanings: "The code of the connoted system is very likely constituted either by a universal symbolic order or by a period rhetoric, in short by a stock of stereotypes (schemes, colors, graphisms, gestures, expressions, arrangements of elements)."

In the documentary pictures of the press, Barthes says, the code of connotation is absent, swallowed up by the denotation, the "analogical plenitude." Thus a painting would be an icon, a photograph an index. Unless his semiotics is merely descriptive, Barthes evidently participates fully in the myth of photographic denotation. But the viewfinder transforms and composes the scene, and the camera encodes the Western perspective embedded in the mechanism.

Decoding pictures requires an analysis of their constituent elements. Although the analysis of form has been recently out of fashion, its use goes back at least to Cézanne.[48] Barthes identifies formal elements as the geometric semes in the semiotic structures of pictorial information. According to Hall, "These formal, compositional and expressive meanings reinforce and amplify the ideological message."[49]

Many of Hine's portraits—including his most famous, a Rembrandtesque portrait of a printer which was widely exhibited—were not published in *Men at Work*. But Hine identified a significant body of work by selecting from his pictures of the previous ten years. A work portrait presents an individual laborer, close enough to show his physical character but far enough to show his tools and machinery. Although *Men at Work* is divided physically between the pictures of the Empire State Building and the work portraits, the pictures themselves are a mix. One or two pictures in the portrait section show a group at a distance or a face at close quarters. In the construction section, roughly one-third of the pictures are portraits. All together, there are twenty-seven work portraits in the book.

In these portraits, the central figure is the male body, placed within the geometry of the frame, the value scale of chiaroscuro, and the linearity of perspective. These abstract elements are in themselves ambiguous. Every left implies a right and likewise up and down, large and small, and so forth. As with language, the parts take meaning from the context as a whole. The principle of simultaneous contrast illustrates the fundamental ambiguity of the parts of vision; a middle gray on a white background will appear much darker than the same gray on a black ground. The complexity of visual grammar is increased by the verbal context as well.

The framing of the work portraits suggests a positive mood. The human face most often appears in the upper left quadrant of the frame, gazing intently toward the right, the positive direction in Western culture. The position and implied direction of the gaze are somewhat modulated because the eyes often look toward the lower right quadrant. A few faces look left from the upper right, contrary to the Western direction of reading. Fewer still look to the right from the lower left quadrant. Only one—the frontispiece—looks down from the lower right. None stares directly out of the frame toward the camera or spectator. This pattern of composition places men in the position of beginnings, opening space to the right, so that reading flows from the left. The faces, with few exceptions, are high in the frame, a dominant, powerful position. This affirmative composition in the form echoes the ambitious tone of the captions.

However, value—the range from white to black—is muted in these portraits, extending from medium-light across the greys to black. The exact position of these grays on the continuum cannot be considered an artifact of reproduction—overinking, spreading on the glossy paper, or the like—because the portraits differ as a group from the higher contrast of the construction shots. Trachtenberg suggests that "the somber tonality of many of the work portraits may in fact register Hine's subliminal doubt about his own optimism."[50] The principle of simultaneous contrast supports Trachtenberg's observation. The more optimistic the text and the composition in the frame, the more somber the gray of the pictures will seem.

Other visual elements in the work portraits suggest tranquility. The scale is moderate—they are less often shown running off the pages, in a so-called full bleed, or as the smallest shot in a group of three, compared to the construction shots. Frames of white space tend to confine or tame the picture, divorcing it from its surroundings and indicating isolation or separation. The horizontal portraits indicate repose, especially in contrast to the slightly more vertical construction shots.

The male form also appears in relation to the geometry of other forms in the frame. Two motifs emerge. The minor motif is the straight line. In about a quarter of the portraits, the body addresses a rigid vertical form (a tool, bar, or machine part). In a few of these, a scatter of exploding shape (sparks or flames) springs from the shaft. A few others—about one-eighth of the portraits—present a body addressing a horizontal linear form (such as a drill, rod, or tool). The major motif, found in about half the pictures, juxtaposes the body and a circle. In roughly half of these, the body and the circle are overlapped or connected by means of one of the rigid linear forms. Two of the circles are small—near the scale of the human head—but most of the circles are very large, engulfing or sometimes dwarfing the body. In all, fully half of the work portraits depict the male form engaged in some way with a large, circular form. Only two of the portraits contain a body without a prominent rod or circle.

The narrowed frames of these portraits do not allow for a clear rendering of linear perspective. This divergence signals the alternative vision of the works, especially in contrast to the construction shots and Hine's documentary pictures. But perspective is still present, an artifact of the camera. In the pictures with larger circles, the perspective lines angle away and the circular forms recede in classic Renaissance fashion. The work portraits are largely controlled by this system of vision, but its effects are somewhat muted and played down in many of the pictures.

The syntax of words and forms in the work portraits sets up a repetitive pattern that is pronounced and emphatic. The pictures are titled much like paintings, with little appeal to the documentary mode. Instead, the language is sweeping and refers to manhood as a theme. The forms are redundant in their presentation not only of the male body but in its position, holding a linear form before an encompassing circle. The muted values set a tone of reverence, and the evidence of perspective is somewhat suppressed. This analysis of form has, in Erwin Panofsky's words, "already overstepped the limits of purely formal perception" and entered the interpretive realm of iconology. As Panofsky suggests, the levels of interpretation are indivisible in practice, but the first would be iconography.[51] The manifest content of the work portraits has but a few icons.

THE HOMOEROTIC ATTIRE

To understand the depiction of the male body, we cannot turn to an extensive literature of male art. Griselda Pollock says, "We never talk of men artists or male art."[52] Although the male has been ubiquitous—perhaps overwhelmingly so—in Western painting, the male presence has been by definition neutral. The male body has been thought problematic only in the work of homosexual artists, such as Leonardo da Vinci, Michelangelo Buonarroti, and the American Thomas Eakins.[53] Definitions of "gay art" usually presuppose a categorical difference that stands outside the generic male perspective as "homoerotic sex-market images."[54]

This attitude is reflected in a particular brand of feminism ascendant in the eighties.[55] Rosemary Betterton wrote that these feminists seek "to explain the position of women as spectators and to account for women's pleasure in images of women."[56] Their analysis served to confuse the fundamental questions about the relationship of spectator and model. The confusion arises from the assumption that any pleasure from viewing a body of the same sex must be explained away. Women's pleasure from looking at women differs from male pleasure because it is homoerotic. The urge to account for this ordinary human response is homophobic. Narcissism is a convenient but misplaced label. The painting is not a mirror or a lake into which one

can gaze and see oneself. The picture is neither the thing nor the reflected thing. Even the model, when peering at the artist's rendering of her, sees not herself but another, and she measures her image of herself against the rendering. The appropriate label is homoeroticism. The feminism of the eighties confused the sign and referent because that particular sexual gaze is proscribed. "Sexual messages are always delivered by the image of an unclothed body," says Hollander,[57] and, according to Weston Naef, "Photographers are the historians of desire, since the camera records only that to which their eyes are attracted."[58]

Because dress is central to the depiction of men, the clothing shown and any degree of undress whatever take on significance. If anything, "The dialectic of clothes and body is more sharply focused when both appear. . . . Conventions in partial exposure further demonstrate how the significance of nudity is created by clothes themselves, not by their absence."[59] The variety and wearing of men's clothing have traditionally been limited and differ only subtly.[60]

Hine's work portraits depict three general patterns of dress. The most common attire, worn by two-thirds of the men pictured, consists of denim overalls with a chambray shirt (or a heavy twill coverall) and a cap. Some also wear a simple twill jacket with widely spaced, rivet-style buttons. Their clothing is soiled and covers all but the face and hands, and even these may be hidden behind gloves and a mask or goggles. Many of their faces are turned away or depicted in shadow or without much detail. Their dress obscures their sexuality and their individuality in practical, functional plainness. They might be called the demure workers.

Another pattern of dress, worn by a quarter of the men, includes a chambray work shirt with the collar open and the sleeves rolled or pushed up to reveal the upper arms (one has removed the shirt to expose a singlet undershirt). The head is uncovered, the hair is mussed, but those who wear a hat choose a fedora instead of a cap. They are shown at closer quarters, their bodies cropped near the waist, but some wear twill work trousers. Although they gaze at their work, their faces, hair, and skin are detailed and individualized. They might be called the dashing workers.

Dashing worker. Untitled work portrait, by Lewis Hine ("Tire Makers: At the control wheel of an enormous calendar, making automobile tires"). From Men at Work *(1932; reprint, New York: Dover, 1977). By permission of George Eastman House.*

The final mode of dress appears only twice. These two men wear a dress shirt with sleeves pushed or rolled up. One has a vest, the other a tie. Both are hatless, but the soft focus removes most of the detail from their faces. Their exposed skin is clean. These specialists are interlopers in the world of work, who have dressed down for the task at hand. They are the romanticized workers.

These categories are not absolutely demarcated, and there is one striking exception. In the frontispiece, the worker is older and wears overalls, but he goes without a shirt, exposing his arms, shoulders, and back. These are smooth and gently curved. He is bent over, closed in on himself, and his limbs overlap. His eyes are averted, looking down but not at his work, and his face has little detail. The skin everywhere is undifferentiated, and the curvature of his arms completes a circle of highlight on the machine. The general effect is one of submission or obeisance. The voyeur is presented with a generalized worker, a male depicted as a conventionalized female. The frontispiece challenges the heterocentric perspective.

Demure men in Hine's first group fare no better than women under the voyeuristic, heterosexual gaze. They are as generalized as women. But rather than being idealized as expressions of nature, they are idealized as part of a mechanism. These men's bodies are desexualized, but the other men's are not. The dashing men who show the skin of their arms and chests and expose

Frontispiece. Untitled work portrait, by Lewis Hine (uncaptioned). From Men at Work *(1932; reprint, New York: Dover, 1977). By permission of George Eastman House.*

their faces and disheveled hair are fully sexual. They concentrate on their work while, aware of the onlooker, they assume a jaunty pose. This self-exposure—eroticism without submission, ordinary sexuality built into the web of quotidian relationships and occupations—comes closest to the feminist ideal that Betterton found in the work of Suzanne Valadon.[61]

THE WORKER'S TOOL

In painting and sculpture since ancient times, men have carried tools in a mannered way. Until the neoclassical period, their tools were implements of war: the sword and the spear. With the rise of nineteenth-century realism, men carried hoes, rakes, or staffs, instruments used in agriculture and travel. The interest in tools carried over into the work of Winslow Homer and the American realists. In portraiture, tools were greatly conventionalized, reflecting the interests and status of the sitter by means of a riding crop, a sword, a scepter, or the like. But after the nineteenth century, tools received little attention in major works of the Impressionists and the succeeding movements into the twentieth century, perhaps in reaction to the conventionality of their previous use.

In contrast, the machine as an icon in painting

reached its apex in Lewis Hine's day. The machine ideal informed the work of Cubists, Futurists, Constructivists, and De Stijl artists before World War I. Ann Ferebee says, "Undecorated and geometric objects symbolized the new machine age."[62] The mass destruction by the war machinery did little to dampen enthusiasm for machines in America. Dada in Europe rebelled against the machine ideal, but when Dada artists came to the United States, their opposition to technology confronted American optimism toward mechanical progress, and their work depicted the machine with a lighter, ironic touch. Francis Picabia's painting *A Young American Girl in a State of Nudity* (1916–17) is one such mechanical depiction. It contains the usual emphasis on the wheel or cog and on geometric precision, but the title also contains a significant allusion to the feminization of the machine. In the early twentieth century, as Jefferson Hunter suggests, "the American felt the machine as an intimate, physical presence, and identified his personal destiny with it."[63] And, as Miles Orvell notes, the union of man and machine had the camera as its offspring.[64]

The combination of men, tools, and machines was captured in the 1932 murals at the Detroit Institute of Arts. Diego Rivera depicted the automobile industry with an assembly line. Workers not only tend the machinery but pull and strain and hunch over intricate objects beneath a complex web of rollers, cogs, wheels, and overlapping curved runners and pulleys. The men are clothed, but free to expose the skin. As they push and pull with force, their muscles bulge.

In the *Men at Work* portraits, five of the men work with a tool such as a drill positioned from the groin; two of these show the buttocks as well (including the frontispiece). Three others are also shown from behind, and all but one of these are overly clad, demure workers. The sexuality of wielding phallic tools from the hip is brutish. Tools are ubiquitous in the other portraits as well. Fully half of the men are depicted using them—a drill, a crowbar, a wrench, a torch, or the like. The tools are not an accidental effect or the natural result of the circumstances of work. In many cases the tool is held, it might be said, ritually. The poses are contrived and the tool is a prop. The manner of engaging the tool has

Demure worker with phallic tool. Untitled work portrait, by Lewis Hine (uncaptioned). From the construction section of Men at Work *(1932; reprint, New York: Dover, 1977). By permission of George Eastman House.*

more to do with its iconic significance than with its use or function. The machine in Hine's work portraits engulfs the man in a web of spokes inscribed in a wheel. The body parts of the man blend into the geometry of the machine, sometimes echoing its parts but more often fading from view in the mechanical recesses and shadows.

Because they are candid, the construction shots reveal what the work portraits hide. Some workers caught in action have their shirts off. They reach out to each other, work in close proximity, and sometimes touch. The candid view catches glimpses of an exposed nipple and a bulge of fabric at the lap. In construction shots

Chummy workers. Untitled construction shot, by Lewis Hine ("Laying a beam"). From the supplement of Men at Work *(1932; reprint, New York: Dover, 1977). By permission of George Eastman House.*

excluded from the original edition but added in the 1977 supplement, men are even chummier. One man appears to embrace another. But they are cut-outs, silhouetted against the city skyline as the sun glints off their muscled arms and shoulders. The candid view objectifies men but reveals a hidden homoeroticism.

The construction shots also contain the icons of the city and the building, a larger frame that can only be touched on here. Hine's book came before what Jonathan Bayer calls the "movement away from the romantic view of the city as a remarkable creation of man, to an alienated view of the city, a destroyer of man."[65] The grand view emphasizes linear perspective; its geometry aligns and regiments the city and the structures. The streets recede to the vanishing point and the beams and buildings in the foreground march back layer after layer in the ideal of masculinist and heterosexist perspective.

THE PHALLUS ENCIRCLED

The straight line is a product of that perspective. Straight lines do not exist in vision, and rarely ever in nature. They are a construct, the product of a particular sort of envisioning that finds its strongest expression in science and engineering. The Parthenon was built with gently curving walls calculated to counteract the curvature of the visual field. In the arts, straight lines are aspired to not only in architecture but also in abstract paintings of the twentieth century, and of course in most paintings representing deep space since the Renaissance. Straight lines are defined as the universal, neutral form within the civilization where men are the universal and generic being. The male perspective dominates but is tacit.

The straight line also invokes the male sexual organ during arousal, further evidence of the link between linear perspective and the dominant view. The penis is never straight but is constructed that way as the epitome of masculine form. The phallus is thus the deeply encoded central construct in Western imagery. "A taboo image in our culture, it is however used instinctively and unconsciously throughout the whole of graphic communication," according to Philip Thompson and Peter Davenport.[66] In Christian iconography, the penis is associated with evil and temptation. The universal spectator cannot make men the object of vision without being "unnatural." The male and the phallus can be represented only indirectly, in the severe and sterile abstraction of the straight line. And male sexual pleasure in ejaculation must be disguised as the exploding or scattering form. Betty Edwards found the starburst pattern to be the analog for human energy and power.[67] The scatter does not always spring from the phallus but is invariably encompassed in circular form.

If men in Western culture must remain tacit and universalized, women, presumably, will be explicit, perhaps in the form of the circle. Although the curved line is a characteristic of the female shape in Western art, the circle is not the symbol of the feminine. Thompson and Davenport identify the triangle as the graphic form for female sexuality, representing the vaginal gate or door.[68] Edwards identifies curved and crossed forms as the essential analogs to femininity among nonartists.[69] These are also found in Griselda Pollock's photo essay on femininity in *Vision and Difference*.[70] The crossing and interlocking of curved forms represent the duality of male and female in Eastern thought as well as in the West.[71] Contrary to our assumption, the woman is not directly or simply evoked in circular form. Instead, the feminine is curvilinear and overlapping, and even the interlacing form may represent family and social bonds.[72] Rather than signaling femininity, the circle is

the symbol of social order. Rings tie women to men in betrothal and matrimony. The circlet, the wreath, crown, and hats generally reflect an encircling of the (generically male) individual and a submission to social and corporate identity.[73] Circles represent social exchange in the form of coins and social organization tied to agriculture and fertility in the Aztec calendar. The circle traditionally symbolizes the heavens.[74] In visual design, Paul Rand also identified the circle as the sign of eternity.[75]

All these elemental visual forms refer tacitly to the male. The straight line as his secret symbol controls the spatial grid and expresses the explosion of his energy. Curved forms that might suggest femininity are subjected to the grid and come to represent family bonds. The circle is the imposition of social constraints, but the feminine is secondary, subjected to the dominant masculine. In the dominant geometry, the female is hardly represented, and she has but the thinnest representation in *Men at Work*. In the work portraits, the iconography of the male body and its surroundings is superimposed on the syntax of line and form. The pattern of forms—the male body addressing, by means of sexual identity or energy, the engulfing realm of social organization or deity—is homocentric, men looking at men as sexual beings (however deeply coded), and referring only tangentially to women as the gender of the social boundaries. This representation, too direct for the comfort of many viewers in its day, signaled the escape from the virgin goddess by means of a mechanical god.

THE ROMANCE OF LABOR

The worker in painting appeared as a symbol of labor with the rise of realism in the nineteenth century. But the realists, who sought to open the subject matter of art to ordinary themes, relied on the language of pictures, which had developed a vocabulary only of nobility and grandeur. The worker depicted in the idiom of nineteenth-century painting was thus ennobled and romanticized. The romance of labor began with the agricultural worker, who in the American sense, labored in the Garden of Eden and was an icon in the pastoral ideal.[76] William Sydney Mount, in

Farmers Nooning (1836), imposes a certain nobility on his laborers and also invokes the feminine by averted gazes and by reclining, posterior, and enclosed poses. The black farmer, asleep with overlapping limbs, is watched by the white men. All the laborers are objectified as the other.

The romance of agriculture began to be transferred to industry by the end of the nineteenth century. Thomas Anshutz, working within the realistic tradition, brought the theme of the worker at rest to the industrial setting with his painting *Steel Workers—Noon Time* (c. 1882). The men are depicted in various poses that emphasize their musculature and exposed skin. Only the young bend over or sit. The male bodies overlap and interlace, appearing almost to embrace. The poses are self-conscious—men play-acting masculinity—but some assume an indifference, perhaps exaggerated, toward the viewer. The eroticism parallels that found in Michael Leonard's paintings of construction workers. But outside of a few examples, industrial labor has not been a central image in painting.

It has been the role of photography—especially the documentary genre, and Lewis Hine's work in particular—to establish the image of the industrial worker. Hine retained the romanticism of labor found in paintings and treated industry as a male preserve, in which anyone but a man becomes a victim. The women and children in his photographs are usually operatives, who tend the spools and looms of textile factories and assembly plants and appear silhouetted against and trapped within the grid of threads or electrical wires—the linear, vertical backdrop of the male perspective. The man as an industrial laborer reveals the analogy of man's muscular labor and the social power of the larger mechanism made from wheels. Hine fixed the image of masculine labor at its apex, before the electrical supplanted the mechanical as the ideal image of power.[77] *Men at Work* may seem unstylish or misguided because it marked the end of this particular, heroic view of labor.

Hine's image of labor developed on a backdrop of the economic forces of the twenties. The end of the Great War and a continuing recession in agriculture created an oversupply of laborers. Instead of the unrest of the previous decade, the twenties saw an increasingly dormant labor movement, and "corporate mastery of American life seemed secure."[78] Hine's insistence on the nobility of labor is poignant, and by depicting construction he pointed to the one industry in which labor was somewhat secure. According to David Montgomery, building projects continued "with little interruption from the turn of the century through the great depression." Construction was not one of the new, electricity-based industries, and "workers' treatment in the 1920s on construction sites . . . differed little from that of the 1880s."

Hine's selection of both a setting and a mode of representation looked backward, to the machine age. His depictions largely contradict the representation of labor by documentary photographers. Evans's pictures may show workplaces, but they are without workers. The men who appear are pointedly not working. Dorothea Lange photographed agricultural workers, male and female, but they were depicted *because* they were idle.[79] Margaret Bourke-White depicts a wide variety of workers, but not many of them are laborers. White-collar workers are more often shown, and agricultural labor almost not at all. One worker appears dwarfed by the round face of a train engine, but that image is the exception in *Say, Is This the U.S.A.*

African-Americans in documentary photography contrast particularly with Hine's Caucasian workers. Edwin Rosskam's overly rhetorical selection of FSA pictures in Richard Wright's *12 Million Black Voices* shows black men digging, toting, harvesting, and walking behind a plow and mule. Otherwise they are idle, sitting around, standing in line. One boy sleeps, another reads, but men either work at backbreaking labor or stand. The machine is notable for its absence. A similar effect is found in Eudora Welty's pictures. Wallace Stegner's effort to fight racial bigotry and bring minorities into *One Nation* still conveys the stereotypical image of the minority laborer. Filipinos and Mexicans do "stoop" labor and are given the same visual treatment of other workers of the depression. "Amerindians" and one black man operate machinery, but the text emphasizes that they are in training, engaging in an activity unnatural to them. Other minorities are equally true to stereotype, and the same pattern holds for Catholics and Jews in the final sections of the book. In Langston Hughes and Roy DeCarava's *The Sweet Flypaper of Life*, only one black man in ten works, predominantly at menial labor.

In subsequent works, American labor plays a tiny role. Robert Frank's photographs of *The Americans* include a single scene with industrial workers—a blurred assembly line with the weaving tubes overhead. The only other factory shot shows idle men seated along a looming brick wall. The automobile, the jukebox, and the television play a more prominent role in the depiction of men. Work, when shown, happens at a desk set deep in the frame—an abstraction, and a tiny one at that, among many more images of leisure. Labor is a deviation from the ideal, depicted just as infrequently as overt homosexuality. Whether the number of laborers who worked in heavy industry with mammoth circular machinery declined throughout the twentieth century is less important than the indication that their representation nearly vanished. George Gerbner argues that "to be 'true to life' in fiction would falsify the deeper truth of cultural and social values served by symbolic functions."[80] Documentary photography is artistic and symbolic, and to the degree laborers are underpresented compared to their actual numbers, the genre exposes the ideal of society, which devalues industrial labor.

Arthur Rothstein shows a virtual litany of occupations—painter, acrobat, store Santa, lifeguard, ice cream man, astronaut—but only a few who could be classed with laborers, including, significantly, convicts sentenced to hard labor. Machines are absent. But in both Frank and Rothstein, the costume of labor begins to appear. Nancy Vickers observed that the Elizabethans became fascinated by the paraphernalia of heraldry once the practical function of knighthood had disappeared from their culture.[81] Men's work finds continued expression in the culture as costume—jeans, undershirts, and work boots flourish in the absence of the laborer. *Men: 1950–1985* by Joan Liffring-Zug reads ironically like an catalog of male costume.

In *Interior America*, Chauncey Hare showed the new image of men, dressed in the garb of the worker and sitting at home, near the television set. The image has supplanted the actuality, at least as it is mediated through the camera. In-

creasingly, the costume is also accompanied by a show of flesh—the ripped jeans, the pushed up sleeves of chambray work shirts, and the tee shirt rolled to expose the deltoid muscles. The male body exposed has become a ubiquitous image in advertising. According to some commentators, Americans are becoming more frank about a man's body, and particularly his genitals, across the cultural range in theater, books, and film, as well as in television and advertising. The new frankness has two faces. One is the demystifying of the male gender, which Todd Gitlin says contributes to equality.[82] But Warhol's *America* suggests another option—the male sexualized and

Objectified worker. "Powerhouse Mechanic," by Lewis Hine. From a postcard (New York: Fotofolio, n.d.). By permission of George Eastman House.

objectified by the media. In Warhol's photographs, nobody is working. The men are famous, or beautiful in the style of homosexual erotica. If Warhol objectifies, other gay artists idealize. The work of Minor White and Robert Mapplethorpe presents the male body as muscular ideal, the pose monumental, the skin unblemished, and the face hidden or decapitated.

In the rush to represent the body and costume of men, the worker image—a man straining with tools to control the encompassing, encircling machine—is ubiquitous. He appears in the choreography of Mark Morris, in the medallions of the American Institute of Graphic Arts, in the advertising for beer and cola. Lewis Hine also plays a part in contemporary representations. Not only is his work being reexamined, but his pictures of men have reappeared along with similar images of the period. Instead of the worker whose sexuality is depicted as an ordinary part of daily activity, postcards from Hine's worker portraits are marketed with the man posing within the circle of the machine, tool erect and flesh exposed with muscles bulging. From the storehouse of Hine's work, these are his most objectified men. They are the icons in the cult of the male body.

THE VIRGIN AND THE DYNAMO

In American cosmology, "the universe is a 'mechanism'" and "the symbol of the machine incorporates a whole metaphysical system."[83] The cult of the machine grew up with the New World and reached its height in the early part of this century, when industry invested enormous amounts of capital into machinery.[84] Industrialists may have described their actions as economic, but their faith was religious. "Since the religious object is that which is uncritically worshipped, technology tends more and more to become the new god."[85]

Henry Adams witnessed the transition from the old to the new religion and recognized their icons. "The Woman had once been supreme," he says. "she was reproduction—the greatest and most mysterious of all energies; all she needed was to be fecund."[86] The virgin of the old religion also wielded another of "the most awesome powers of women, the power to nourish."[87] But the old symbolism of the virgin had no power in America, according to Adams. After attending the Great Exposition of 1900, he described the new religion, founded on the dynamo's spiritual effect.

To understand the virgin and the dynamo, he turned to art, and in the deepest of ironies—revealing a prescience that informs his whole work—he found the American expression of the power of sexuality in the work of Walt Whitman. Adams calls most other American art sexless and says that he "cared nothing for the sex of the dynamo until he could measure its energy."[88] This sentiment reveals the dominant vision of the world, which was built by and for heterosexual men on the foundations of linear perspective. This male-centered vision, which values the efficiency of the straight line and the mechanisms of geometry and hierarchy, controlled all other texts and conceptions in the culture. The machine was the inevitable expression of that form of vision. As Jacques Ellul insists, "Technique has penetrated the deepest recesses of the human being."[89] We even talk of the "machinery of the imagination."[90] In the dominant picture,

"machinery" stands for a principle, or perspective, or system of value . . . trace[d] through every department of thought and expression . . . each category [revealing] the same tendency: an excessive emphasis upon means as against ends, a preoccupation with the external arrangement of human affairs as against their inner meaning and consequences.[91]

Richard Hoggart restates the principle as, "whatever serves and suits the machine is right."[92] In this way the machine was greeted as a god, with ecstasy and dread.[93] The technical view overtook even organized religion in the theological debates about science in the twenties and thirties in America.[94] But its ascendancy was to be its own undoing.

Lewis Hine took up the camera in 1904, the year Frank Lloyd Wright argued that "this transforming force, whose outward sign is the . . . machine, is now grown to the point that the artist must take it up . . . although there is involved an adjustment to cherished gods."[95] Like Wright and Herbert Read,[96] Hine set out to conform the

Female worker. "A Madonna of the Machine," by Lewis Hine. From Women at Work, *ed. Jonathan L. Doherty (New York: Dover, 1981). By permission of George Eastman House.*

gods of Renaissance perspective, as embedded in the camera, to the new religion. Allan Sekula called him a mystic whose "mysticism corresponds to the status of the photograph as spiritual expression."[97]

Scholars have noted the religious quality of *Men at Work*. Trachtenberg suggested that Hine built up "a modern version of the cathedral."[98] Stott says the book "portrayed construction workers and engine builders as the selfless priests . . . in the modern cult of the machine."[99] That these men are priests can be seen in contrast to Hine's photographs of women. Of the

153 pictures in the posthumous collection *Women at Work*, only a few present the female form ministering to the machine. The only image of a woman composed like the majority of work portraits in *Men at Work* is a picture titled "A Madonna of the Machine." This particular representation has the homoerotic force of a related work described by Mary Ann Caws—"the tale of how woman harmonizes with her partner . . . She is in complete understanding of her mechanical lover" in the act of "metallic reproduction."[100]

In his "Madonna" and in *Men at Work*, Hine served the cult of the machine, but in the work portraits he moved further, from showing god through the machine to showing the god himself: man. Rather than being the link in the history of documentary style, the work portraits are a link in art's representation of manhood which began earlier in the century with Egon Schiele's drawn and painted self-portraits. Hine's images took part in the burst of male representation after World War I that included the beginnings of nudism, the founding of bodybuilding magazines, and the marketing of homosexual erotica.[101] According to Mircea Eliade, "Through the mediation of artistic expression, the attributes of a religious abstraction are revealed. . . . Sacred art seeks to represent the invisible by means of the visible."[102]

The machine icon of masculinist culture turned on man himself to reveal its maker. As Hine observed in *Men at Work*, machines do not make themselves: "The character of the men is being put into the motors, the airplane, the dynamos upon which the life and happiness of millions of us depend." In the dominant discourse, the other had been defined as female, the force of social constraint. The escape from the power of the woman was made by means of the machine, which seemed to provide reproduction and nourishment of its own. But in escaping the woman, man confronted himself. The story of the death of the machine age is an echo of Oedipus and Narcissus. If the self and the other are the same, mythology suggests only two alternatives, to kill the other or to waste the self in futile confusion. These alternatives are played out in all the cultural representations of women and homosexuality and in actual and mediated violence against them and against minorities.[103] The existence of the racial, sexual, and cultural other confronts the mechanical vision that, in Lewis Mumford's phrase, "anesthetizes every part of the personality that will not easily conform to its mechanical needs."[104]

THE ALTERNATIVE VISION

But there is an alternative. It incorporates the insights of feminism and gay liberation, without their limitations. Feminism offers a mode of representation that sees the body as simultaneously aesthetic, sexual, and sharply individual. The alternative vision shares that mode without the homophobia, common in the eighties, that must justify the woman's pleasure in seeing her own gender. Gay liberation suggests the possibility that beholding homoerotically is a simple, common experience requiring no justification. The alternative vision shares that freedom, without participating in the objectification and idealization of men's bodies typical of homosexual erotica. The alternative vision replaces mechanism with imagination. Instead of the ideology of objectivity, which encourages a fixed perspective and a rigid canon based on hierarchy and stereotyping, the alternative proposes the ideology of particularity. This mode of vision was identified by William James, who

> noted our marked indifference to forms of existence other than our own, our habitual and pervasive intolerance of what is alien, in short, our characteristic inability through an act of imagination to get outside our own skins, to put ourselves in the place of others, to understand that the only hope of escaping from the prison of self-regarding egotism, is by learning how to imagine, acknowledge, and value what is distinctly individual and other.[105]

The new way of seeing focuses on the self and the vagaries of vision. Its central metaphor, human sight, suggests the primary role of the interpreter, the I in the eye. Knowing is then a creative act, and communication is essentially persuasive. Because knowledge is inherently limited and constructed, particularism replaces orthodoxy, and individuals participate in their own repre-

sentation. We do so by forming and reforming groups. In the face of politics, we create interest groups that share our goals. To confront the media, we join audiences that reflect our geography and taste. Within the academy, we form departments of women's, African-American, gay, Caribbean, labor, and cultural studies. This particularism eschews the deductive logic of science and engineering in favor of artistic vision, which explores the specific, working inductively until a larger pattern emerges.

Much that critics decry in the new visual culture is not new but a return to the complexity of vision, unaided by linear perspective that organizes the culture hierarchically "while the true structure of privilege remains unnamed."[106] Instead of efficiency, the new vision offers the paradoxes inherent in the thing and in the image, prying the referent from the sign as experienced in vision. The ambiguities of scale and luminosity, which trouble those who compare paintings and photographs to television, are present in human eyesight. The alternative vision acknowledges the ambiguity rather than longing for the old certainty. Finally, the new vision accepts the central paradox of seeing and believing, for sight is never twice the same—light and color are fluid. Instead of diving in to swim, the critics seek the solid ground of pigments, chemistry, and pictures. It is a world that never existed, since those very pictures, within the field of vision, are as inconstant and mutable as all things seen.

Hine's work portraits gave an early glimpse of the alternative. The critics of his vision demonstrate what Susan Sontag calls "the American impatience with reality."[107] His images of male bodies make us uncomfortable to the degree we see from the dominant perspective, and in doing so, they suggest the alternative. What Hine explicitly, like Henry Adams unknowingly, foresaw was a vision of the dominant I of Western culture as the self and as the other at once. The only way out of male dominance is through examining men. In so doing, we may come to the dead ends of homophobia or sex-market homoerotica. But it is possible that we may acquire the alternative vision, which finds pleasure in imagining ourselves in others—because (not in spite) of our sexual, racial, or cultural difference. This image, present in *Men at Work*, is a fully realized portrait, at once sexual and social, self and other, with all its inherent paradox.[108]

NOTES

1. Lewis W. Hine, *Men at Work* (New York: Dover, 1977), n. p. Others appeared posthumously.

2. For a summary of Hine's career, see Naomi Rosenblum, "Biographical Notes," *America and Lewis Hine: Photographs, 1904–1940* (New York: Aperture, 1977), 16–25, and Daile Kaplan, ed., *Photo Story: Selected Letters and Photographs of Lewis W. Hine* (Washington, D.C.: Smithsonian Institution Press, 1992).

3. See, for example, David Macaulay's *Unbuilding* (London: Hamilton, 1981).

4. The photographs were better accepted by collectors.

5. Judith Mara Guttman, *Lewis W. Hine and the American Social Conscience* (New York: Walker, 1967), 38.

6. Alan Trachtenberg, *Reading American Photographs: Images as History, Mathew Brady to Walker Evans* (New York: Hill and Wang, 1989), 133.

7. Susan Meyer, "In Anxious Celebration: Lewis Hine's *Men at Work*," *Prospects* 17 (1992): 319–52.

8. Trachtenberg, *Reading American Photographs*, 204.

9. Don Gifford, *The Farther Shore: A Natural History of Perception* (New York: Atlantic Monthly Press, 1990), 187–88.

10. Guttman, *Lewis W. Hine*, 23.

11. John Berger, *Ways of Seeing* (London: BBC and Penguin, 1972), 47.

12. Berger, *Ways of Seeing*, 269.

13. See Carol M. Armstrong, "Edgar Degas and the Representation of the Female Body" in *The Female Body in Western Culture: Contemporary Perspectives*, ed. Susan Rubin Suleiman (Cambridge: Harvard University Press, 1986), 223–42; and Colleen McNally and Arnold S. Wolfe, "Deconstructing Images: Understanding the Role of Images in the Social Production of Meaning," *Investigating Visual Literacy*, ed. Darrell G. Beauchamp, Judy Clark-Baca, and Robert A. Braden (Blacksburg, Va.: International Visual Literacy Association, 1991), 291–300.

14. Anne Hollander, *Seeing through Clothes* (New York: Viking, 1978), 209.

15. For example, see Francois de Louville, *The Male Nude: A Modern View* (New York: Rozzoli, 1985); and Peter Weiermair, *The Hidden Image: Photographs of the Male Nude in the Nineteenth and Twentieth Centuries*, trans. Claus Nielander (Cambridge: MIT Press, 1988).

16. Hollander, *Seeing through Clothes*, 234–39.

17. In *Say, Is This the U.S.A.*, Margaret Bourke-White (with Erskine Caldwell) shows most people as emblematic of roles or places, in typical costume, but the men are nonchalant, the women ornamental. Men who do not face the camera often gaze at women. In *An American Exodus*, Dorothea Lange represents mostly men; women, when shown, are depicted in the gestures of nurturing others, often presenting their backs to the camera.

18. Critics identified documentary style in the 1930s but, as Trachtenberg argues, actually lionized pictorialism by finding expressive form in documentary pictures and displaying them in museums (*Reading American Photographs*, 169). These stylistic distinctions were passed down in subsequent histories and reverberated in the institutional forms of photographic practice. See Beaumont Newhall, *The History of Photography from 1939 to the Present* (New York: Museum of Modern Art, 1982), for example, and compare Helmut Gersheim, *The History of Photography from the Camera Obscura to the Beginning of the Modern Era* (New York: McGraw-Hill, 1969).

19. William Stott, *Documentary Expression and Thirties America* (Chicago: University of Chicago Press, 1973), 21.

20. John Fiske and John Hartley, *Reading Television*, New Accents (London: Methuen, 1978), 24.

21. Seeing and belief are explored in R. L. Gregory, *The Intelligent Eye* (New York: McGraw-Hill, 1970).

22. C. L. Hardin, *Color for Philosophers: Unweaving the Rainbow* (Indianapolis, Ind.: Hackett, 1989), 8–10.

23. Hardin, *Color for Philosophers*, 7.

24. Stott, *Documentary Expression*, 31.

25. Natural vision seems cameralike to us, just as other forms of vision seemed natural in earlier cultures, as noted by Arnold Hauser in *The Philosophy of Art History* (New York: Knopf, 1959), 399ff. Our modern camera vision is an invention of greater significance than any machine. "By conditioning the audience, the photograph became the norm in the appearance of everything. It was not long before men began to think photographically," says William M. Ivins, Jr., in *Prints and Visual Communication*, Graphic Art 10 (New York: Da Capo Press, 1969), 138.

26. One description of the visual literacy approach is in Len Masterman, *Teaching about Television* (New York: Macmillan, 1980).

27. Roland Barthes, *Camera Lucida: Reflections on Photography*, trans. Richard Howard (New York: Hill and Wang, 1981), 14.

28. Quotations are from Alan Trachtenberg, ed., *Classic Essays on Photography* (New Haven: Leete's Island Books, 1980), 111–12.

29. In Pliny's story of a competition between artists, the winner painted a curtain so real that his opponent asked him to pull it back and show his work. See Norman Bryson, *Vision and Painting: The Logic of the Gaze* (New Haven: Yale University Press, 1983).

30. Erwin Panofsky, *Perspective as Symbolic Form* (New York: Zone, 1991), 27.

31. Joel Snyder, "Picturing Vision," *The Language of Images*, ed. W. J. T. Mitchell (Chicago: University of Chicago Press, 1980), 230–40.

32. "If we took some of the theories of the Renaissance at their face value we should have to conclude that beauty ... can be constructed with a rule and compass," writes Irving Babbitt, *The New Laokoon: An Essay on the Confusion of the Arts* (Boston: Houghton Mifflin, 1910), 218.

33. Trachtenberg, *Reading American Photographs*, 230; Maren Stange, *Symbols of Ideal Life: Social Documentary Photography in America 1890–1950* (Cambridge: Cambridge University Press, 1989), 87.

34. Guttman, *Lewis W. Hine*, 42.

35. Gisèle Freund, *Photography and Society* (Boston: Godine, 1980).

36. Berger, *Ways of Seeing*, 86–87.

37. See John R. Whiting, *Photography Is a Language* (New York: Ziff-Davis, 1946), 5–10, for example.

38. Michel Foucault, *The Order of Things: An Archaeology of the Human Sciences* (New York: Vintage, 1973), 9–10.

39. Ulrich Keller, "Photographs in Context," *Image* 19, no. 4 (1976): 1.

40. Walter Benjamin, "The Work of Art in the Age of

Mechanical Reproduction," *Illuminations*, ed. Hannah Arendt (New York: Schocken, 1986), 226.

41. Hall, "The Determinations of News Photographs," in *The Manufacture of News: Social Problems, Deviance and the Mass Media*, rev., ed. Stanley Cohen and Jock Young, Communication and Society (London: Constable, 1981), 227.

42. Benjamin, "The Work of Art," 226.

43. Trachtenberg, *Reading American Photographs*, 225.

44. See the example cited by Stange, *Symbols of Ideal Life*, 78.

45. Stange, *Symbols*, 81.

46. Roland Barthes, *Image, Music, Text*, trans. Stephen Heath (New York: Noonday, 1977), 36.

47. The quotations of Barthes in this section are from *Image*, 16–18.

48. Gyorgy Kepes, in *Language of Vision* (Chicago: Theobald, 1945), asserted the unified grammar of pictures. Heinrich Wolfflin used formal elements to discover the patterns of historic styles in his 1932 classic *Principles of Art History: The Problem of the Development of Style in Later Art* (New York: Dover, 1950), 13–16.

49. Stuart Hall, "The Determinations of News Photographs," 242.

50. Trachtenberg, *Reading American Photographs*, 223.

51. Erwin Panofsky, *Meaning in the Visual Arts* (New York: Doubleday, 1955), 26, 39.

52. Griselda Pollock, "Women, Art and Ideology: Questions for Feminist Art Historians," in *Visibly Female: Feminism and Art Today*, ed. Hilary Robinson (London: Camden, 1987), 203–21.

53. Emmanuel Cooper, *The Sexual Perspective: Homosexuality and Art in the Last 100 Years in the West* (London: Routledge and Kegan Paul, 1986), 2–12, 31–35.

54. Nicolas A. Moufarrege, "Lavender: On Homosexuality and Art," *Arts Magazine* 57, no. 2 (1982): 80.

55. The state of thought in the field is summarized in a special issue, The Spectatrix, edited by Janet Bergstrom and Mary Ann Doane, of *Camera Obscura* (May–September 1989).

56. Rosemary Betterton, "How Do Women Look?: The Female Nude in the Work of Suzanne Valadon," Robinson, *Visibly Female*, 255 (note no. 52).

57. Hollander, *Seeing through Clothes*, 178.

58. Weston J. Naef, *Counterparts: Form and Emotion in Photographs* (New York: Dutton, n.d.), 65.

59. Hollander, *Seeing through Clothes*, 236.

60. Hollander, *Seeing through Clothes*, 348.

61. Betterton, *How Do Women Look*, 250–71.

62. Ann Ferebee, *A History of Design from the Victorian Era to the Present* (New York: Van Nostrand Reinhold, 1970), 78.

63. Jefferson Hunter, *Image and Word: The Interaction of Twentieth-Century Photographs and Texts* (Cambridge: Harvard University Press, 1987), 66, 73.

64. Miles Orvell, *The Real Thing: Imitation and Authenticity in American Culture, 1880–1940* (Chapel Hill: University of North Carolina Press, 1989), 201.

65. Jonathan Bayer, *Reading Photographs: Understanding the Aesthetics of Photography* (New York: Pantheon, 1977), 60.

66. Philip Thompson and Peter Davenport, *The Dictionary of Graphic Images* (New York: St. Martin's Press, 1980), 179.

67. Betty Edwards, *Drawing on the Artist Within* (New York: Simon and Schuster, 1986), 85.

68. Thompson and Davenport, *Dictionary*, 245.

69. Edwards, *Drawing*, 91.

70. Griselda Pollock, *Vision and Difference: Femininity, Feminism and Histories of Art* (London: Routledge, 1988).

71. Germano Facetti and Alan Fletcher, *Identity Kits: A Pictorial Survey of Visual Signals* (New York: Van Nostrand Reinhold, 1971), 41.

72. As in, for example, the Japanese family arms listed by Adrian Frutiger, *Signs and Symbols: Their Design and Meaning* (New York: Van Nostrand Reinhold, 1989), 317.

73. Facetti and Fletcher, *Identity Kits*, 3.

74. Thompson and Davenport, *Dictionary*, 110.

75. Paul Rand, *A Designer's Art* (New Haven: Yale University Press, 1985), 14.

76. Leo Marx, *The Machine in the Garden* (New York: Oxford University Press, 1964), 88–98.

77. Marshall McLuhan, *Understanding Media: The Extensions of Man* (New York: New American Library, 1964), 175.

78. Quotations in this paragraph are from David Montgomery, *The Fall of the House of Labor: The Workplace, the State, and American Labor Activism, 1865–1925* (New York: Cambridge University Press, 1987), 7, 176, 110.

79. In her 1969 addendum, unemployment still is shown, but shopping has replaced loitering.

80. George Gerbner, "Teacher Image in Mass Culture: Symbolic Function of the 'Hidden Curriculum,'" *Communications Technology and Social Policy: Understanding the New "Cultural Revolution,"* ed. George Gerbner, Larry P. Gross, and William H. Melody (New York: Wiley-Interscience, 1973), 268.

81. Nancy J. Vickers, "This Heraldry in Lucrece's Face," in Suleiman, 210 (see note 13).

82. Lena Williams, "Bodies Go Public: The Nature of Privacy Changes for Men, Too," *New York Times*, 31 Oct. 1990, natl. ed.: B1, 8.

83. Marx, *Machine in the Garden*, 165.

84. Montgomery, *Fall of the House*, 215.

85. John Wilkinson, "Translator's Introduction," in Jacques Ellul, *The Technological Society* (New York: Knopf, 1964), xi.

86. Henry Adams, *The Education of Henry Adams*, (1918; reprint, Boston: Houghton Mifflin, 1961), 384.

87. Margaret R. Miles, "The Virgin's One Bare Breast: Female Nudity and Religious Meaning in Tuscan Early Renaissance Culture," Suleiman, 207 (see note 13).

88. Adams, *Education of Henry Adams*, 385.

89. Jacques Ellul, *The Technological Society* (New York: Knopf, 1964), 325.

90. John Brumfield, "Apples and Oranges There May Be; and May Be Not-Photography, Too," in *Photography and Language*, ed. Lew Thomas (Berkeley: University of California Press, 1979), 35.

91. Marx, *Machine in the Garden*, 171.

92. Richard Hoggart, *Speaking to Each Other: Essays by Richard Hoggart*, vol. 1 of *About Society*, 2 vols. (London: Chatto and Windus, 1970), 112.

93. Orvell, *The Real Thing*, 158.

94. Giles Gunn, *The Interpretation of Otherness: Literature, Religion, and the American Imagination* (New York: Oxford University Press, 1979), 13.

95. Herbert Read, *Art and Industry* (New York: Horizon, 1953), frontispiece.

96. Read, *Art and Industry*, xi.

97. Allan Sekula, "On the Invention of Photographic Meaning," *Photography in Print: Writings from 1816 to the*

Present, ed. Vicki Goldberg (New York: Simon and Schuster, 1981), 472.

98. Trachtenberg, *Reading American Photographs*, 224.

99. Stott, *Documentary Expression*, 213.

100. Mary Ann Caws, "Ladies Shot and Painted: Female Embodiment in Surrealist Art," in Suleiman, 278 (see note 13).

101. Weiermair, *The Hidden Image*, 15.

102. Mircea Eliade, *Symbolism, the Sacred, and the Arts*, ed. Dian Apostolos-Cappadona (New York: Crossroad, 1986), 55.

103. Marshall McLuhan, *The Mechanical Bride: Folklore of Industrial Man* (Boston: Beacon, 1951), 98.

104. Lewis Mumford, *Art and Technics* (New York: Columbia University Press, 1952), 10.

105. Gunn, *Interpretation of Otherness*, 176.

106. Carol Shloss, *In Visible Light: Photography and the American Writer, 1840–1940* (New York: Oxford University Press, 1987), 267.

107. Susan Sontag, *On Photography* (New York: Farrar, Straus & Giroux, 1977), 59.

108. This chapter was presented to the Commission on Visual Communication at the Speech Communication Association Convention, Atlanta, November 1991.

6

Auden and the "Arctic Stare": Documentary as Public Collage *in* Letters from Iceland

Marsha Bryant

*L*ETTERS FROM ICELAND, A COLLABORATION BEtween W. H. Auden and Louis MacNeice as well as between photographs and the written word, has been unjustly relegated to the margins of Auden criticism since it first appeared in 1937.[1] Appreciated for its wit but often dismissed for its lack of conventional structure, the book is generally regarded as an entertaining travelogue or "literary holiday" by critics of Auden's poetry. At the same time, *Letters from Iceland* has been assigned to a marginal position by critics of travel literature. For example, Paul Fussell claims that it "marks the decadent stage in the course of the between-the-wars travel book."[2] I believe that the lack of critical attention to this text is partly due to the "travel book" label. While Auden certainly devotes some attention to describing Iceland and its inhabitants, his primary concern in *Letters from Iceland* is a more fundamental one—the politics of representation. The "travel book" label fails to address the purposeful disjunction Auden achieves by mixing genres and dislocating perspective through his poems, prose letters to various friends, quotations from previous travelers, and his own photographs.[3] A more productive approach to this text would take into

account the fact that Auden had just ended his six-month's job with a documentary film collective before traveling to Iceland. This acknowledgement certainly calls for more attention to the book's photographs. Initially Auden's borrowings from documentary were empowering, allowing him to expand the frame of his vision to include Iceland's workers and industry. But this very power proved to be politically suspect. Auden's first-hand experience with film made him aware of the politics of visual representation, so that he experimented with camera framing and with collage form in order to blur the line between observer and observed in *Letters from Iceland*. As creating images with pen and camera made him more self-conscious about representation, Auden came to recognize the inherent authority of documentary. He became distrustful of its eye-witness accounts and class inequality, anticipating by several decades such revisionist critiques as Bill Nichols's and John Tagg's. *Letters from Iceland* is the first literary text in which Auden negotiated his problematic relationship with documentary representation—a process he would continue through the end of the thirties. Examining this text as a response to documentary reveals its importance in understanding Auden's eventual disillusionment with socially conscious art.

It would be impossible for me to provide a thorough account of the entire book in the limited space of this essay. However, a brief chapter-by-chapter summary gives some indication of its radical disjunction, along with the portions I will emphasize in my discussion. Most chapters are individual "letters"—in verse, prose, or both—which do not make up a continuous narration. The majority of the book's illustrations are Auden's photographs, usually printed two to a page. Scattered throughout the book, these and other illustrations are often but not always located near related verbal text. Chapter 1 presents the first part of *Letter to Lord Byron*, a long poem which Auden divides into five separate chapters. Since *Letter to Lord Byron* has received far more critical attention than any other part of *Letters from Iceland*, I will refer to it only in the context of the book's relation to documentary and collage. The next chapter is addressed to Christopher Isherwood and contains Auden's poem "Journey to Iceland." MacNeice's first contribution, chapter 3, justifies the writers' decision to make their journey. The following chapter, "For Tourists," provides typical guidebook information about such matters as currency and transportation. Chapter 5 continues *Letter to Lord Byron*, followed by an unusual chapter containing quotations from various travel books on Iceland (Auden entitles it "Sheaves from Sagaland"). Significant because of its public collage, "Sheaves" demonstrates the ways Auden revises High Modernist collage to create a double exposure of Icelanders and foreign observers. In chapter 7, "Letter to R. H. S. Crossman," Auden explores the concept of framing by pitting documentary and poetic vision against each other. After another installment to Byron, Auden begins his series of prose letters to Erika Mann Auden in which he discusses photography and travel writing.[4] Interrupting the two Mann letters is MacNeice's poem "Eclogue from Iceland." Another of MacNeice's chapters, "Hetty to Nancy," parodies travel diaries with a gender reversal. Calling himself "Hetty" and Auden "Maisie," MacNeice gives a prose account of a camping expedition the authors made with a group of En-

glish schoolboys. More important for my essay, the chapter describes Auden's experiments with camera angles. The autobiographical fourth part of *Letter to Lord Byron* comes next, followed by Auden's chapter addressed to Kristian Andreirsson, an Icelander. In chapter 15 Auden writes to his film colleague William Coldstream. The Coldstream letter is the culminating attempt to represent the totality of his Iceland experience, and Auden employs a highly self-conscious, disjointed form which simulates the unedited rushes of a documentary film. The book's final chapters are the last segment of *Letter to Lord Byron*, and Auden and MacNeice's terza rima "Last Will and Testament." One cannot help but find *Letters from Iceland*'s physical appearance more jarring than that of many High Modernist fragmented texts such as Eliot's *The Waste Land*, Pound's *Cantos*, or Auden's own *The Orators*.

Letters from Iceland has usually been read as either pure entertainment or as a commentary on the England of the late 1930s from the vantage point of a remote country.[5] In both cases it has been classified as a travel book—a label that has survived in more recent studies such as Fussell's *Abroad* (1980) and Edward Callan's *Auden: A Carnival of Intellect* (1983), as well as in the book's paperback reissue in Paragon House's Armchair Traveller Series (1990). However, these standard readings and the "travel book" label fail to account for *Letters from Iceland*'s radically disjunctive form. Edwin Muir, one of the first reviewers, called it "a pleasantly formless book"; more recently, A. T. Tolley largely dismisses it as a travel book because he finds it "too filled out with extraneous material."[6] In a more perceptive comment about form, George T. Wright argues that Auden's text demands an active reader: "The audience as well as the poet is supposed to think, instead of passively receiving picturesque descriptions. So the book shifts from one kind of writing to another, from one author to another, with the abruptness of fantasies or dreams."[7] Again, I find a comparison with documentary useful in engaging with this text. Rather than dislocating travelogue with "fantasies or dreams," Auden disrupts the expository structure of documentary with unanchored montage. The book lacks the authoritative voice-over that lends structure to conventional documentaries.

By creating loosely edited rushes instead of a linear sequence, Auden invites the reader/viewer to construct meaningful relationships among the book's competing parts. In fact, we can say that *Letters from Iceland* calls into question the very possibility of representing that country, not only for the reader but for Auden as well.

Auden adapted much of the book's political vision and his photographs' style from the General Post Office (G.P.O.) Film Unit. He had just ended his six-month's job working for the G.P.O. Unit and its affiliates before coming to Iceland. Considering the Unit's rapid production rate, this time was substantial; Auden wrote verse and prose commentary for five documentary films: *Coal Face* (1935), *Night Mail* (1936), *The Way to the Sea* (1937), *The Londoners* (1939), and *God's Chillun* (1939). Besides writing, he occasionally served as directorial assistant and learned how films were edited. In addition, Auden examined the medium's potential and limitations in his review of Paul Rotha's book *Documentary Film*.

British documentary filmmaking was still in its first decade when Auden began his employment with the G.P.O. Unit. Its practitioners and sponsors saw much promise in the medium's ability to educate the general public. For many, documentary was also a potential force in leftist politics. As Samuel Hynes comments in *The Auden Generation*, this kind of film "was to serve as an instrument for spreading political, sociological, and economic knowledge, and as a counter-force to the bourgeois propaganda media—the national newspapers, commercial entertainment-films, and public education."[8] One can see its appeal to the young Auden, who had written in *The Poet's Tongue* that poetry's concern is with "extending our knowledge of good and evil, perhaps making the necessity for action more urgent and its nature more clear, but only leading us to the point where it is possible for us to make a rational and moral choice."[9]

The G.P.O. Unit, under documentary pioneer John Grierson's direction from 1933 to 1937, had its beginnings in the Empire Marketing Board (E.M.B.) Film Unit. At the E.M.B., Grierson formed a team of collaborators whose "mission" was to depict the British empire's different regions and industries to one another. Their best-known films are *Drifters* (1929), *Industrial Britain* (1931), and *Granton Trawler* (1934). When the E.M.B. was closed, its Film Unit was moved to the G.P.O. to publicize that agency's various communications and technologies. This government support allowed the film collective to continue experimenting with recording on-location sound and integrating film music and verse commentaries with the flow of images. In addition, the G.P.O. headquarters provided a base for promoting documentary filmmaking. Harry Watt, codirector of *Night Mail*, recalls such missionary zeal in an interview: "We all of us went round lecturing at film societies, raising enthusiasm for this type of film and running films." Auden gave a brief lecture on "Poetry and Film" to the North London Film Society in 1936.[10]

Working on films about mail trains and coal mining prompted Auden to revise his approach to representing industry. One of Grierson's goals for both the E.M.B. and the G.P.O. was to make the working class visible to the British general public. Defending his early thirties films in "The Course of Realism," he writes: "The workers' portraits of *Industrial Britain* were cheered in the West End of London. The strange fact was that the West End had never seen workmen's portraits before—certainly not on the screen."[11] Auden always had an eye for northern England's industrial landscape, but the "Auden country" of his earlier career was a landscape in which people were often intruders—full of wrecked machinery and abandoned mines.[12] In contrast, the Iceland book shows a populated landscape full of farmers, haymakers, fishers, and herring gutters. Auden's photographs do not depict people labeled "writer," "attorney," or "banker." Like his colleagues at the G.P.O. Unit, Auden finds workers not merely suitable but necessary subjects to show his readers. Only in two photographs, "Herring Factory" and "Whaling Station during the Lunch-hour," do we see industrial machinery without the people who operate it. This focus on workers reflects the G.P.O. Unit's belief that on-location recording allows the documentary artist to depict them "realistically." As his comments reveal, Grierson does not doubt the authenticity of his "workmen's portraits." In the same essay he faults early filmmakers for lacking "social confidence and an easy acceptance of the right to social observation."[13] So de-

gave one an extraordinary vision of the cold controlled ferocity of the human species.[14]

One detects similar emotions in the three photographs, which Auden presents more confidently. The first, entitled "Whaling Station during the Lunch-hour," shows a large saw on a mechanical arm cutting across the background of whale pieces, rails, and ladders (*Letters* 148).[15] By fore-

"Whaling Station during the Lunch-hour," by W. H. Auden. From Letters from Iceland *(London: Faber, 1937). Photographs from* Letters from Iceland *are reprinted by permission of the Estate of W. H. Auden; ©1937 by W. H. Auden; copyright renewed 1965 by W. H. Auden.*

spite the G.P.O. Unit's attention to the working class, the privileged eye is the one *behind* the camera.

In some of his photographs for *Letters from Iceland,* Auden displays a similar visual authority in organizing and presenting labor. The images that most closely resemble a conventional documentary sequence are grouped together in the chapter "W. H. Auden to Erika Mann Auden No. 2." Here Auden's depiction of a whaling station emulates the G.P.O.'s focus on workers and machines, yet his use of image and text also criticizes that industry. After questioning the ability of his words to represent the proposed subject, Auden writes Mann a compelling, emotionally charged description:

> A seventy-ton one [whale] was lying on the slip-way like a large and very dignified duchess being got ready for the ball by beetles. To see it torn to pieces with steam winches and cranes is enough to make one a vegetarian for life. . . . A bell suddenly clanged and everyone stuck their spades in the carcase and went off for lunch. The body remained alone in the sun, the flesh still steaming a little. It

W. H. Auden, "Flensing by Steam-winch" and "The Corpse," by W. H. Auden. From Letters from Iceland *(London: Faber, 1937).*

grounding the saw and making it the only diagonal line in the shot, Auden depicts it as a
monstrous instrument of torture. Later in the
book he explains to Coldstream that the saw "is
for cutting up jaw-bones" (*Letters* 223). The next
image, "Flensing by Steam-winch," presents a
group of men removing a whale's skin (*Letters*
149). Auden shoots them behind the whale,
dwarfing them so that they do seem like beetles
in comparison. The final shot, on the same page,
shows what appears to be the same men and
whale, but from a different angle and a greater
distance. A cross-section has been removed from
the whale, and the angle makes the men seem
much larger. Auden entitles this photograph
"The Corpse." Placing the two images together
demonstrates how perspective influences perception; he manipulates the way we see the whal-

ing station. Moreover, his photographs and
captions signal his trust in the documentary
method for conveying "the cold controlled ferocity" he saw. While he was not a "professional"
photographer—a factor that has unjustly excluded his images from critical analysis—Auden
clearly comprehended the politics of framing
and camera angles.[16] It is this knowledge that
would lead to his eventual distrust of documentary representation.

Auden also invokes documentary when he
represents Iceland's economically disadvan-
taged—further evidence of the G.P.O. Unit's influence. The best example is a photograph from
the chapter "Letter to Kristian Andreirsson." In
a classically composed shot, Auden foregrounds
two children, a clothesline, and a boat in a shore-
side community (*Letters* 218). The children are

"What the Tourist does not see," by W. H. Auden. From
Letters from Iceland *(London: Faber, 1937).*

positioned slightly below the frame's horizontal center, following the rule of thirds. Captioned "What the Tourist does not see,"[17] the photograph invests Auden with documentary authority by implying he sees more than "mere" tourists do. He makes the same distinction in his remarks to Andreirsson three pages earlier:

> It is an observation frequently made by bourgeois visitors that in Iceland there are no rich and no poor. At first sight this seems to be true. There are no mansions like those in Mayfair, and no hovels like those in the East End. Wages and the general standard of living are high in comparison with other countries; and there is less apparent class distinction than in any other capitalist country. But when one remembers that Iceland has an area larger than Ireland, a population smaller than Brighton, and some of the richest fishing grounds in the world, one is not convinced that the wages could not be higher and the differences less. I saw plenty of people whose standard of living I should not like to have to share. (*Letters* 216)

Note how Auden valorizes his eye-witness account and elevates his observations above those of less socially conscious visitors. Both the remarks and the photograph reveal the problematic nature of documentary representation, which is further complicated when the observer and observed are of different classes, races, genders, or nationalities. Part of our response is to credit Auden for addressing such issues as class division. Unlike "the invasion" of French tourists whom MacNeice describes "taking cine-photos of four or five unhappy little native children togged up in pseudo-national dress and standing in awkward dumbcrambo attitudes against a blank wall," Auden strives for a more "authentic" representation (*Letters* 195, 194).

Yet the photograph's appropriateness is questionable. Its depiction of the scantily-draped clothesline and the close-set houses in the distance, coupled with the caption, indicates that these children are poor. Moreover, Auden caught them unawares. The camera's distance which allows this surprise also dwarfs the children between the clothesline's wooden poles and the boat. Unlike his close-up photographs of people who present themselves as they wish to be seen, this long shot makes the children appear

vulnerable—the girl awkwardly hitches up the back of her dress while the boy peers from behind the clothesline. While the documentary artist may defend such representations by asserting objectivity or by appealing to the human condition, Susan Sontag points out that they are not neutral: "Gazing at other people's reality with curiosity, with detachment, with professionalism, the ubiquitous photographer operates as if that activity transcends class interests, as if its perspective is universal."[18] "What the Tourist does not see" creates rigid demarcations between the privileged photographer who observes and reports and the human subjects who are observed and captured. Such a division works against whatever socially conscious aim the photographer may have intended. This contradiction, along with other problems, fueled Auden's criticism of the G.P.O. Unit.

Auden's borrowing from documentary in *Letters from Iceland* does not indicate blind acceptance of that mode of representation. Four months before he sailed to Iceland, his review of G.P.O. colleague Paul Rotha's *Documentary Film* appeared in *The Listener.* In it Auden sharply criticized documentary filmmakers' failure to question the assumptions behind their practice. As Edward Mendelson comments, Auden saw a contradiction between advocating social reform and receiving financial support from government and industry.[19] More important, Auden's review points out the unequal class positions of observer and observed. He writes: "It is doubtful whether an artist can ever deal more than superficially (and cinema is not a superficial art) with characters outside his own class, and most British documentary directors are upper middle."[20] This discrepancy generated a crucial part of Auden's critique, and he tried to counter such inequality in several of *Letters from Iceland's* photographs. Again, what especially troubled Auden was not so much the obstacles in achieving a socially conscious vision but his G.P.O. colleagues' refusal to acknowledge them. While Rotha's book proposes a Marxist "dialectic method" for filmmaking, it also contains such unreflective characterizations of the documentarist as this one: "His is a job of presenting one half of the populace to the other."[21] Despite his socialist aims, then, Rotha reinforces class division by assigning the privileged viewer's position to the middle and upper classes. In Tagg's terms, focusing the camera on the working and under classes degrades them because such a practice "turn[s] on a social division between the power and privilege of *producing* and *possessing* and the burden of *being* meaning."[22]

Auden saw that documentary's segregation of observer and observed granted filmmakers this other form of power—that of knowing or "possessing" their subjects. Indeed, Rotha asserts that "the power of making things known that need to be known is the principal promise of documentary to-day."[23] In "The Course of Realism" Grierson describes the act of recording in imperialist, almost militaristic terms. He praises the G.P.O. Unit's progress in "giving each new slice of raw material a perspective and a life, leading us in each new adventure of observation to a wider and more powerful command of medium and material alike."[24] This "raw material," which is often human subjects, gains significance through voice-over's exposition. Auden's review articulates this subordination by dubbing in a voice for the filmmakers behind the camera: "'We must abandon the story and report facts, i.e., we must show you people at their daily work, show you how modern industry is organised, show you what people do for their living, not what they feel.'" Chastising the G.P.O. Unit's restricted vision, Auden counters that "the private life and the emotions are facts like any others, and one cannot understand the public life of action without them" (Review 354–55). He recognizes that representing people as workers does not necessarily grant them the power of a reciprocal gaze. Defining someone solely by occupation does not allow his or her image to resonate a plurality. In *Ideology and the Image,* Nichols addresses this issue when he discusses ethnographic films:

> Such films normally depict individual characters, but they focus their attention upon a level of abstraction beyond the individual. This is not only their strength but also their potential weakness. Individual social actors risk becoming no more than examples . . . with their value assessed solely by the quality of their exemplification.[25]

In other words, portraying a group of men as coal miners in order to comment on their working conditions reduces them to a category, *the coal miner*—which in turn allows the viewer to process their images as ready-made information.

Although Auden's critique of documentary is not as sophisticated as more recent ones such as Tagg's and Nichols's, his review of *Documentary Film* shows a remarkable degree of suspicion for someone writing at a time when the genre held its highest promise. His fundamental objection to the movement was its advocates' confidence in their ability to know their subject. Toward the end of the review he states, "No reputable novelist would dare write his novel before he has spent years acquiring and digesting his material, and no first-class documentary will be made until the director does not begin shooting before he has the same degree of familiarity with his" (Review 369). Auden's experiments in *Letters from Iceland* prompt his doubt that any "degree of familiarity" is adequate in constructing an "authentic" or "true" representation. Questioning his G.P.O. colleagues' investment in realism, Auden apprehends the slippage between his representations and what they signify.

In *Letters from Iceland* Auden often counters documentary's privileged gaze by blurring the line between observer and observed. Two strategies he employs in decentering documentary authority are exposing the observer and dislocating the viewer. Each strategy involves fragmentation. The chapter "Sheaves from Sagaland," a compilation of travel-book selections about Iceland, demonstrates the first method. Many of the travelers that Auden cites do not allow a counterperspective from the Icelanders; they subjugate native people and customs to their own sensibility. Auden subverts such appropriating vision by arranging the quotations under his own headings. His strategy becomes a political act as he exposes the travelers' judgments of Iceland as unintended self-portraits. For example, the section entitled "The Natives" indicates as much about the observers as it does about its ostensible subject. Here are Auden's selections from Sir George McKenzie's *Travels in Iceland* (1812):

Concerning their lack of education
"It is not uncommon in Iceland for people of all ranks, ages and sexes to sleep in the same apartment. Their notions of decency are unavoidably not very refined; but we had sufficient proof that

the instances of this which we witnessed proceeded from ignorance, and expressed nothing but perfect innocence."

Concerning their high-grade living
"Publications connected with practical morality are very common in Iceland, and several excellent books of this kind have lately appeared in the island, adapted chiefly to the use of farmers or those of the middle-classes; in which moral instruction is judiciously blended with amusing information in various branches of knowledge. The most valuable of these writings is a work called *Evening Hours.*" (*Letters* 67)

Although he purports to assess Icelandic values, McKenzie inadvertently comments on his own—revealing upper-class British ideology to be repressive and self-righteous. His narrowly focused, aggressive gaze creates such hierarchical oppositions as decent and indecent, sophisticated and ignorant, English and Icelandic. Unable to perceive his own political investment in such labels, McKenzie sees native customs as inversions of more "civilized" British ones. However, in *Letters from Iceland* Auden turns the camera the other way to allow us a look at the observers: McKenzie is exposed along with his observations.

Auden's excerpts in "Sheaves from Sagaland" also reflect the radical disjunction which structures the entire book. In creating this form, he revises High-Modernist collage. While collage offers a strategy for unsettling the documentary viewer's privileged position, this form, which Auden inherited from Modernism, does not address the general public. *Letters from Iceland* combines the fragmentation of collage and the popular appeal of documentary to achieve a more socially conscious, less aggressive gaze than either genre alone. By dislocating the viewer as well as his own position, Auden defuses both genres' authority. He calls the book a collage in part 1 of *Letter to Lord Byron*, warning that it will defy genre expectations:

Every exciting letter has enclosures,
    And so shall this—a bunch of photographs,
Some out of focus, some with wrong
    exposures,
    Press cuttings, gossip, maps, statistics, graphs;
    I don't intend to do the thing by halves.
I'm going to be very up to date indeed.
It is a collage that you're going to read.
(*Letters* 21)

This announcement deliberately invokes the "up to date" fragmentation of Auden's immediate predecessors Eliot and Pound. But Auden recognizes that collage can only partially counter authoritative vision. *The Orators* (1932), with its highly fragmented and cryptic "Journal of an Airman," taught him that disjunction alone does not ensure political pluralism. Auden's foreword to the 1966 reprint of *The Orators* states that his "name on the title-page seems a pseudonym for someone else, someone talented but near the border of sanity, who might well, in a year or two, become a Nazi."[26] In a similar fashion, *The Waste Land*'s disjunction does not prevent Elizabeth and Leicester in their "gilded shell / Red and gold" from standing out as the most empowered image in Eliot's poem—a center of authority.[27] The term *collage* must be qualified if it is to address adequately Auden's radical play with genre.

Auden's collage reclaims the form as public domain. Demystifying the technique, he presents collage so that it does not restrict its audience to artists and academics (*Letters from Iceland* was a Book Society selection). Instead of citing canonical passages from Homer, Dante, Baudelaire, Wagner—materials of High Modernist collage—Auden invokes both verbal and visual forms of mass media. *Letters from Iceland*'s public collage does contain some literary allusions—including the long poem addressed to Lord Byron (as much a public as a literary figure). Two photocaptions allude to John Bunyan and Wilfred Owen, respectively.[28] But the balance of sources is certainly less academic than Eliot's in *The Waste Land*, which for all its Shakespeherian Rags and Mrs. Porters relies mostly on canonical texts. As Auden tells Lord Byron,

Parnassus after all is not a mountain,
    Reserved for A.1. climbers such as you;
It's got a park, it's got a public fountain.
(*Letters* 22)

A collage need not be an alienated artist's esoteric vision, but may offer instead a necessary and accessible way of representing the external world. In this sense Auden agrees with Rotha that "it is surely fatal for an artist to attempt to divorce himself from the community and retire into a private world where he can create merely

for his own pleasure or for that of a limited minority."[29] But Auden disagrees with the orderly,
expository approach that characterized many
documentary films. Therefore, he chooses a
more disruptive form. Just as readers form an
impression of their own culture from the disjointed parts of newspapers and magazines,
Auden's readers must construct their vision of
Iceland from the book's fragmented accounts.

In *Letters from Iceland* Auden occasionally stops
to ridicule High Modernist techniques that
alienate the general public. For example, in a
stanza of *Letter to Lord Byron* he includes lines of
German, French, Greek, and the fragment
"glubit. che . . ." commenting: "What this may
mean / I do not know, but rather like the sound /
Of foreign languages like Ezra Pound." "Letter
to William Coldstream" presents a comic portrait
of MacNeice standing "on the quay muttering
Greek in his beard / Like a character out of the
Cantos—"(*Letters* 18, 226). Auden even includes
a playful pastiche of *The Waste Land* in his poem
"Journey to Iceland":

> Then let the good citizen here find natural
>   marvels:
> The horse-shoe ravine, the issue of steam from a
>   cleft
>   In the rock, and rocks, and waterfalls
>   brushing the
> Rocks, and among the rocks birds.
>
>   (*Letters* 25)

Unlike Eliot's mythical, sterile desert in "What
the Thunder Said," Auden's landscape reflects a
specific location—the "natural marvel" of Iceland's wet, rocky terrain (as depicted in several
of the book's photographs). Its inhabitants are
citizens, not fisher kings. As Tom Paulin asserts,
Letters from Iceland reflects Auden's belief that the
artist "has a duty to be responsible both in the
content of his work and in his relation to society."[30] I would add that the artist must be also
responsible in choosing a form.

The book's most striking example of public
collage is the chapter "Sheaves from Sagaland."
Besides exposing the travelers, this anthology
also inverts the High Modernist collages of Eliot
and Pound by featuring its borrowings as the
main text. In fact, one of the citations provides

a parodic analogy to quotation-filled works such
as *The Waste Land:*

Mr. X.

  "I discovered a curious fact about Mr. X. which
accounted for that gentleman's occasional readi-
ness in making a quotation. Every night he
wrapped himself in a large grey plaid of which he
was very proud; it had been, he said, his companion in the mountains of Mexico. I now happened
to examine some scarlet letters on the plaid and,
to my amazement, discovered whole passages from
Shakespeare and other poets embroidered in red
silk. In fact Mr. X. slept in a book and could always
refresh his memory by studying when he woke."—
Umbra (*Letters* 71–72)[31]

The High Modernist collage's author and reader
become the anonymous Mr. X cloaking himself
in others' words to appear erudite. On the other
hand, "Sheaves from Sagaland" quotes mostly
from lesser-known sources instead of the "clas-
sics." Auden undercuts his two canonical authorities. Shakespeare's "'Pish for thee, Iceland
dog. Thou prick-eared cur of Iceland'" is hardly
inspiring—especially when introduced with "*The
Immortal Bard proves that nothing escapes him.*" Neither does Auden spare much reverence for Richard Burton's unflattering remark about the
Icelandic woman's "'habitual frown'" with the
heading "*The translator of the Arabian Nights gets
the raspberry*" (*Letters* 62, 73). The "Sheaves from
Sagaland" collage celebrates anarchic disorder,
not authority.

Auden's photographs form another important
element of *Letters from Iceland*'s public collage.
Like the documentary films on which he worked,
they were intended to reach the general public.
Auden explains his position on photography in
the second letter to Mann, stressing that the medium is not the property of an artistic elite: "It is
the democratic art, i.e. technical skill is practically
eliminated—the more fool-proof cameras be-
come with focusing and exposure gadgets the
better—and artistic quality depends only on
choice of subject" (*Letters* 137). Both the definition of *artist* and *art* are broadened as Auden
emphasizes photography's availability to the
masses. He also plays with photography, borrowing collage's fragmented perspective to confuse spatial relations. Several of these images

disorient not only the viewer's position but also his own. In this way, Auden fractures the authoritative gaze of both documentary and High-Modernism. The resulting instability is often quite comical. For example, the photograph entitled "The Student of Prose and Conduct" shows MacNeice from the chest up looking through a man's pants legs, or perhaps through a tent flap (*Letters* 32). MacNeice takes up most of the photograph's left side, while the cloth in question cuts across the center in an uneven diagonal line and is cropped at the right by the camera. A lighter-colored object that also appears to be cloth cuts across the upper left corner, doubly framing MacNeice. What exactly is he "studying" in this photograph? The caption comes from "Journey to Iceland," which characterizes various kinds of travelers and what they seek. Auden's speaker bestows on them their respective wishes, giving "the student of prose and conduct" these locations to visit:

> The site of a church where a bishop was put
> in a bag,
> The bath of a great historian, the rock where
> An outlaw dreaded the dark.
>
> (*Letters* 25–26)

This list of attractions is as disjointed as the photograph; both fragment their representations. Like the collage in "Sheaves from Sagaland," such disorientation does not require academic knowledge to decipher. As John Fuller points out, these sites are standard tourist attractions in Iceland (113–14).[32] But MacNeice is not looking at any of these things; he regards Auden through narrowed eyes, his mouth compressed in a smirk. Again Auden blurs the line between observer and observed—this time by making himself the object of the "student's" gaze. By comically placing himself under scrutiny, he undermines his own authority.

An even more jarring photograph, "Stella's Boot," appears in MacNeice's chapter "Hetty to Nancy" (*Letters* 156). The title reflects his camp spirit in transforming the male riding party into a group of schoolgirls. Through MacNeice (Hetty) we learn that Auden (Maisie) likes to "tak[e] art shots of people through each other's legs" (*Letters* 173). "Stella's Boot" depicts a pair

"The Student of Prose and Conduct," by W. H. Auden. From Letters from Iceland *(London: Faber, 1937).*

of riding boots cutting across the foreground and the lower half of a horse across the whole top of the foreground; framed by this partial torso, an entire horse appears in the background. By showing only the boots, Auden masks the wearer's gender so he can attribute them to MacNeice's character "Stella." More important, "Stella's Boot" raises questions about the photographer's subject and position. Displacing the viewer, Auden's photograph is composed so

"Stella's Boot," by W. H. Auden. From Letters from
Iceland *(London: Faber, 1937).*

that this subject is indeterminable; only the caption makes us select the boots as a focal point.
Where is Auden in relation to the boots? Possibly,
he twisted his body to include his own legs, which
would make the photograph a fragmented self-
portrait—another send-up of High Modernism.
This "portrait of the artist" can boast of fashionable fragmentation; yet the viewer needs no
"footnotes" to appreciate its comic incoherence.

Auden explored the powers and limits of
documentary not only through experimenting
with *Letters from Iceland*'s photographs, but also
with his poetry. As we have seen with "Journey
to Iceland," this experimentation includes cross-
referencing poems and photographs—often by
drawing photo-captions from a particular line of
poetry. Jefferson Hunter points out in *Image and
Word* that placing poetry and photographs together allows the reader/viewer to question the
poet's visual authority.[33] In the case of *Letters from
Iceland*, Auden is questioning not just his own
observations, but the very acts of seeing and recording. More specifically, he interrogates the

model of social engagement popularized by
documentary film and photography—one that
appealed to many socially conscious artists in
the thirties.

With their invocations of "the camera's eye,"
the poems "Letter to R. H. S. Crossman, Esq."
and "Letter to William Coldstream" reveal how
working with film and photography made
Auden more self-conscious about representation. Auden's poem to Crossman has received
considerable discussion (of the poems in *Letters
from Iceland*, only *Letter to Lord Byron* has generated more).[34] Most critics agree on its preoccupation with perceiving and recording, concluding
that Auden rejects "abstract" for "concrete" vision.[35] I find these assessments limiting in two
ways. First, they divorce the poem from its context in *Letters from Iceland*. After all, Auden's
omission of these poems from collected volumes
indicates that they are incomplete when excised
from their accompanying photographs and
other related portions of the book. Second and
most significant, standard readings fail to ques-

tion the dichotomy they establish with the terms *unique* or *real* and *abstract* or *imaginary*, just as Grierson and Rotha fail to examine their assumptions about documentary realism versus studio fiction. Both adherents of "concreteness" reveal an underlying faith in artistic representation to capture an unmediated fragment of "actuality." But, as we have seen, Auden understands documentary's inability to depict Greenberg's "uniqueness of individuals." The companion poems to Crossman and Coldstream demonstrate the visual instability at the center of *Letters from Iceland.* In doing so, they show why Auden found documentary a partially useful, but ultimately inadequate means of representing his engagement with Iceland.

Previous accounts of "Letter to R. H. S. Crossman" have not identified the external event that Auden's poem tries to describe—a sports festival mentioned briefly in his second letter to Mann: "The sport-fest was a primitive affair. Some part singing by middle-aged men in blue suits with brass buttons which was barely audible, male and female high jumping, and a swimming race in a shallow and very dirty-looking pond" (*Letters* 147). Auden also represents the sport-fest with two photographs entitled "Local swimming Sports" (*Letters* 145). Once again he blurs the line between observer and observed, this time with an upper image depicting the crowd of spectators followed by a double eye-line match of the swimmers (one of them turns his head over his shoulder toward the shore). The photographer observes Icelanders observing Icelanders. This sequence is jarring because in order to align the spectators' and swimmer's gazes, Auden would need to reverse the angle on the lower image. In cinematic terms, he has violated the 180–degree line.

An equally disorienting progression occurs in the Crossman poem, one which destabilizes distinctions between concrete and abstract. The first stanza situates the sporting event in its distinctly Icelandic landscape, but Auden's ambiguous pronouns begin to blur this initial subject:

"Local swimming Sports," by W. H. Auden. From Letters from Iceland *(London: Faber, 1937).*

> A glacier brilliant in the heights of summer
> Feeding a putty-coloured river: a field,
> A countryside collected in a field
> To appreciate or try its strength;
> The two flags twitter at the entrance gates.
>
> (*Letters* 91)

Does *countryside* refer to the field's topographical features or to the local inhabitants? Does *its* indicate the field battling with the glacier or the athletes competing with each other? Only the image of the flags clearly evokes a human context. Such a description complicates claims that Auden is advocating concreteness in this poem.

Our next clue that its literal references are to the sport-fest comes in the following stanza:

> I walk among them taking photographs;
> The children stare and follow, think of questions
> To prove the stranger real.
>
> (*Letters* 91)

These lines are especially significant because they comment on the documentary artist's engaged stance. While his on-location recording reflects Auden's eye-witness account, the reference to the camera places the resulting representations under the guise of an "objective" mechanical device. The children's stares fracture the "stranger's" organizing gaze, and their engagement through dialogue acknowledges the mediation of their subjectivity in "knowing" him. One photograph related to these lines acknowledges this reciprocal gaze. In Auden's medium close-up shot "The Arctic Stare," an Icelandic boy peers under a railing at the viewer (*Letters* 144). The gazing boy is doubly framed by the joining rails' triangular shape, emphasizing his act of looking. Staring at Auden with wide eyes, he does not appear uncomfortable but coolly regards Auden, who seems to be below him. However, Auden fools the viewer with this perspective. If we turn the book on its left side to

reorient the image to its original position, we see that the boy sits in someone's lap and looks *up* at the camera. Auden's choice in framing the image and in presenting it sideways empowers the subject, as does the caption "The Arctic Stare." Instead of privileging the photographer's eye, he repositions an image that would otherwise empower himself.

At other moments in the Crossman poem, Auden does not so readily yield to the camera but combats its images with his captions. *Letters from Iceland* contains three other photographs related to the festival which appear in the Crossman poem. He captions them with lines from the third stanza:

> Nevertheless let the camera's eye record it:
> Groups in confabulation on the grass,
> The shuffling couples in their heavy boots,
> The young men leaping, the accordion playing.
> Justice or not, it is a world.
>
> (*Letters* 91)

Again Auden turns to "the camera's eye" for a supposedly objective representation, which he invokes with the verb "record." But note the almost grudging tone of "Nevertheless," as if he senses that his words must compete with his photographs. In fact, some of the stanza's lines double as deliberately misleading captions which call both representations into question. For example, the photograph entitled "The shuffling Couples in their heavy Boots" depicts a crowd of people greeting each other (*Letters* 96). The caption suggests that they are dancing, yet only the couples in the right foreground adopt such a posture. Moreover the people are cropped at the waist, so the viewer questions the caption's authority in asserting that they wear boots. The photograph "Back to the Hands, the Feet, the Faces" poses similar questions with its framing; we see faces but no hands and feet (*Letters* 96). Which form of representation is the "accurate" one? Roland Barthes's epigraph to *Empire of Signs* provides an appropriate description of Auden's effect: "The text does not 'gloss' the images, which do not 'illustrate' the text. For me, each has been no more than the onset of a kind of visual uncertainty."[36] Like the Crossman poem's confusion of "concrete" and "abstract" vision, its opposing photographs and captions disorient our vision.

"The Arctic Stare," by W. H. Auden. From Letters from Iceland *(London: Faber, 1937).*

And the artist prays ever so gently—

"Let me find pure all that can happen.
Only uniqueness is success! For instance,
Let me perceive the images of history,
All that I push away with doubt and travel,
To-day's and yesterday's, alike like bodies."

Yes, just like that. . . .

(Letters 92)

I find this prayer highly ironic; surely it is not to be taken as a prescription. First, Auden frames the prayer with the almost comical "ever so gentle" artist and the reductive summation that begins stanza six.[37] Moreover, this artist makes impossible demands on artistic vision. The prayer begins with a peculiar tension between the "pure" and the "unique"—the former implying a distillation of the latter into something like the images in Plato's cave. Auden's artist asks for both, equating the two. In the stanza's next line, the artist asks to "perceive the images of history," which is to see a representation twice removed from its signified. This circular vision evades the literal object of one's gaze, conflating the removed "images of history," the engaged perspective of "doubt and travel," and the linear progress of "To-day's and yesterday's"—what we might call collage, documentary, and travelogue. Rather than achieving "uniqueness," then, this artist collapses plural perspectives into a vague rendition in which all is "alike like bodies"—a vision that anticipates *Spain*. Unlike the gentle artist, Auden knows that vision is always already mediated.

In fact, we can read the entire poem as an allegory of representation—one that demonstrates the inevitable intrusion of one's subjectivity on his or her perceptions and, by extension, art. In the poem's final stanzas, Auden extends the initial frame to blend the sport-fest with Icelandic sagas, that week's events, human nature in general, and the political crisis in Europe. He returns to the "glacier brilliant" of stanza one, but its boundaries now extend in all directions:

Until indeed the Markafljōt I see
Wasting these fields, is no glacial flood
But history, hostile, Time the destroyer
Everywhere washing our will, winding
  through Europe

"The shuffling Couples in their heavy Boots" and "Back to the Hands, the Feet, the Faces," by W. H. Auden. From Letters from Iceland *(London: Faber, 1937).*

Most critics anchor their claims about concrete vision in the artist's prayer of stanza five—which they assume to be straightforward. The stanza's call for a renewed vision unsettles the kind of delineations we make between abstract and concrete, imaginary and actual:

An attack, a division, shifting its fords.

He imagines the glacier-as-History "Flowing through Oxford too, past dons of good will" like Crossman (*Letters* 93). Iceland's landscape opens into the broader terrain of the human psyche and European social change (*Letters from Iceland* contains several comments on the Nazis). This representation explodes the very concept of framing, exposing the limitations of a realist belief in concreteness or a reportorial claim of objectivity. According to Mendelson, this passage shows that "the artistic price a poet pays for a resonant abstraction like History is the forfeiture of truth."[38] I do not read the glacier's transformation as a fall from grace. Instead, I contend that Auden's poem achieves a more resonant representation of the sport-fest and its surroundings *because* of its tensions. The plural images of the glacier undermine any assumptions that one of them qualifies as "truth."

Auden's struggle with representation reaches its crisis in the highly self-conscious poem "Letter to William Coldstream."[39] While Beach dismisses it as "mostly an account of what the tourist had observed in a fortnight," this poem in fact addresses Auden's major dilemma in constructing *Letters from Iceland*.[40] For it is the eyewitness account that he is questioning—both in the Coldstream poem and in the book as a whole. Significantly, Auden chooses another colleague at the G.P.O. Unit who was "suspected, quite rightly, of being disloyal" to the documentary movement (*Letters* 222). Coldstream, painter, and Auden, poet, each had a vested interest in testing the validity of documentary representation with respect to their own more traditional artistic media. Perhaps because of these outside careers, Auden and Coldstream were more distrustful of documentary than were some of their colleagues.

"Letter to William Coldstream's" emphasis on seeing is even more extensive than the Crossman poem's, including references to G.P.O. filmmakers Basil Wright, Stuart Legg, and R. Q. McNaughton, as well as to Grierson. In effect, the poem to Coldstream becomes a disassembled documentary on Auden's engagement with Iceland. Disconnecting his observations, Auden creates loosely edited rushes by dividing the poem into a series of events and a collection of images—what he calls "telling" and "perceiving." These sections correspond roughly to a film's sound and image tracks, respectively.[41] Conventionally, the soundtrack of a G.P.O. documentary anchors the flow of images through expository voice-over. Nichols points out that in classic thirties documentaries, sequencing depends on the sound track: "Each sequence sets in place a block of argumentation that the image track illustrates."[42] On the other hand, Auden's poem to Coldstream removes most of these connectives. In this way the poem—and, by implication, the entire book—reveals both the layers of mediation involved in documentary filmmaking and Auden's final attempts to overcome them.

"Letter to William Coldstream" begins with a humorous opening paragraph exposing the arbitrariness of narrative conventions, part of the poem's section on "telling." Auden offers an account of what he, MacNeice, and Michael Yates did after their camping expedition with the schoolboys:[43] Now the three ride from Hraensnef to Reykholt where they stayed two nights. Thence they went to Reykjavik and took ship to Isafjordur. Joachim was the vice-consul, a man well spoken of. He found them a motor-boat to take them to Melgraseyri in Isafjördardjup" (*Letters* 220). By the end of the paragraph this stilted pastiche of Icelandic sagas gives way to contemporary, colloquial language. But Auden rigidly adheres to the convention of chronological order, calling his efforts "a little donnish experiment in objective narrative" (*Letters* 220). Of course, chronology is a principle of selection crucial to maintaining narrative's linear structure; narrative can hardly be "objective." The "experts" Auden parodies in the poem's next section fail to recognize the ridiculousness of holding together this series of events by chronology alone. One critic from the Literary Supplement cries that Auden's story lacks landscape while "the professional novelist" complains, "'Too easy. No dialogue.'" Another reviewer rejects the story because "'It's simply not Tolstoi'" (*Letters* 221, 220). Their contradictory advice in pinpointing the crucial element in narrative writing undermines these conventions and justifies Auden's decision to subvert them. *Letters from Iceland* rejects the false order that narrative imposes on the world.

Recognizing the artificiality of one structural device makes Auden more self-conscious about using others. As with the Crossman poem, this awareness makes the task of determining and representing his subject difficult, but constructing the Coldstream poem becomes an almost crippling enterprise. The initial obstacle is how to begin:

> I'm bringing a problem.
> Call it as Henry James might have done in a
>   preface
>   The Presentation of the Given Subject
> The problem of every writer of travels;
> For Life and his publisher hand him his theme
>   on a plate:
> "You went to such and such places with so-
>   and-so
> And such and such things occurred.
>
>   Now do what you can."
> But I can't.
>
> (*Letters* 222)

How does one position the frame? The travel-book formula, with its reliance on chronology and events, becomes another grossly inadequate means of organizing the book. Earlier, Auden had explained to Mann that travelogue proves unsatisfactory because "the actual events are all extremely like each other—meals—sleeping accommodation—fleas—dangers, etc., and the repetition becomes boring" (*Letters* 142). The Coldstream poem is an unusual place to elaborate on this problem of organization, since it appears in one of the book's final chapters. Conventionally, we would expect the author to construct a resolution, but Auden disassembles his text.

Auden investigates the dilemma of perception and representation by returning once more to documentary. In this final attempt to revise the genre into a resonant plurality, he pushes its claims of objectivity to the limits by impersonating a camera. This exercise both assumes and rejects documentary authority. While it dispenses with poetic conventions in favor of a more cinematic order, it also exaggerates the documentary stance to parodic proportions. Auden portrays documentary as some form of divine objectivity:

> Very well then, let's start with perceiving
> Let me pretend that I'm the impersonal eye
>   of the camera
> Sent out by God to shoot on location
> And we'll look at the rushes together.

Earlier in the poem he had admitted, "The poet's eye is not one from which nothing is hid" (*Letters* 223, 221). But here Auden simulates the kind of representation a documentary might achieve if such an unmediated "on-location" perspective were possible. As he reviews his photographs for *Letters from Iceland,* Auden constructs a string of images loosely connected by cinematic terms:

> Now a pan round a typical sitting-room
> Bowl of postcards on table—Harmonium with
>   Brahm's [sic] Sapphic Ode
> Pi-picture—little girl crosses broken ravine
>   bridge protected by angel.
> Cut to saddling ponies—close up of farmer's
>   hands at a girth strap
> Dissolve to long shot of Reykholt school . . .
>
> (*Letters* 223)

The camera's eye is attractive to Auden because it allows him to connect random images and events while avoiding both the causal logic of narrative and the rhetorical logic of expository prose and documentary. Yet replacing chronological and spatial transitions with editing instructions still involves mediation, even though Auden attributes the editing process to an "impersonal eye." As Rotha asserts in his book, editing is the primary process by which filmmakers interpret what they observed: "Nothing photographed, or recorded on to celluloid, has meaning until it comes to the cutting-bench."[44]

Two of the final photographs that Auden examines in the poem's "perceiving" section provide his penultimate comment on documentary (they appear on the book's next-to-last photo-page). I find them especially significant in assessing Auden's engagement with documentary representation. The photograph to which he devotes the most attention simulates Grierson's *Drifters,* a film about fishermen for Britain's herring industry. It appears opposite the page containing this verse description:

> And here's a shot for the Chief—epic, the
>   *Drifters* tradition

"The Motorboat cost 40 *kronur" and "Epic, the* Drifters *tradition," by W. H. Auden. From* Letters from Iceland *(London: Faber, 1937).*

The end of a visit, the motor-boat's out of the
  screen on the left
It was blowing a hurricane.

(*Letters* 224)

Auden's photograph, also entitled "Epic, the *Drifters* tradition," shows two oarsmen, medium close-up, and the head and shoulders of a man standing behind them in the boat's stern.[45] We see the boat's starboard in the extreme lower-left corner, and a portion of the sea in the lower-right corner. The oarsmen look intent on their task (neither one faces Auden), while the man in the back looks grimly forward but seems unaware of the camera. This "epic" shot shows men battling the elements, a dominant idea in Grierson's *Drifters.* The director writes of his film that "it had a theme in social observation—the ardor and bravery of common labor. . . . I remember the effort it took to convince showmen of the time that an industrialized fishing fleet might be as brave to the sight as the brown sails of sentiment and that the rigors of work were worth the emphasis in detail."[46] Auden's photograph reflects Grierson's spirit in finding its drama in the oarsmen's labor rather than in the rising waves. More important, his "epic" label acknowledges that Grierson's "social observation" still imposes an ordering vision on the fishermen—"ardor and bravery" are ingredients of heroic characters. In fact, Grierson portrays documentary filmmakers as brave by association. He inflects his description of filmmaking with self-empowering language, casting his team of directors as imperialistic explorers: "We have set up our tripods among the Yahoos themselves, and schools have gathered round us. Our realist showing, if secondary to the main growth of cinema, has assumed a certain bravery."[47] Adventurers in observation, documentarists engage with "the more difficult territory" of the working class, the underclass, and people of foreign cultures. Auden's own description of his photographic tribute to Grierson heightens this "bravery" by pointing out that the shot was taken during a hurricane. In this sense, documentary photographs signify not only Barthes's "That-has-been," but also I-was-there.[48] The adventuring I/eye inflects the image with its mediating presence, so that a neutral photograph is impossible.

While Auden offers Grierson his thanks and respect in *Letters from Iceland*'s final chapter, "Last Will and Testament," his allusions to Grierson in the Coldstream poem imply that documentary engagement does not lead to any fuller apprehension of the subject than other modes of vision. He makes this point photographically by pairing his "Epic" shot with another image entitled "The Motorboat cost *40* kronur." This caption also comes from the Coldstream poem:

> Now going up Isafjördup—the motorboat cost
> 40 kronur.
> The hills are a curious shape—like vaulting-
> horses in a gymnasium
> The light was rotten.
>
>   (*Letters* 224)

In this shot Yates and MacNeice sit on top of another boat, leaning against a short wall. Cluttered with the pipe that juts in the center and the pile of luggage and equipment in the bottom foreground, "The Motorboat" opposes a tourist's snapshot with the more polished allusion to Grierson, causing the latter to appear staged. Auden's pairing invokes Barthes's "onset of visual uncertainty," reflecting the book as a whole. *Letters from Iceland* questions the organizing eye and voice-over of British documentaries, just as it questions the judgmental gaze of travel books and the allusive fragmentation of High Modernist collage.

After listing his shots, Auden wonders how to arrange them:

> Well. That's the lot.
> As you see, no crisis, no continuity.
> Only heroic cutting could save it
> Perhaps MacNaughten might do it
>   Or Legge.[49] [sic]
> But I've cut a few stills out, in case they'd
> amuse you.
>
>   (*Letters* 224)

As we have seen, Auden's G.P.O. colleagues may solve this dilemma by imposing "heroic" editing. But Auden opts for a discontinuous collection of stills and rushes. The "crisis" his book reflects is not narrative climax but the act of representation. In his introduction to *The Burden of Representation*, Tagg includes this kind of instability in his characterization of the thirties, calling the period "a moment of crisis not only of social and economic relations, and social identities, but, crucially, of representation itself: of the means of making the sense we call social experience."[50] For Auden, his precarious arrangement of *Letters from Iceland* makes grouping its parts into a cohesive whole a deliberately impossible task not only for him, but for the reader as well.

I find *Letters from Iceland* significant because it reveals a more plural, more distrustful engagement with documentary than does the work of many of Auden's contemporaries. With its eye-witness authority, documentary became prominent during the social turmoil of the 1930s as artists searched for ways to represent such crises as the American Depression and the Spanish Civil War. But *Letters from Iceland* does not grant as much credence to this genre as do Grierson's films, George Orwell's book *The Road to Wigan Pier* (1937), or Joris Ivens and Ernest Hemingway's film *The Spanish Earth* (1937). As Auden continues to experiment with combining photographs and words in *Journey to a War* (an account of the Sino-Japanese War), he further questions the validity of documentary representation. When Fussell complains about the self-consciousness in *Letters from Iceland* and *Journey to a War* and that "nothing is rounded off," he misses their value.[51] Auden's self-consciousness is generated in part by his desire to create equal power relations between observer and observed.

Examining Auden's photographs complicates the conventional argument that his stylistic changes after the thirties indicate an abandonment of political conviction.[52] By looking through his viewfinder we see his strategies for framing his perceptions. He retreats from documentary representation because he becomes disillusioned with art's ability to capture social crises. Yet he also rejects the High Modernist position of political disengagement by addressing the world around him with pen and camera. Orwell points out the political limits of the High Modernist gaze in *Inside the Whale*:

> Our eyes are directed to Rome, to Byzantium, to Montparnasse, to Mexico, to the Etruscans, to the Subconscious, to the Solar plexus—to everywhere except the places where things are actually happening. When one looks back at the twenties, nothing is queerer than the way in which every important event in Europe escaped the notice of the English intelligentsia.[53]

If documentary is art at its most engaged, then we must credit Auden with exploring its powers and limits in the loosely edited rushes of *Letters from Iceland*. Auden's public collage provides a paradigm for the diverse, fragmented means by which we go about making partial, tentative sense of our world.

NOTES

This essay originally appeared in *Journal of Modern Literature* 17.4.

1. This study focuses on Auden's contributions to *Letters from Iceland*, which comprise most of the book. The Bloomfield-Mendelson bibliography cites Auden's remark that MacNeice wrote eighty-one pages, but all sections bearing his initials add up to sixty-four pages. When we count MacNeice's contributions to "Last Will and Testament," the total still does not add up to eighty-one (unless Auden was referring to manuscript pages). Possibly, MacNeice assisted with the chapters "For Tourists" and "Sheaves from Sagaland."

2. See Frederick Buell, *W. H. Auden as a Social Poet* (Ithaca: Cornell University Press, 1973), 139; Paul Fussell, *Abroad: British Literary Traveling between the Wars* (New York: Oxford University Press, 1980), 219.

3. The latter have received surprisingly little attention, although some critics occasionally use photographic terms to characterize some of Auden's verbal texts. For example, Margaret Moan Rowe describes *Letter to Lord Byron* as a collection of slides in "Travels with a Poet," *Modern British Literature* 4 (1979): 128–36. To my knowledge, only Frederick Buell and Tom Paulin (see note 5) incorporate readings of a photograph in their criticism on *Letters from Iceland*. More recently, Valentine Cunningham notes two of Auden's ironic photo-captions in *British Writers of the Thirties* (New York: Oxford University Press, 1989), 329.

4. Auden married Erika Mann so she could receive a British passport and escape Nazi Germany.

5. As his review title "On Being Mainly Amused" indicates, Edward Sackville-West takes the former position and praises both authors for being "funny" in *New Statesman & Nation* (7 August 1937): 226. Of those who read *Letters from Iceland* as political commentary, Tom Paulin provides the most insightful analysis. See his *"Letters from Iceland:* Going North," *Renaissance and Modern Studies* 20 (1976): 65–80. Frederick Buell takes a middle position, asserting that the book's political commentary is tempered by comedy.

6. Edwin Muir, review of *Letters from Iceland*, by W. H. Auden and Louis MacNeice, *Criterion* (October 1937): 154; A. T. Tolley, *The Poetry of the Thirties* (New York: St. Martins, 1975), 305.

7. See George T. Wright, *W. H. Auden* (New York: Twayne, 1969), 76.

8. Samuel Hynes, *The Auden Generation: Literature and Politics in England in the 1930s* (Princeton: Princeton University Press, 1976), 212–13.

9. W. H. Auden, introduction to *The Poet's Tongue*, in *The English Auden*, ed. Edward Mendelson (New York: Random, 1977), 327–30.

10. Elizabeth Sussex, *The Rise and Fall of British Documentary* (Berkeley: University of California Press, 1975), 60. Sussex's book offers an informative account of the people involved with the G.P.O. Unit in chapters 3 through 5. An "authorized report" of Auden's lecture appears in *Janus* (May 1936): 11–12.

11. John Grierson, "The Course of Realism," in *Grierson on Documentary*, ed. Forsyth Hardy (New York: Harcourt Brace Jovanovich, 1947), 167.

12. For example, see the poems "Who stands, the crux left of the watershed" and "Who will endure / Heat of day and winter danger."

13. Grierson, *Grierson on Documentary* 162.

14. W. H. Auden and Louis MacNeice, *Letters from Iceland* (London: Faber, 1937), 149. All quotations from *Letters from Iceland* reprinted by Permission of Paragon House Publishers. Further references cited within the text as *Letters*.

15. In a letter to the author (1 August 1987), Edward Mendelson states that "it's fairly safe to conclude that Auden wrote the captions for the photos in *Letters from Iceland*," referring to a letter in Faber's files in which "someone complains that Auden has written so heavily on the back of the *Iceland* photos that the impression shows through on the front." Photographs appear opposite the page cited in the text.

16. In *Image and Word: The Interaction of Twentieth-Century Photographs and Texts* (Cambridge: Harvard University Press, 1987), for example, Jefferson Hunter groups Auden and Isherwood's documentary book *Journey to a War* with travel books by such diverse writers as Graham Greene and Peter Fleming. Hunter claims that these texts "make little real use of their illustrations," pointing out that Fleming's and Auden's contain "amateurish photographs . . . by the authors" (157). Not only does this pronouncement ignore Auden's experience with film, but it also fails to acknowledge the images' deliberate instability. I find it interesting that Hunter does not dismiss photo-texts by photographers who were not "professional" writers.

17. Here, as in the rest of this essay, I follow Auden's often eccentric capitalization.

18. Susan Sontag, *On Photography* (New York: Farrar, Straus & Giroux, 1977), 55.

19. For a useful discussion of Auden and the G.P.O. Unit, see Edward Mendelson, *Early Auden* (Cambridge: Harvard University Press, 1983), 281–84.

20. W. H. Auden, review of *Documentary Film*, by Paul Rotha, *The Listener* (19 February 1936): 368–69. All further references cited within the text as Review.

21. Paul Rotha, *Documentary Film* (London: Faber, 1936), 130.

22. John Tagg, *The Burden of Representation: Essays on Photographies and Histories* (Amherst: University of Massachusetts Press, 1988), 6.

23. Rotha, *Documentary Film*, 7.

24. Grierson, *Grierson on Documentary*, 167.

25. Bill Nichols, *Ideology and the Image: Social Representation in the Cinema and Other Media* (Bloomington: Indiana University Press, 1981), 238.

26. W. H. Auden, *The Orators* (1932; reprint, London: Faber, 1966), 7.

27. T. S. Eliot, *The Complete Poems and Plays, 1909–1950* (New York: Harcourt Brace, 1971), 45.

28. These captions are "Christian and Mr. Worldly Wiseman," an allusion to *Pilgrim's Progress*, and "With Paucity that never was Simplicity," from Owen's poem "Insensibility." Not surprisingly, these pairings of image/text belittle their human subjects—just as Eliot's juxtaposition of the pub women and Ophelia denigrates the former in *The Waste Land*. Auden's first caption appropriates two men as Bunyan's representative types, divorcing them from any relation to Iceland. The second caption comes from the opening

lines of "Insensibility's" final stanza, where Owen contends that hardened soldiers who repress emotion to survive are more fortunate than those blissfully unaware of war's atrocities. By using this line as a photo-caption, Auden causes the three people he caught unaware to appear obtuse and provincial.

29. Rotha, *Documentary Film*, 62.

30. Paulin, "*Letters from Iceland:* Going North," 76.

31. The passage comes from Clifford Umbra's *Travels*, 1865.

32. John Fuller, *A Reader's Guide to W. H. Auden* (New York: Farrar, Straus & Giroux, 1970), 113–14.

33. Hunter, *Image and Word*, 169.

34. Auden knew Richard Crossman at Oxford and had contributed to Crossman's essay collection *Oxford and the Groups* (1934). Crossman was an Oxford don at the time *Letters from Iceland* was written.

35. For example, Joseph Warren Beach finds Auden lamenting our predisposition to "interpret individuals in terms of abstract categories in the vain hope of making them 'real'" in *The Making of the Auden Canon* (Minneapolis: University of Minnesota Press, 1957), 139. Similarly, Herbert Greenberg sees Auden appreciating "the uniqueness of individuals and events" in *Quest for the Necessary: W. H. Auden and the Dilemma of Divided Consciousness* (Cambridge: Harvard University Press, 1968), 80. Mendelson sums up the poem's structure as contrasting "the real world of unique particulars and the imaginary world of abstract historical forces" in *Early Auden* (311, see note 19).

36. Roland Barthes, *Empire of Signs*, trans. Richard Howard (New York: Hill and Wang, 1982), xi.

37. This gentle artist anticipates the whispering poet in *Spain* (London: Faber, 1937), another amusing figure. Auden wrote *Spain* eight months after "Letter to R. H. S. Crossman."

38. Mendelson, *Early Auden*, 314.

39. Sir William Coldstream returned to painting after leaving the G.P.O. Film Unit and served as professor of Fine Art at the Slade School of Art.

40. Beach, *Making of the Auden Canon*, 140.

41. Auden also designates as the poem's "orchestral background" the radio news from Europe. While *Letters from Iceland* was published a year before Archibald MacLeish's *Land of the Free*, the latter American book is more often cited as pioneering in its filmic conception of image/text relations. This is probably because MacLeish borrows from film to create a visual unity. The first page of MacLeish's poem is headed with "The Sound Track" and a bold line. This line continues across the top of every left page, each containing the next section of the poem. On every right page is a single photograph.

42. Nichols, *Ideology and the Image*, 197.

43. Yates, a schoolboy at the time, spent three weeks traveling with Auden and MacNeice in Iceland. His account of this trip appears in *W. H. Auden: A Tribute*, ed. Stephen Spender (New York: Macmillan, 1975), 59–68.

44. Rotha, *Documentary Film*, 77.

45. I see more at stake here than the "ribbing of Grierson" that Cunningham points out (329, see note 3).

46. Grierson, *Grierson on Documentary*, 167.

47. Grierson, *Grierson on Documentary*, 164.

48. See Roland Barthes, *Camera Lucida: Reflections on Photography*, trans. Richard Howard (New York: Hill and Wang, 1981), sections 32–33 for a discussion of this "inimitable feature" of photographs.

49. R. Q. McNaughton and Basil Wright edited *Night Mail*. Stuart Legg was a sound supervisor for *Coal Face*.

50. Tagg, *Burden of Representation*, 8.

51. Fussell, *Abroad*, 220.

52. For a succinct, lively critique of this dualistic conception, see the opening pages of Stan Smith's *W. H. Auden* (Oxford: Basil Blackwell, 1985).

53. George Orwell, *Inside the Whale and Other Essays* (Harmondsworth: Penguin, 1957), 156.

7

Demythologizing Facts and Photographs
in Three Guineas

Julia Duffy and Lloyd Davis

*T*HREE GUINEAS IS A FEMINIST, PACIFIST TRACT WRITten by Virginia Woolf and first published in June 1938. It reflects upon and condemns the European arms buildup and the imminence of war. Further, it surveys British social institutions such as the crown, the law, the church, the military, and the family, in order to consider the relations between fascism and these elements of patriarchal culture. In her introduction to the text, Hermione Lee notes that through the 1930s Woolf's feminism "became increasingly involved with her horror of Fascism."[1] By connecting political critique to a feminist perspective, Woolf questions a nostalgic patriotism that emerged in Britain in response to developments in Europe. Leonard Woolf had published the polemical pamphlet *Quack, Quack!* in 1935. It maintained that a reversion to savagery was taking place and juxtaposed pictures of Hitler and Mussolini with those of primitive war gods. *Three Guineas* continues this argument but replaces images of primitive deities with those of contemporary British totems, "absurd photographs of generals and judges in full regalia."[2] Woolf thereby questions a complacent acceptance of domestic institutions that would construct Continental fascism as their

antithesis. The "absurd" function of the photographs is one of the main ways in which the text interrogates this basic nationalistic move.

It is therefore surprising to realize that in the publishing history of *Three Guineas* the illustrations have at times been left out.[3] A year after first thinking of writing the work as a sequel to *A Room of One's Own,* Woolf decided, "It is to have 4 pictures."[4] Though it was eventually published with five, photographs were envisaged as an integral part of the text from very early on, more than four years before Woolf started to write it on 24 November 1936.[5] The omission of the pictures affects the ways in which the text can work and be read. In particular, their absence serves to diminish connections that Woolf strives to make between fascism and patriarchy, foreign and domestic politics, and dominance and hierarchy in the public and private spheres.[6]

The five plates were included in the first two issues of the English edition, printed by the Hogarth Press in June 1938 and November 1943, and also in the first American edition, brought out by Harcourt, Brace and Company in August 1938. However, the second editions in both countries—in America, a Harbinger Book by Harcourt, Brace & World in 1963, and in England, a Penguin Book in 1977—dropped the "illustrations." Subsequent Hogarth reprints have reduced the size of the pictures, and recent Harvest editions by Harcourt Brace Jovanovich continue to leave them out.[7]

Apart from *Three Guineas*, Woolf's other books with illustrations are all "biographies": *Orlando: A Biography, Flush: A Biography*, and *Roger Fry: A Biography*. Over the years, reprints and new editions of these works have also randomly omitted the pictures or changed their number and size. Occasionally, later editions have restored the original pictures (for example, the 1973 Harvest edition of *Orlando*) or added extra ones (the 1976 Harvest *Roger Fry* includes three more than the fifteen plates of the two 1940 first editions). In no instance are the photographers identified, though Woolf's sister, the painter Vanessa Bell, is sometimes credited with line drawings (as for *Flush* in 1933) and jacket design (for the 1938 *Three Guineas*). The source of the pictures is noted irregularly—*Flush* acknowledges permission for reproduction from the National Portrait Gallery, but *Three Guineas* gives no such indication. Instead, a marked mistaking of the origin and subject matter of its photographs becomes a central strategy of Woolf's critique.

The place of pictures in the publishing of Woolf's work is therefore an uncertain one. There seems to be no policy in either the United States or England for reissuing the texts with a full complement of illustrations. Motives for the changes could be speculated upon. It is more fruitful, however, to consider the generic and interpretive effects of including and omitting the pictures.

The exclusion of the photographs implies that they are viewed as expendable—a subsidiary part of the text, illustrative of and dependent on the written word. A generic hierarchy is constructed and enforced, in which a dominant verbal medium is asserted. Moreover, there is pressure to fix the reader and her reading practice within this hierarchy. How could she begin to think that the copy of *Three Guineas* she is reading is not *the* copy? How might she question whether the way that the pictureless version encourages her to read is but *one* way of responding to the text? The tacit removal of the photographs smooths

out processes of response and interpretation. With the grounds for a range of different readings foreclosed, the verbal text is naturalized and its editorial discretion concealed.

When the photographs are included in *Three Guineas*, a range of textual complexities arises. The photographs can be read thematically, in "absurd" or parodic terms, but they also initiate a set of intertextual processes. The written text—its ambiguity increasing despite its recurrent reference to "the facts"—is further complicated as it engages with a different and at times resistant medium. Any presumption of the word's authority over the visual image is disrupted.

A multiplicity of meanings is triggered by the ironic inclusion of the photographs ("ironic" since the narrator refers to other pictures but never to these ones, uncannily anticipating their omission). Woolf writes against patriarchal war not simply by producing facts, figures, and photographs but "by exposing the relativity of supposed absolutes and endorsing pluralism of meaning."[8] Her critique has two targets, one historically contextual, the other transhistorical and generic. *Three Guineas* reproduces the referential and polemical features of a political tract to challenge, on the one hand, traditional and contemporary practices in patriarchal culture, and on the other, the textual conventions through which that culture is represented and understood. In short, Woolf focuses on "the social work that representation can and does do," both depicting and challenging conventions deriving from a patriarchal system.[9]

These challenges take place in various ways—from direct criticism of social and military violence, to satire of dominant social institutions, to reconsiderations of discursive effects on readers. For example, in using pictures to destabilize the verbal text, *Three Guineas* seems to contest an influential theoretical emphasis on the role of vision in producing "the subject." This schema proposes that social identity is established while a person enacts reciprocal roles of seer and seen. The observer is "caught, manipulated, captured, in the field of vision,"[10] through an "imaginary misrecognition of the 'ego', i.e. in the ideological formations in which it 'recognizes' itself."[11] When seen by others, this selfhood marks "the principle of [its] own subjection," for "the techniques

"A General." From Three Guineas *(London: Hogarth, 1938). Courtesy of The Hogarth Press and the Estate of Virginia Woolf.*

that make it possible to see induce effects of power."[12] In both roles, the subject finds a visually determined position.

The photographs in Woolf's text precipitate a different process. In viewing them, our reading of the written work's nationalistic and positivist tropes is disturbed. The "field of vision" undermines rather than settles the reader's position. This disruption starts with the first picture, an ornately costumed and decorated, military male. His eyes are level with our own, and in meeting his gaze we seem to be located within a traditional world of arms and man. Our vision would

subject us to his sight and the old regime he metonymically represents. Yet the age of the figure fragments this position, accentuating the outdatedness of his order. The general looks past it, and we look past, or through, him.

The photograph elicits resistance to the social hierarchies that it signifies. It invites us to pressure the text, to crack its symbolic dignity into a grin. Peering at the general's eyes, half-closed with wrinkles, we wonder whether he isn't in fact glancing away. Something has drawn his flickering consciousness elsewhere; he seems to smile absent-mindedly, maybe recalling a witty remark about the Crimea, or perhaps stirring at an old feeling within, a bodily rhythm that softens the arteries. His expression triggers a counterreading. The picture starts not only to confront icons of tradition and power but also to destabilize the framing written text.

These effects are analogous to what Julia Kristeva has called the "semiotic" process of discourse. The interactive, verbal-pictorial discourse that comprises *Three Guineas* becomes a source of disruption to patriarchal values and meanings. Numerous critics have suggested that Woolf's language exemplifies Kristeva's concept of the semiotic.[13] This notion reworks the ideological and psychoanalytic theory, noted above, that would locate the subject with a fixed identity. Kristeva theorizes a prepatriarchal, presymbolic discourse which emerges through a reciprocal relationship between child and mother. This mutuality produces the rhythmic, multivalent semiotic that escapes circumscription within patriarchal discourse.

While critics have studied linguistic functions of the semiotic in Woolf's fiction, they have not noted its heightened operation in the interaction between the photographic and verbal texts in *Three Guineas*. Following Kristeva, we can see this discursive process as integral to the ideological and semiotic challenge of Woolf's text: "The text is a practice that could be compared to political revolution: the one brings about in the subject what the other introduces into society"; the semiotic "destroy[s] not only accepted beliefs and signification, but, in radical experiments, syntax itself."[14] The interaction between the pictorial and written parts of *Three Guineas* disrupts conventions of syntax, signification, and genre, as well as the traditional social orders they may represent and reinforce.

Thus the aim of this paper is to unpack the semiotic and ideological processes of Woolf's text. In the first place, this interaction suggests that the visual structure which Jacques Lacan and others have identified may only produce a masculinist subject. Woolf's text shows that visual registers may subvert the position of such a figure and thereby participate within feminist critique. At the same time, the relation between the photographs and written text serves to complicate their generic significance. *Three Guineas* does not reify the visual but demythologizes the authority that its photographs of male figures appear to exude. The seemingly timeless value of their roles and status is questioned by juxtaposing them with descriptions of 1930s fascism. Through relocating the photographs, the text interrogates their iconic grandeur and pomp. It is these destabilizations of visual and verbal conventions and expectations that distinguish Woolf's text.

In the first Hogarth Press edition of *Three Guineas*, a list of illustrations at the front of the book reads as follows: "1. A General, 2. Heralds, 3. A University Procession, 4. A Judge, 5. An Archbishop." These five, full-page, black-and-white photographs are, however, only obliquely referred to within the written text. For instance, on the page opposite the picture of the general we read:

> Every button, rosette and stripe seems to have some symbolical meaning. Some have the right to wear plain buttons only; some may wear a single stripe; others three, four, five or six. And each curl or stripe is sewn on at precisely the right distance apart. (23;19)

The photograph prompts amazement as the accoutrements are revealed in a strict hierarchy of meaning. The uniform suggests a nonnegotiable code. As with all the pictures, the actual presence of this one within the pamphlet is never specifically mentioned; yet the photograph illustrates one of the social institutions that is being directly criticized.

Throughout *Three Guineas* Woolf blames institutions such as the military, the crown, the universities, the law, and the church for upholding and furthering the cause of patriarchal fascism, in England and all of Europe. The attack against these institutions is based on their traditional social dominance. Yet Woolf's critique also extends to the symbolic function of such "ideological state apparatuses." Their inflexible, univocal discourse is signified by the precise placement of stripes and buttons on the old general's uniform. Each ribbon and badge denotes an official meaning—rank, affiliation, a national history, and personal record of military deeds. The exactness of their positions seeks to eliminate the possibility of differing responses, and the esoteric symbolism excludes those cut off from the martial codes of "dictated, regimented, official pageantry, in which only one sex takes an active part" (131;114).

Woolf later describes patriarchal institutions and societies as fostering

> a monstrous male, loud of voice, hard of fist, childishly intent upon scoring the floor of the earth with chalk marks, within whose mystic boundaries human beings are penned, rigidly, separately, artificially. (121;105)

His aggressive discourse is inscribed upon the natural and social worlds, "the floor of the earth," as well as on the bodies of those whom it *pens*. The similarity of this "male" to leading dictators and patriarchs of the time (or of any time) is not to go unnoticed.[15] For here, as in *A Room of One's Own*, Woolf urges women to protest against the oppression imposed by masculinist social institutions. Whether in the home and family, or in the state, in the form of the military, such institutions are founded upon repression and violence.[16] Woolf proposes a general definition of the male "Dictator . . . who believes that he has the right . . . to dictate to other human beings how they shall live," whether he "speak[s] English or German" (62;53).[17]

Women are no longer to be "locked in the private house without share in the many societies of which his society is composed" (121;105). This forced domesticity represents a loss of selfhood, "For by so doing we should merge our identity in yours." Accordingly, Woolf suggests that women are to found their own "society," to be called the "Society of Outsiders." This group will deny the patriarchal presumptions of patriotic identity and feeling for "'our' country," which "throughout the greater part of its history has treated me as a slave" (125;108). It is based on radical "indifference" that will have practical and (anti-)structural implications, producing a society "without office, meetings, leaders, or any hierarchy, without so much as a form to be filled up"; the model for this society, "far from sitting still to be painted, dodges and disappears" (132;115).[18]

The outsiders' society is not to be a counter-society that would place women in the powerful positions which men traditionally occupy, nor is it to be governed by patriarchal law. Rather, it is to be located in the margins of mainstream culture, which it influences and disrupts while maintaining the integrity of its outsider's role. It is a society that cannot be conclusively described because what sets it apart is its paradoxical place and energy, "a passive experiment . . . [which] seems to show that to be passive is to be active; those also serve who remain outside" (135–36;118–19).[19] This society will be constantly in process, and its relativizing effects on the dominant culture seem to parallel the influence of the marginalized photographs on the central written text.

Through the narration, then, Woolf can be seen to be criticizing the aggression inherent in patriarchal institutions. As an alternative to their systemic violence, she proposes her Society of Outsiders. But if *Three Guineas* challenges the order of patriarchy only through this call to action, by describing and censuring social circumstances and events, the impact would be somewhat predictable. Instead, its disruptive effects also occur by representing the subversive interaction of the visual and verbal texts.

To describe *Three Guineas* as a "political tract" implies its exclusion from the fictive genres of literature which are typically considered to be Woolf's primary domain. Yet throughout this polemical work, Woolf envisages social "experiments [that] will not be merely critical but creative" (130;113). When describing the Society of Outsiders, she stresses that it wishes "to help the human mind to create and to prevent it from scoring the same rut repeatedly" (132;114). Woolf extols an imaginative activity over mindless conformity. She sees creativity not as anti- or

asocial but aimed at subverting traditional cultural and discursive forms. In reworking the genre of the political tract, Woolf pressures a restrictive opposition between fictional and non-fictional discourse. The pressure begins through a revision of the role of the photographs.

While the content of these pictures, like the general's medals, is sometimes described, their presence in the book is never mentioned after the initial list of illustrations. There is, however, another set of photographs which is repeatedly referred to, "photographs of dead bodies and ruined houses that the Spanish Government sends almost weekly" (79;68). In introducing these pictures, Woolf underlines the apparent reality of their reference, which is made all the more truthful by the violence of the images:

> There are also other pictures—pictures of actual facts: photographs. Photographs, of course, are not arguments addressed to the reason; they are simply statements of fact addressed to the eye. But in that very simplicity there may be some help. Let us see then whether when we look at the same photographs we feel the same things. . . . They are not pleasant photographs to look upon. They are photographs of dead bodies for the most part. This morning's collection contains the photograph of what might be a man's body, or a woman's; it is so mutilated that it might, on the other hand, be the body of a pig. But those certainly are dead children, and that undoubtedly is the section of a house. . . . Those photographs are not an argument; they are simply a crude statement of fact addressed to the eye. . . . They are violent. (13–14;10–11)[20]

The meaning of these pictures is unequivocal "'horror and disgust'" (14;11). The denoted facts seem to fuse all viewers' interpretations into a singularly truthful, moral response. As Stuart Hall has noted, such pictures (like the news photographs of which he writes) construct effects of reality and truth by disguising their ideological dimensions under the documentary image, "offering themselves as literal-visual transcriptions of the 'real world.' . . . They seek a warrant in that ever pre-given, neutral structure, which is beyond question, beyond interpretation: the 'real world.'"[21]

Initially Woolf appears to endorse the ideological and moral consensus produced by the photographs. The reader is repeatedly asked to look at them. There is an insistence upon the actuality of the images, the events they depict, and the meanings of those events. The result is patriotic solidarity, as readers recoil before the horror of foreign fascism.

Yet these are not the photographs reproduced in *Three Guineas*. Substituted for the pictures of dead bodies and ruined dwellings are ones of Englishmen dressed in uniforms. The atrocities we are continually told to look at are transformed into emblems of British patriarchy. Comforting oppositions between England and Europe, democracy and fascism, are undercut, and a consensual response of horror and disgust is confounded. The connections argued for in the written text among patriarchy, militarism, and atrocity are reinforced by the paradoxical links between the photographs constantly referred to and the different ones that are presented. If both sets of images are the products of patriarchy, then the target of judgment is disconcertingly redirected to the home front. And it is the social differences between men and women that preclude a single patriotic, moral viewpoint and afford this critical perspective: "Though we see the same world, we see it through different eyes" (22;18).

The ambiguity over which pictures the narrator is talking about is orchestrated by the repetitious, rhythmical refrain of "Look also at the photographs." The conflation of both sets of pictures under the one heading of "dead bodies and ruined houses" disrupts the informative function of the list of illustrations at the front of the book. Any patriotic reassurance is further pressured by attacks on the pictures' denotations. These reversals in meaning—and the breakdown of relations between the pictorial and written media—mark a more detailed questioning of social values and facts.

Woolf develops the equivocal denotations of the photographs by reviewing the idea of what a fact is. She starts by arguing against patriotism as a natural reason for war. This "fact" is instead a sign of patriarchal social structures:

> To prove this . . . we can appeal to facts. Take the fact of education. . . . Take the fact of property. . . . It would seem to follow then as an indisputable

fact that "we" . . . must still differ in some essential respects from "you." . . . (21–22;17–18)

The repeated invoking of the facts by Woolf's narrator and her male correspondent—"Now we are here to consider facts. . . . Let us return to facts," he writes (70–73;60–63)—parallels the constant referral to the pictures. Facts and images are related in terms of naturalized truth: "Those photographs . . . are simply a crude statement of fact addressed to the eye" (14;11); "Fix our eyes upon the photograph again: the fact" (163;143). This obsessive reference to the facts, with its emphasis on "evidence" (for example, "the evidence of the letter and of the photographs when combined with the facts" [79;68]), undermines its own positivist bent and reveals itself as an ideological and rhetorical ploy, the strategic attempt of patriarchal discourse and power "to reinject realness and referentiality everywhere."[22] "Facts" become tropes which echo through the text but have no truth value. Like the pictures, they question the premise of their own consensus: "But these facts, as facts so often do, prove double-faced" (30;26).

Accordingly, the rhetoric of facts, photographs and evidence, reinforced by the punctilious footnotes, suggests that the narrator is trying to convince the male addressee of her feminist viewpoints through using his own language. Her excessive appeals work, however, to parody his discourse and to question the mythology of facts and photographs.

Anticipating Stuart Hall's analysis of news pictures is Roland Barthes's discussion of the myths of photography:

> Of all the structures of information, the photograph appears as the only one that is exclusively constituted and occupied by a "denoted" message, a message which totally exhausts its mode of existence.

Barthes adds that the insistence that "the photographer had to be there" is the "mystical definition of denotation."[23] It invests the photographer with a kind of presence which compels the viewer to believe what he or she sees. The photograph relies upon and reinforces a system of factuality—the presence of the photographer, the accuracy of vision, the denotative function of the photograph, and the truth of its image. This naturalized discourse—fusing notions of self-hood, vision, and meaning—is contested by Woolf's text.

In *Three Guineas* the rhetoric of facts is in part expressed through appealing to the indisputable truth of biography: "Biography proves," "the greatest testimony . . . which biography provides," "consult biography," "the answer of biography" (29–31;24–26). For Woolf, biography is a masculinist genre, linked to the family patriarch, Leslie Stephen, who compiled the Victorian *Dictionary of National Biography*. With its self-assured negligence in not naming which "nation" it refers to and in almost totally excluding women—"It is much to be regretted that no lives of maids . . . are to be found in the Dictionary of National Biography" (186;166)—this work exemplifies the masculinist arrogance of Victorian imperialism. In *Three Guineas* Woolf invokes biographical truth in hyperbolic terms only to warn us of the alluring myths of the genre: "We must not be baffled by the evasions of biography or seduced by its charm" (31;26).

Of Woolf's biographical works (the genre in which she regularly used photographs), *Orlando* most notably challenges the mythology of biographical fact. This story of a person who lives for a period of several hundred years and changes sex every now and then includes photographs of the protagonist. Yet by presenting deliberately posed and misleading pictures (of Vita Sackville-West), Woolf's novel questions the conventional notion of facts and photographs, demonstrating that their truth value is culturally determined rather than absolute. The persistence of this determination is illustrated by the story Woolf tells in her diary of the difficulty of persuading booksellers to display *Orlando* with their collections of fiction. Instead it was placed amidst biographies of famous people.[24]

Like Leslie Stephen's conception of biography, photography often functioned for Victorian England as a patriotic and patriarchal icon. This occurred in foreign and domestic settings. Judith Williamson, for example, has considered the parallel development of photography and the nineteenth-century bourgeois family. She argues that photography quickly became a strategic means of representing, synthesizing, and naturalizing the State and the family:

Queen Victoria was the first monarch to realize the marvellous ideological opportunities offered by photography and insisted on being always represented as a wife and mother, rather than a ruler.[25]

Through the same period, we also find that "the camera became a coloniser, a preparer of the route to European expansion in the late nineteenth century."[26] This colonial function is still evident in Leonard Woolf's choice of photographs in *Quack, Quack!* and suggests a crucial difference between that work and *Three Guineas*. John MacKenzie notes that "a fresh wave of patriotic, militarist material appeared with the Second World War, and if the imperial content was now rather more muted, it was nevertheless still present."[27] No doubt there occurs a rise in representations of the national family in war time as well—the famous recruiting poster in which a little girl asks her father what he did in the war springs to mind.

Written in the years before World War II, *Three Guineas* works against these traditions of family and national portraits. The photographs it includes seem to offer evidence of British dominance. They make power reassuringly perceivable, helping to consolidate the "bourgeois Imaginary" of Victorian culture.[28] This imaginary realm comprised two types of images: those which displayed the objects of imperialization (the indigenous peoples of Asia and Africa, the natural environment, harnessed to the demands of industry), and those depicting the agents of imperialism (statesmen, armies, and industrial machinery).

The photographs in *Three Guineas* fall into this second category, displaying the colonizing agents—the army, the church, the monarchy, the universities, and the law—in their full might and glory. Such were the cultural myths of photographic denotation and fact. Yet by placing such images in a context that characterizes these male figures as imperial patriarchs, Woolf undermines the denotative conventions of the photographs. In their narcissistic finery, the figures become objects of ridicule. They are stripped of their power: a uniformed man "is not to us a pleasing or an impressive spectacle. He is on the contrary a ridiculous, a barbarous, a displeasing spectacle" (25;21).

As Williamson's comments on Victorian por-

Three photographs ("Orlando as Ambassador," "Orlando, about the year 1840," "Orlando on her return to England") from Orlando: A Biography *(London: Hogarth, 1928). Courtesy of The Hogarth Press.*

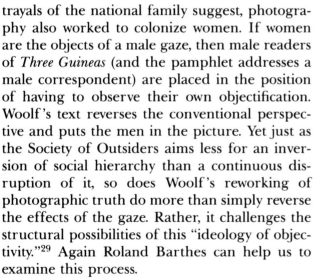

trayals of the national family suggest, photography also worked to colonize women. If women are the objects of a male gaze, then male readers of *Three Guineas* (and the pamphlet addresses a male correspondent) are placed in the position of having to observe their own objectification. Woolf's text reverses the conventional perspective and puts the men in the picture. Yet just as the Society of Outsiders aims less for an inversion of social hierarchy than a continuous disruption of it, so does Woolf's reworking of photographic truth do more than simply reverse the effects of the gaze. Rather, it challenges the structural possibilities of this "ideology of objectivity."[29] Again Roland Barthes can help us to examine this process.

In the essay "The Third Meaning," Barthes outlines three levels of meaning within the photograph. The first two meanings are the informational and symbolic. Applied to the picture of the general in *Three Guineas,* the informational meaning would be that we see a "general," while the symbolic meaning would be constituted by what the "general" connotes in a social context.

Barthes then posits a "third meaning," related to Woolf's demythologizing discourse of facts and photographs, one

> of signifiance . . . a semiotics of the text. . . . It seems to open the field of the meaning totally. . . . It belongs to the family of the pun, buffoonery, useless expenditure. Indifferent to moral aesthetic categories . . . it is on the side of the carnival.[30]

The "moral aesthetic" indifference of the third meaning links it to the feminist indifference of the Outsiders to martial patriotism. There are additional effects of "signifiance" in *Three Guineas*. The photographs function in the "field of the signifier," in that each picture is arbitrarily placed in the text. At one level the content of the photographs seems impressive; more notable, however, are the contradictory relationships between the pictures and the written text, pomp juxtaposed with corpses and ruins. As unanchored signifiers, the pictures undercut any "informational" or "symbolic" meanings. The selection and placement are never explained, and they become increasingly ludicrous and offbeat. Their "third meaning" disrupts and relativizes the informational and symbolic effects of patriarchal identity and authority.

With the exception of the picture of the general, the camera angles position the viewers into looking up at the men, and so imply a relationship of inferiority. In these photographs the males, from their hierarchical dominance, deign not to look at us. The university professors, the judge, and particularly the archbishop look away from the camera in disregard of their audience. In each case the status of these figures seems to be confirmed by the presence of an attentive entourage. The attendance of these groups is obediently restrained.

Such restraint is most evident in the picture of the archbishop. The altar boys, dutifully following their leader, seem to avert their eyes from him, in recognition of the visual grandeur of his

"Heralds." From Three Guineas *(London: Hogarth, 1938). Courtesy of The Hogarth Press and the Estate of Virginia Woolf.*

"A University Procession." From Three Guineas
*(London: Hogarth, 1938). Courtesy of The Hogarth
Press and the Estate of Virginia Woolf.*

"A Judge." From Three Guineas *(London: Hogarth,
1938). Courtesy of The Hogarth Press and the Estate
of Virginia Woolf.*

"An Archbishop." From Three Guineas *(London: Hogarth, 1938). Courtesy of The Hogarth Press and the Estate of Virginia Woolf.*

presence. The power of his position, coded in his lavish garb, defies the apprehension of any would-be onlooker. The belligerence of the judge's expression and his physical isolation suggest an inviolability which likewise forestalls any potential onlooker from gazing on his visage (the two men on the right glance at him furtively as if in fear of being caught). The photograph of the heralds similarly serves to exalt the sovereign

whom they represent. In this case, rather than deferring perception, the king has totally absented himself from the photograph, perhaps to observe the observers of his entourage. His absence implies his presence, producing a power at once "visible and unverifiable."[31]

The photograph of the general differs from these others in that we are openly invited to inspect every ribbon, braid, and insignia on his overcrowded uniform. His legs and his hands are cut out of the photograph, and his decorated torso demands our complete attention. He forces our eyes into focus, reaffirming his authority in the realm of military affairs.

Three Guineas disrupts these patriarchal, symbolic meanings first, as noted earlier, by equating them with the photographs of dead bodies and ruined houses. More importantly, the contradictory syntax of verbal and pictorial texts questions their symbolic value by making the "third meaning" increasingly operative. Once the photographs are placed in this disruptive context, unpredictable incongruities emerge, such as discordant, farcical intrusions from the background. For example, in the photograph of the general the paraphernalia of cords and rods surrounding his hat, collar and coat combine with his advanced age to look more like a medical neck brace than tokens of military might. The feather on his hat, in its phallic defiance of gravity, begins to mock its aged possessor. All of a sudden the general appears senile and impotent, a signifier of superseded masculinity.

In the picture of the heralds, the position of the trumpeters next to the horse's arse—with the inflated cheeks of the man second from the left and the eyes of the one next to him concentrated skywards—leads us to wonder who blows harder.[32] The background of the photograph of the archbishop discloses an enigmatic figure in plain clothes and dark glasses. He seems self-consciously out of place, and Zelig-like, having wandered into the wrong photograph, tries to catch our attention. Looking at the procession of academics, we hold our breath, awaiting the slapstick clash of maces on mortarboards.[33]

The insertion of photographs of corpses and ruined houses would have been a polemical tactic in conventional political rhetoric, as practiced, for example, by the Spanish government. This political intention devalues and translates the dead into tropes. In contrast, *Three Guineas*'s photographs of old men unsettle the generic seriousness of political discourse and reject its traditional decorum by using icons that carnivalize that gravity and beg the question of its motives. It is hard to decide whether the pictures are irrelevant, horrific, or ludicrous. For they are all of these at once, signifying textual and ideological challenge.

In this light, the omission or reduction of the pictures in reprints of *Three Guineas* raises important questions. Lowering production costs seems only a partial explanation. Perhaps the photographs were considered insignificant or auxiliary to the written text. Their denotative relevance could be considered minimal, their parodic function not grasped. On the other hand, perhaps the inclusion of the photographs was found to be generically and ideologically transgressive. As discussed earlier, the discrepant relationship of the photographs to the written text unsettles conventional expectations of discursive coherence and order.

In any case, this editorial practice realizes a form of censorship that restores the stability of the discourse. In "The Ethics of Linguistics," Kristeva addresses the question of censorship, noting that "a (any) society may be stabilized only if it excludes poetic language," and that:

> The poet is put to death because he wants to turn rhythm into a dominant element; because he wants to make language perceive what it doesn't want to say, provide it with its matter independently of the sign, and free it from the denotation. For it is this eminently parodic gesture that changes the system.[34]

Censorship of discourse is a repressive act. The exclusion of the pictures in *Three Guineas* would help to reimpose a system of denotative discourse.

Anticipating Kristeva's hypothesis, Woolf also considers discourse as political action and censorship as oppression. In an essay entitled "The Artist and Politics," she writes of the constraints imposed upon the artist both by a totalitarian regime and by a state at war, again questioning any distinction between foreign and domestic governments.[35] In such periods the writer is in

constant threat of being silenced if she does not provide a voice for official views. Elsewhere Woolf defends the political force of art against charges of decadent aestheticism, writing in 1939 that, though not involved in any public action concerning war, "by writing I am doing what is far more necessary than anything else."[36] She conceives of her writing as action against fascism.

Three Guineas articulates the social and historical marginalization of women, proposing that they belong to a Society of Outsiders. This society functions analogously to semiotic discourse in that it disrupts and unsettles the ruling system while escaping definition by that system. Moreover, *Three Guineas* attacks traditional order not only at an explicit level but also at a structural level. It subverts a nationalistic rhetoric of consensus and truth by revealing its masculinist and militaristic premises. This ideological challenge can be perceived most strikingly in the interaction between the visual and verbal registers of the text, its demythologizing of the denotative, patriarchal discourse of facts and photographs.

NOTES

1. Hermione Lee, introduction to *Three Guineas*, by Virginia Woolf (London: Hogarth, 1986), xii.

2. Lee, introduction, xii.

3. For the publication details of *Three Guineas* see B. J. Kirkpatrick, *A Bibliography of Virginia Woolf*, 3rd ed. (Oxford: Clarendon, 1980), 65–67.

4. *The Diary of Virginia Woolf*, 5 vols., ed. Anne Olivier Bell (London: Hogarth, 1982), 4:77, the entry for 16 Feb. 1932. Woolf conceived of the work on 20 Jan. 1931 (*Diary*, 4:6).

5. *Diary*, 5:35.

6. Cf. Brenda R. Silver, "The Authority of Anger: *Three Guineas* as Case Study," *Signs* 16 (1991): 342–43.

7. Quotations from *Three Guineas* are from the accessible Hogarth (1986) and Harvest (1966) reprints. They are cited parenthetically, with Hogarth page numbers placed first. The photographs are reproduced from a 1947 Hogarth "New Edition" (so labeled on the title page), which is not listed in Kirkpatrick's *Bibliography* but has the same pagination as the 1943 issue described there (see 66–67).

8. Victoria Middleton, "*Three Guineas*: Subversion and Survival in the Professions," *Twentieth Century Literature* 28 (1982): 406.

9. Frank Lentricchia, *Criticism and Social Change* (Chicago: University of Chicago Press, 1983), 50. Woolf's notebooks from the 1930s indicate the wide-ranging issues she considered while writing *Three Guineas*. There are three volumes of press cuttings and copied extracts that relate to the text. See *Virginia Woolf's Reading Notebooks*, ed. Brenda R. Silver (Princeton: Princeton University Press, 1983);

pieces from English newspapers that are linked to the pictures include "Women and Gladiators" (266); "Equality of the Sexes only a Myth / Wives the Law's Favourites / By His Honour Judge McCleary" (267); "Young Women and the Church / A Suspicion that They Are Not Wanted" (272); "The Fellows [sic] attitude to Oxford and women" (302–3).

10. Jacques Lacan, *The Four Fundamental Concepts of Psycho-Analysis*, trans. Alan Sheridan (New York: Norton, 1981), 92.

11. Louis Althusser, *Lenin and Philosophy and Other Essays*, trans. Ben Brewster (New York: Monthly Review Press, 1971), 219.

12. Michel Foucault, *Discipline and Punish: The Birth of the Prison*, trans. Alan Sheridan (New York: Vintage, 1979), 203, 170–71.

13. For example, Jane Marcus, *Virginia Woolf and the Languages of Patriarchy* (Bloomington: Indiana University Press, 1987); Makiko Minow-Pinkey, *Virginia Woolf and the Problem of the Subject* (New Brunswick, N.J.: Rutgers University Press, 1987); and Toril Moi, *Sexual/Textual Politics: Feminist Literary Theory* (London: Methuen, 1985). For Julia Kristeva's concept see especially "From One Identity to Another," in *Desire in Language: A Semiotic Approach to Literature and Art*, ed. Leon S. Roudiez (New York: Columbia University Press, 1980), 124–47; and *Revolution in Poetic Language*, trans. Margaret Waller (New York: Columbia University Press, 1984).

14. Kristeva, *Revolution in Poetic Language*, 17, 133. Woolf was highly conscious of her text's feminist ideological charge: "If I say what I mean in 3 Guineas I must expect considerable hostility" (*Diary*, 5:84). The response of her nephew and biographer, Quentin Bell, exemplifies the anticipated reaction: "What really seemed wrong with the book . . . was the attempt to involve a discussion of women's rights with the far more agonising and immediate question of what we were to do in order to meet the ever-growing menace of Fascism and war. The connection between the two questions seemed tenuous," *Virginia Woolf: A Biography*, 2 vols. (San Diego: Harvest, 1972), 2:205.

15. Cf. Woolf's remarks on hearing Hitler speak on the radio: "Hitler boasted & boomed. . . . Mere violent rant. . . . A savage howl like a person excruciated. . . . Then another bark" (*Diary*, 5:169); "We listened to the ravings, the strangled hysterical sobbing swearing ranting of Hitler at the Beer Hall" (5:245).

16. Woolf's portrait of the petulant tyrant echoes in her recollections of her father's "violent temper" and "violent rages" in *A Sketch of the Past* (in *Moments of Being*, ed. Jeanne Schulkind [San Diego: Harcourt Brace Jovanovich, 1985]). She contrasts the terms of family memories: compared to her mother, recalled as "a general presence rather than a particular person" (83), Leslie Stephen dictates a definite memory, "all contained and complete and already summed up" (109). Woolf made notes on two newspaper articles from 1 Aug. 1936 on dictatorship in Germany and in the family (*Reading Notebooks*, 250, 293).

17. Cf. *Diary*: "These dictators & their lust for power— they cant [sic] stop" (5:177).

18. As she was finishing *Three Guineas*, Woolf contemplated starting "an illustrated sheet to be called The Outsider" (*Diary*, 5:128); later in 1938 she mused, "I'm fundamentally, I think, an outsider" (5:189).

19. Woolf's "outsiders" could be compared to Kristeva's "'new generation of women,'" who have "two attitudes— *insertion* into history and the radical *refusal* of the subjective limitations imposed by this history's time on an experiment carried out in the name of . . . irreducible difference": see "Women's Time," *Signs* 7 (1981): 20.

20. Woolf refers to similar photographs in a notebook entry, "The horror of war. / The Spanish photographs" (*Reading Notebooks*, 254), and in a letter to her nephew Julian Bell (dated 14 Nov. 1936): "This morning I got a packet of photographs from Spain all of dead children, killed by bombs—a cheerful present," *Leave the Letters Till We're Dead: The Letters of Virginia Woolf*, vol. 6: 1936–1941, ed. Nigel Nicolson (London: Hogarth, 1980), 85. Her impressions of the Spanish Civil War were intensified by seeing refugees in London (*Diary*, 5:97), and by the death of Julian Bell in Spain. At one point she suggests that she sublimated part of her grief for him into "incessant writing, thinking about 3 Gs" (see *Diary*, 5:125).

21. Stuart Hall, "The Determinations of News Photographs," in *The Manufacture of News: Social Problems, Deviance, and the Mass Media*, rev., ed. Stanley Cohen and Jock Young (London: Constable, 1981), 241.

22. Jean Baudrillard, *Simulations*, trans. Paul Foss et al. (New York: Semiotext(e), 1983), 42.

23. Roland Barthes, "The Photographic Message," in *A Barthes Reader*, ed. Susan Sontag (New York: Hill and Wang, 1982), 197, 208.

24. *The Diary of Virginia Woolf*, vol. 3: 1925–1930, ed. Anne Olivier Bell (London: Hogarth, 1980), 193.

25. Judith Williamson, *Consuming Passions: The Dynamics of Popular Culture* (London: Marion Boyars, 1986), 116.

26. John M. MacKenzie, *Propaganda and Empire: The Manipulation of British Public Opinion, 1880–1960* (Manchester: Manchester University Press, 1984), 19.

27. *Propaganda*, 23. Woolf kept two such articles: "Lord Hewart on England—Home of Liberty / A Castle That Will Be Defended to the Last" and "The Lord Mayor's Show / City Pageantry in Sunshine / Tableaux of Empire" (*Reading Notebooks*, 279, 313).

28. Peter Stallybrass and Allon White, *The Politics and Poetics of Transgression* (London: Methuen, 1986), 126.

29. Hall, "Determinations," 242.

30. "The Third Meaning: Research Notes on Some Eisenstein Stills," in *A Barthes Reader*, 320.

31. Foucault, *Discipline and Punish*, 201.

32. Woolf kept news photographs of heralds "Proclaiming the Coronation of King Edward in London" (*Reading Notebooks*, 291).

33. Woolf records having seen such a procession at Cambridge University when T. S. Eliot was awarded an honorary degree. Lord Baldwin, the chancellor who conferred the degree, is in this picture, and as Woolf writes, "If anyone reads it [*Three Guineas*], the illustration is pat to hand" (*Diary*, 5:149–50).

34. Kristeva, "The Ethics of Linguistics," in *Desire in Language*, 31.

35. Virginia Woolf, *Collected Essays*, 4 vols. (New York: Harcourt, Brace & World, 1966–67), 2:230–32.

36. Woolf, *Sketch*, in *Moments of Being*, 73.

8

Double-Crossing Frontiers:
Literature, Photography, and the Politics of Displacement

Carol Shloss

On PAGE 45 OF *A SEVENTH MAN: MIGRANT WORKERS in Europe,* there is an uncanny image: it is the torn photograph of an unknown man. The rip cuts the face diagonally. The upper left half shows a cap, one ear, one eye, the nose, and a fraction of a shoulder. The lower right half contains the other ear and eye, the mouth, and is printed in enough detail to let us see that the man is poorly shaved and that his shirt is worn. The two fragments are separated from each other by several lines of type; and because of their position on the page, they usurp space that might otherwise have been used for the text. The white space is neither economical nor aesthetic, and yet this lack of economy and beauty is poetic: it is, for me, a visual metaphor for work shared in the lives of the writer John Berger and the photographer Jean Mohr.

On one level, this is nonsense. The photograph was probably not taken by Jean Mohr—it is a common identity photograph of a Portuguese migrant worker—and the page was almost certainly not laid out by John Berger. Either Sven Blomberg, a painter, or Richard Hollis, a designer, would more probably be responsible for the *mise en page,* but it does not matter. With its fragments and gaps, photographs and text, the page speaks eloquently about the dialectic between separation and reunion and about art as a "reassembly of what has been scattered."[1] It announces its labor, it addresses the issue of pain, and it asks us to attend to the irrepressibly political nature of the world.

These are far-reaching concerns, and at first it is difficult to see their connection. Literally the torn photograph is an emblem of peasant cunning in the face of duplicity. It was devised by Portuguese migrants who needed secretly to cross both the Spanish and French frontiers in order to find "guest work" in more industrialized countries than their own. Their guides would often take exorbitant sums of money and then abandon them on the mountains just across the Spanish border, where they would become lost and sometimes die.[2] The photograph became their defense: half of it was given to the guide; half was mailed home after the migrant had reached France safely. By taking his half to each migrant's family, the smuggler could prove the completion of his mission and then claim his fee. I imagine Berger to have included this information in order to show one of the many

141

per capita income in Portugal – an average which included the incomes of the upper class – was $370.) So the migrants devised a system to protect themselves. Before leaving they had their photographs taken. They tore the photograph in half, giving one

half to their 'guide' and keeping the other themselves. When they reached France they sent their half of the photograph back to their family in Portugal to show that they had been safely escorted across the frontiers; the 'guide' came to the family with his half of the photograph to prove that it was he who had escorted them, and it was only then that the family paid the $350. The migrants crossed in groups of a hundred or so. Mostly they travelled by night. Hidden in lorries. And on foot.

After nine days he reached Paris. He had the address of a Portuguese friend, but he knew no directions. To find the address he must take a taxi. Before letting him open the door, the taxi

"Portuguese migrant," by Jean Mohr. From A Seventh Man: Migrant Workers in Europe *(New York: Viking, 1975). By permission of Penguin Books Ltd.*

difficulties of a border crossing for those in "underdeveloped" countries. "It isn't the geographical frontier that counts," he tells us. "The frontier is simply where [the emigrant] is liable to be stopped and his intention to leave thwarted" (*Seventh* 43). But there is more to this anecdote than its literal explanation, for it is also the result of another kind of cunning. We could say, in fact, that it stands as an emblem of Berger's and Mohr's careers, which have both involved a prolonged confrontation with frontiers, with how they exclude, and with the excluded. In the case of these Portuguese peasants, the exclusion is literal, and their intention to breach a national barrier becomes an act of courage because the danger to their lives is real. But any-

thing that serves as a barrier can pose a similar threshold experience, where crossing can bring either suffering or trans-formation: transport and change of structure and hope. These are the attributes of art as Berger and Mohr practice it, and they are the attributes that make page 45 of *A Seventh Man* a poem. The page brings together, by the labor of artists, what political force has fragmented and torn apart.

I can think of no better way to represent the dismemberment of human wholeness more eloquently than with a torn photograph. Where the image in its entirety announces, "I am present to sight and to memory," the halved image says, "I am divided from myself by the necessity of this crossing." Like the paper that is mailed back home to complete the picture, the migrant hopes one day to be reunited with his family, with his homeland, and with his own integrity. He hopes to be healed from the wrench of circumstances that have required him to work abroad. Whether he can do this or not in actuality remains in question. But what we can see on this page is Berger and Mohr's gesture of defiance: no reparation can be made to the person who is represented in the image. But "the space which separates" him from himself can be represented by the space of the page (*Our Faces* 96), the text of his life can be articulated in words, and the issue of wholeness can be addressed. If the life represented is fractured, the possibility of ending its division is suggested to us by the invisible intelligences which have reassembled its parts and put them together on the page. Like a poem, the page suggests the hope of an existence which is indivisible.

* * *

We can now see that the principles which have guided the construction of this single page are the principles which govern the entire book. Two modes of production are pitted against one another throughout as Berger and Mohr work together on behalf of what is indivisible in life and against monopoly capitalism—whose labor alienates people and, in the case of migrant workers, displaces them from their homes in "underdeveloped" countries. Years after the publication of *A Seventh Man*, Berger would continue to insist on the centrality of this concern: "Never before our time," he would write in *And Our Faces, My Heart, Brief as Photos,* "have so many people been uprooted. Emigration, forced or chosen, across national frontiers or from village to metropolis, is the quintessential experience of our time" (55).

A Seventh Man focuses on geopolitics and on the actual and symbolic meanings of the frontier itself. Like Michel Foucault, the underlying premise of Berger and Mohr's work is a view of history as a dialectic of opposed forces which provoke a "complex interaction between uneven economies, societies and ideologies."[3] National frontiers are, for them, one of the sites of this power play. They are places that allow the "advanced" industrial nations of Europe to practice a supervisory authority over those who desire entry; they also allow national definitions that are based on a process of exclusion, although one of Berger's major points is that those who are allowed entry into Germany, France, Belgium, and Switzerland remain excluded Others anyway.

Several of Jean Mohr's photos show how the bodies of the workers become subject to this exercise of power. In one image, a German doctor is examining Turkish workers in a recruitment station in Istanbul. Six men ("You yourself must be the seventh") stand stripped to their shorts while he inspects each in turn. The two men at the right end of the line have been "done." Their shoulders are stooped, their heads hang, and their eyes are turned to the floor. The third man bears the doctor's scrutiny (he has pulled down

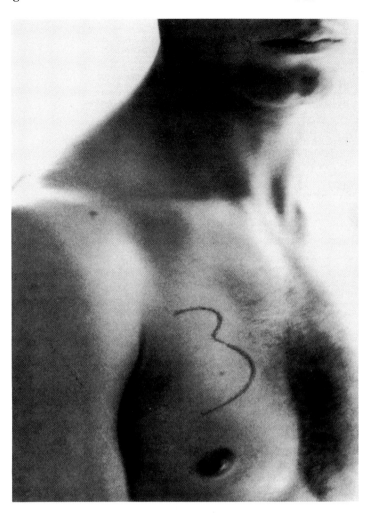

"Each man examined has his number marked in ink on chest and wrist," by Jean Mohr. From A Seventh Man *(New York: Viking, 1975). By permission of Penguin Books Ltd.*

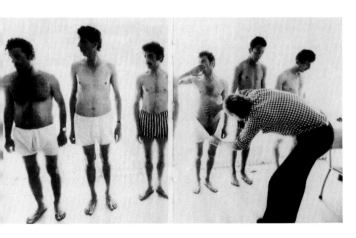

"Medical examination, Istanbul," by Jean Mohr. From A Seventh Man *(New York: Viking, 1975). By permission of Penguin Books Ltd.*

the man's underwear, exposing him while he palpitates the abdomen) with the gesture one makes at the scene of a violent crime. His mouth is open, his head is turned away, and his hand is raised as if to stop himself from retching. The three remaining men stand with their heads averted. In another photograph, a man whose face is not imaged bears the number "3" on his shoulder. We do not need to be told in words that crossing the border into Germany is also a crossing into namelessness and humiliation. The photograph speaks just as clearly as John Berger, who describes this threshold experience as a kind of birth: "He passed [the medical exam] and was born" (*Seventh* 58). But his further comments show the irony of such new life, for the peasant is "born again" into a single function: his body's labor power.

> He is admitted to do a certain kind of job. He has no rights, claims or reality outside his filling of that job. While he fills it, he is paid and accommodated. If he no longer does so, he is sent back to where he came from. It is not men who immigrate but machine minders, sweepers, diggers, cement mixers, cleaners, drillers, etc. . . . To rebecome a man (husband, father, citizen, patriot) a migrant must return home. The home he left because it held no future for him. (*Seventh* 58)

Of the meaning of their experience, as Berger represents it, the emigrants have little understanding, or rather they have a self-understanding that does not accord with the immensity of their predicament. For them, the decision to migrate was made consciously in order to achieve specific goals. Whatever the isolation, strangeness, and discomfort of their foreign status, their going was an expression of will.

It is here, in dealing with the issue of consciousness that is incommensurate with experience, that Berger encounters a major narrative dilemma. European migrant workers are painfully aware of their fragmented home lives, for they live in barracks where lovers, children, wives, and other family members are unmistakably absent. But they cannot see the discrepancy between these experiences which derive from their objective historical moment and the subjective way they explain experience. Berger wants, in writing about them, both to respect their own self-understanding and to demonstrate its insufficiencies, to create, as it were, a double emplotment.

He achieves this through the trope of dreaming, using as metaphor the process which brings together the two dimensions of psychic life—conscious and unconscious thought. If lack of consciousness can act narratively as an alazon or blocking character, standing in the way of social change that might alleviate suffering, then the dream can act narratively as a messenger from the unconscious, offering the possibility of psychic integration. It is not, however, the dream of an individual that we are asked to imagine, but the dream of collective humanity:

> This book concerns a dream/nightmare. By what right can we call the lived experience of others a dream/nightmare? Not because the facts are so oppressive that they can weakly be termed nightmarish; nor because hopes can weakly be termed dreams.
>
> In a dream, the dreamer wills, acts, reacts, speaks and yet submits to the unfolding of a story which he scarcely influences. The dream happens to him. Afterward he may ask another to interpret it [or] . . . break his dream by deliberately waking himself up. (*Seventh* n.p.)

Berger's metaphor explains both a mode of emplotment and a set of oppositions. By identifying the migrant's life as part of a dream story he did not write, Berger has found a way to represent a dichotomy between the seeming autonomy of the subject and the real power of social structures and their force. In the same way that trauma in psychic life is caused by a conflict between conscious and unconscious impulses, the migrant's experience could be said to be gripped by a "political unconscious." That is, the trope places history itself as the unseen mover of events, the invisible cause of the emigration of workers across national frontiers. "As a figure in a dream," Berger continues, "dreamt by an unknown sleeper, he appears to act autonomously, at times unexpectedly; but everything he does . . . is determined by the needs of the dreamer's mind. Abandon the metaphor. The migrant's intentionality is permeated by historical necessities of which neither he nor anybody he meets is aware." (*Seventh* 43)

Although Berger forsakes his own tropological language at this point, I would like to remain with it a moment longer, for it can help to clarify the migrant's place within the industrial nations which are his "host" countries, and it can also explain more specifically the role Berger and Mohr, writer and photographer, propose to play in relation to their subject.

If the migrant workers are unconscious and if they are sabotaged by what they do not yet know, they can also be said to *be* the unconscious of Europe in the sense that their absence from official histories—their status as the refuse or "Abfall" or the rejected Other—is the result of willful cultural repression.

"Working conditions of migrant workers constructing a tunnel under Geneva, Switzerland," by Jean Mohr. From A Seventh Man *(New York: Viking, 1975). By permission of Penguin Books Ltd.*

Nowhere is this idea represented more forcefully than in a section of *A Seventh Man* called "A Report from under Geneva." In it, Berger tells about Geneva's decision to upgrade its infrastructure by installing a new drainage system to serve the right bank of the lake. Located approximately thirty meters underground—one tunnel running five kilometers, the other (for utility cables) running half that length—the work was done by migrant labor from Yugoslavia, Spain, and southern Italy. Because of the high risk of accident, the threat to health posed by silicosis, and the low pay of these manual jobs, no Swiss workers wanted them. Mohr's photographs are dark, with poor contrast of black and white; they show men working underground

with shovels and pneumatic drills or operating a rotary cutting machine called a "mechanical mole."

As they bore under the city, buried beneath the sight of the community the tunnels will support, they serve as visual metaphors of their own political lives. They are that which the Swiss do not want to see about themselves, that which is pushed down into the unconscious: the uncomfortable knowledge that their lives are built upon the labor of "underdeveloped" men. As Berger says, migrant workers go from being unknown to being unknowable to being beneath understanding.

Language and images function, then, in the same way that displacement functions in dreams: as representations of what is latent in social consciousness. The very act of expression helps to accomplish the "dream work," for it turns what is latent knowledge to the Swiss into languages that have a manifest content to us. Indeed, the revelation of the buried contents of the unconscious double-crosses or subverts it. What is hidden in actual social life is displaced into art and made available for scrutiny and change.

Indeed, it is by continuing to follow the logic of this psychological trope that we can begin to draw the various threads of *A Seventh Man* together and to specify another aspect of art that is implicit in Berger and Mohr's collaboration. If the logic of historical materialism is to hide its existence as if in the unconscious, then the function of this book, in addition to the act of assembling, is to show forth what seems to be absent. As Berger says, "To see the experience of another, one must do more than dismantle and reassemble the world with him at its center. One must interrogate his situation to learn about that part of his experience which derives from the historical moment" (*Seventh* 104).

Against the migrant workers' absence of historical perspective, the writer and photographer pose their understanding of monopoly capitalism's intent to appear "absent" as a source of human alienation. Another way to say this is that for them, as for Marx, Freud, and Nietzsche, "the process of hiding is the structure of truth."[4] Given this understanding, their work moves toward a double disclosure: (1) toward naming real historical forces that operate invisibly in order to disguise their domination, and (2) toward naming those histories that official "History" would leave in silence and darkness. Left to official notice, the story of these guest workers would remain below the threshold of discourse. No camera eye of History would follow them into their subterranean existence, nor would any text contextualize their lives. The tunnel—the economic infrastructure—would exist, but it would exist in darkness, without revelation. "Officially," Berger observes, "apologists for the system argue that . . . emigration benefits underdeveloped countries" (*Seventh* 75). "Behind this curtain of argument," he counters, using as metaphor the cloth which obscures vision through windows, "reality remains unchanged" (*Seventh* 78). Mohr contributes to this theme of exposing purposeful obscurity with photographs of migrants working as window washers in Vienna, Austria. Like Berger's narrative, the images have a double function: (1) to show that the official view from such windows is obstructed, and (2) to show that the bodies of the workers are the agents of better vision. By seeing them, instead of simply looking out of the clear glass, we can attend to the full story of labor relations in Austria; we can understand how official knowledge that wants to appear transparent and self-evident is often—like glass—constructed, mystifying, and in need of cleaning.

* * *

When Berger and Mohr work in this manner—with disclosure of political "secrets" as a motive force—they are dealing with a more general problem of representation that has remained a concern through their careers. How can the Other be represented in culture without committing violence or distortions that are analogous to those already perpetrated by supervisory authorities on the political level? How can art become a mode of production that has integrity in the face of its subject? And how can we read what Fredric Jameson has called the "ideology of form": "the symbolic messages transmitted to us by the coexistence of various sign systems which are themselves traces or anticipations of modes of production"?[5]

Several ways of addressing these questions can be provided by thinking of (1) the principles of inclusion and exclusion that guide the selections of texts and images in *A Seventh Man*, (2) the constellation provided by the photographs and texts which, taken together as a system, operate according to a discernable syntax, and (3) the self-reflectiveness of the artists themselves.

When we consider the principles of inclusion in *A Seventh Man*, it becomes clear that the book functions in a way that is similar to Theodor Adorno's description of negative dialectics:

Adorno . . . inscribes in his philosophy of negative dialectics the same originary movement that Freud claims as the origin not only of negation, but implicitly of all propositions and thus of all thinking: the opposition, differentiation and rhythm of acceptance and rejection: "This I want to introduce into me, this I want to exclude from me."[6]

A Seventh Man begins with rejection: it rejects the frontiers or boundaries that are customarily used by industrial nations for excluding guest workers either from entering their countries or from being given full status as citizens and human beings. The book includes the rejected. Implicit in its choice of subject is, then, intellectual and artistic labor which resists the existing social order because of its own alternative vantage point. Unabashedly utopian, Berger would later identify this creative stance with the central cosmological myths of Western thought:

Many previous cosmological explanations of the world proposed . . . an ideal original state and afterwards, for man, a continually deteriorating situation. The Golden Age, the Garden of Eden, the Time of the Gods . . . all were far away from the misery of the present. That life may be seen as a Fall is intrinsic to the human faculty of imagination. To imagine is to conceive of that height from which the Fall becomes possible. (*Our Faces* 39)

To see the possibility of wholeness is also to know the pain and negativity of the present and to understand how it is inscribed in the bodies of the oppressed. To return to Adorno's language, "the corporeal moment announce[s] to cognition that suffering should not be, that it should become different."[7]

If *A Seventh Man* criticizes and negates, it also

concerns itself, as does a doctor or psychoanalyst, with healing. We might say that pain is the motor of Berger and Mohr's efforts but not their destination. In absolute terms, their goal is the political and economic transformation of the world, and their art is made in the service of that transformation. They do not see their book—with photographs and texts—in opposition to life, but as a speech act within life, a part of the imagination's dialogue with the conditions of its own existence.

What acts of imagination are capable of answering oppressive circumstances? One of them has already been accomplished in *A Seventh Man* by its attention to the issue of repression. The book fulfills Adorno's injunction to "let suffering speak [as] the condition of all truth."[8] But further work is done by the combinations that lace Berger's text and Mohr's photographs into a sequential whole. As if answering Adorno ("The constitutive wound of all thought is the inadequacy of concept and truth"), Berger and Mohr constantly work with the idea of "montage" or "constellation" ("But thought is also the attempt to heal the wound through concepts in their constellation").[9]

How can we describe that constellation? What guides its particular formation? The single most important aspect of their collaboration is its balance of power. *A Seventh Man* is not an illustrated text: to illustrate means to supplement, to add to, to enhance as if by giving examples of something else which is primary: "Here is a picture of the pneumatic drill I have just described to you in words." To collaborate is to contribute work that is unique but of commensurate weight. And indeed, this equity is made quite explicit. In "A Note to the Reader," Berger explains,

> The book consists of images and words. Both should be read in their own terms. Only occasionally is an image used to illustrate the text. The photographs, taken over a period of years by Jean Mohr, say things which are beyond the reach of words. The pictures in sequence make a statement: a statement which is equal and comparable to, but different from, that of the text. (*Seventh* n.p.)

The significance of this way of working is simply that it balances tensions: the book does not try to homogenize pictures and text, nor does it try to avoid contradictions. It does not subordinate the vision of one artist to the intelligence of the other; it avoids hierarchies. Tropologically we might say that Berger's domain is the domain of speech as Mohr's domain is that of image, but it would be equally important to observe that the border is open and that free passage from one mode of perception to the other is encouraged. Gilles Deleuze, in writing about Michel Foucault, uses the image of combat between enemies to help us imagine the interaction between saying and seeing in a text:

> Between the figure and the text, we must admit a whole series of crisscrossings, or rather between the one and the other attacks are launched and arrows fly against the enemy target, campaigns designed to undermine and destroy; wounds and blows from the lance, a battle . . . images falling into the midst of words, verbal flashes crisscrossing drawings . . . discourse cutting into the forms of things.[10]

This is not a naive descriptive language, and it is predicated on a premise that I share—that "the sciences of man" are inseparable from the power relations which make them possible.[11] But it seems impossible for Deleuze to imagine a peaceable kingdom. The existence of two realms of perception creates in his mind the image of political frontiers where the strong dominate the weak, and where issues of "capitalization" and "underdevelopment" come into play in deciding the fates of warring art forms.

If Berger and Mohr are waging war, they are waging it together. Dynamic passage from one state to another need not be conflictual and need not involve the deployment of unequal power. It seems not at all unimportant to me that two of the most intensely self-reflective writers of our time who have worked with Mohr—John Berger and Edward Said (*After the Last Sky: Palestinian Lives*)—have both used the language of transport to describe the function of photographs in their lives and in their thinking about the possible effects of art.

Berger tells us that "a friend came to see me in a dream. From far away. And I asked in the dream: 'Did you come by photograph or train?' All photographs are a form of transport and an expression of absence" (*Seventh* 13). Similarly in

After the Last Sky, Said reflects, "How easily trav-
elled the photos make it seem and how possible
to suspend the barriers keeping me from the
scenes they portray."[12] What is dispersed in life,
Mohr's photographs gather together and transport into a recontextualized present that is represented to us by the physical structure of the
book itself. It is a resettlement of images, even
for those, like Said, who live in exile and without
a state to return to.

One of the most eloquent twentieth-century
spokesmen for the dispossessed, Said has seen
in Palestinian lives the extreme example of the
homelessness and dislocation which is Berger's
subject; and he has also understood it within the
tendency of "orientalism" to control and ma-
nipulate "manifestly different world[s]."[13] In
working with Mohr, his aim was very similar to
Berger's: to find a writing stance which neither
reduplicated this structure of knowledge nor reduced the Other to exoticism. The situation of
Palestinians is, he claims, also made visible at national frontiers where

> [w]e are . . . stopped at borders, or herded into
> new camps or denied reentry or residence or
> barred from travel from one place to another,
> more of our land is taken, our lives are interfered
> with arbitrarily, our voices are prevented from
> reaching each other, our identity is confined to
> frightened little islands in an inhospitable environ-
> ment of superior military force sanitized by the
> clinical jargon of pure administration. (*Last Sky* 19)

For Said, the alternative to this "jargon" is another kind of mimetic posture which refuses an
authoritative, aggressive narrative in favor of
"constructed and deconstructed" ephemera or
narratives which occur as fragmentary compositions. "All cultures," he tells us, "spin out a dialectic of self and other, the subject 'I' who is
native, authentic, at home, and the object 'it' or
'you' who is foreign, perhaps threatening, different out there" (*Last Sky* 19). What is unique to
Palestinian culture, he claims, is the extent to
which Palestinians have bought into this perception of themselves as Other and the extent to
which, finding no official places for themselves,
their genius expresses itself in "crossing-over and
clearing hurdles" (*Last Sky* 16). Given this predicament of "difference," Said considers that

*"Tel Sheva, 1979. A village of settled nomads near
Bersheeba," by Jean Mohr. From* After the Last Sky:
Palestinian Lives *(New York: Pantheon, 1986). Pho-
tographs from* After the Last Sky © *1986 by Edward
W. Said. Reprinted by permission of Pantheon Books,
a division of Random House, Inc.*

Mohr's photographs—"taken from the outside"—render the Palestinian in an appropriate
way as Other. "Thus the insider becomes the outsider" (*Last Sky* 41). "Many Palestinian friends
who saw Jean Mohr's pictures," he reflects,
"thought that he saw us as no one else has. But
we also felt that he saw us as we would have seen
ourselves—at once inside and outside our world.
The same double vision informs my text" (*Last
Sky* 6).

sociated with "official" supervision, he could at least avoid stereotyping the Palestinians as fighters, terrorists, or "lawless pariahs" (*Last Sky* 4). Many of his images are highly self-reflective; that is, they speak imagistically of the situation of their own composition as in "The Photographer Photographed" or indirectly in images which manifest themselves as thresholds. In "Palestinian Boy and Israeli Soldier," for example, the photograph uses its own framing as a device for indicating the cultural exclusion of the boy and his marginal place in the Middle Eastern world.

"*Amman, 1984. A visit to the former mayor of Jerusalem and his wife, in exile in Jordan,*" by Jean Mohr. *From* After the Last Sky *(New York: Pantheon, 1986).*

Looking at images of people and places to which he is legally denied access because of his nationality, Said reflects on the strangeness of a world in which knowledge of his own people has to be brought to him by a European photographer who saw for him and who probably communicated through an interpreter. From the faces of those photographed, Said decides that Mohr was treated politely, but skeptically "as someone who came from or perhaps acted at the direction of those who put them where they so miserably are. There was the embarrassment of people uncertain why they were being looked at and recorded" (*Last Sky* 12).

If Mohr could not completely avoid being as-

"*Jerusalem, 1979. The photographer photographed,*" by Jean Mohr. *From* After the Last Sky *(New York: Pantheon, 1986).*

"Kalandia (near Ramallah), 1967. A few days after the end of the June War: in the foreground, an Israeli officer, lost in thought. Behind the window, a young villager," by Jean Mohr. From After the Last Sky *(New York: Pantheon, 1986).*

"We are the periphery," says Said, "the image that will not go away" (*Last Sky* 41).

Mohr's awareness participates in a self-reflectiveness that is general to all three artists, for all ask themselves what interest has guided their own curiosity. This self-scrutiny—laying bare their own motives to the same extent that they expose the quality of their subjects' lives—is the third aspect of a mode of artistic production that is common to Mohr, Berger, and now Said. They have all attended to issues of incorporation/exclusion that are common both

to definitions of nationalism and to predatory structures of knowledge; they have all considered the importance of "constellating" thought as Adorno defines it, that is, as a grouping of "concepts" which, by regrouping the constellations of history, functions as an answer to that history. And they have also understood that true human equity allows scrutiny to be reciprocal. "I would like to think," Said says at the end of *After the Last Sky*, "that such a book not only tells the reader about us, but in some way also reads the reader. . . . We are also looking at our observers" (*Last Sky* 166).

By making the structure of observation explicit, Mohr, Berger, and Said offer their art as an alternative to the invisible strategies of political domination. Said, writing as an insider who is giving strangers access to experience that would otherwise remain private, joins with his subject to look outward to those who observe in order to remind them that Others have a viewpoint and that their seeming marginality does not condemn them always to be the objects of history. Judgment is a mutual activity.

Unlike Said, Mohr and Berger stand as outsiders to their subjects, united to them by some qualities that make community possible, but separated, too, by the circumstances of their birth. In *After the Last Sky*, Mohr is explicit about the origins of his interest in questions about Palestine, telling us of his German nationality, his family's resettlement in Switzerland, their request for Swiss nationalization, his first assignment to photograph Palestinians, and the thirty years that passed before he understood that he had used the outrages of a few Palestinian extremists to justify turning his back on the rest of them (*Last Sky* 8). In 1979 Berger would use a similar catalog of traits to sort out how he was like and unlike the French peasants who were the subject of the first part of his trilogy, *Into Their Labours*.

What is unnamed, but all the more powerful for that reason, is the homelessness that these artists share with their subjects. Given the economic and political organization of the late twentieth century under capitalism, there are rarely places for human beings to be whole. In this sense, without ignoring the specific historical situations of either group, both migrant workers and Palestinians can serve as figures for an intellectual and emotional displacement that is more general in our time: like torn photo graphs, we are ripped apart from ourselves, subject to the violence of history and prey to social definitions that divide one individual from another.

In response to this violence, art, as Mohr, Berger and Said practice it, can serve as a teleological shelter, an alternate home for the spirit. It can be the place where the double-crossing of history is itself double-crossed.

> *To double-cross is to betray—as national frontiers betray the workers and cultural groups who traverse them.

> *To double-cross is to cross together—as Mohr and Berger, and Mohr and Said have done in their respective books. If we look for the ideology of form in these texts, we find artists whose collaboration between seeing and saying shows us that a mode of production need not diminish or oppress its subjects.

> *To double-cross is to subvert—as the life of the interior subverts fragmentation by imaginatively reassembling and arranging parts broken by historical circumstances.

> *To double-cross is to go and to return home—as guest workers and Palestinians hope to do but frequently cannot. As Berger says, "An assured place for him no longer exists in his village. Such an end can be subsumed under several generalizing categories in order to render it normal: The Road to Development; The Unification of Europe; The History of Capitalism; even The Oncoming Revolutionary Struggle. But the categories do not make him less homeless, in space and time" (*Seventh* n.p).

In the face of this displacement, Berger, Mohr, and Said offer us their books in whose form we find restored the possibility of double-crossing—returning home—in another sense. Like poets, these men use images and words to "bring [us] together-into-intimacy" with people who are usually forgotten or ignored because of the barriers we normally erect to separate ourselves from the uncomfortable knowledge of their pain (*Our Faces* 97). It is as if the books themselves become the vehicles for crossing frontiers, bringing us "home" to a place where, at the moment of revelation provoked by the constellation of what we see and read, we "lose all sense of exclusion; [we find ourselves] at the center" (*Our Faces* 51).

Theodor Adorno also had this sense of the-book-as-home and was criticized for it—as if the exercise of imaginative life were an inadequate response to external force. But I agree with him that "in his text, the writer sets up house."[14] When this housekeeping involves a writer and a photographer, the arrangements become more complicated, but the principle remains the same:

> Just as he trundles papers, books, pencils, documents untidily from room to room, he creates the same disorder in his thoughts. They become pieces of furniture that he sinks into, content or irritable. He strokes them affectionately, wears them out, mixes them up, rearranges, ruins them. For a man who no longer has a homeland, writing becomes a place to live.[15]

NOTES

1. John Berger, *And Our Faces, My Heart, Brief as Photos* (New York: Pantheon, 1984), 96. All further references cited within the text as *Our Faces*.

2. John Berger, *A Seventh Man* (New York: Viking, 1975), 44. All further references cited within the text as *Seventh*.

3. Edward Said, "Criticism between Culture and System," in *The World, the Text, and the Critic* (Cambridge: Harvard University Press, 1983), 216.

4. Rainer Nagele, "The Scene of the Other: Theodor Adorno's Negative Dialectic in the Context of Poststructuralism," in *Postmodernism and Politics*, ed. Jonathan Arac (Minneapolis: Minnesota University Press, 1986), 105.

5. Fredric Jameson, *The Political Unconscious* (Ithaca: Cornell University Press, 1981), 76.

6. Nagele, "Scene of the Other," 98.

7. Theodor Adorno, *Negative Dialectics* (New York: Seabury, 1973), 203.

8. Adorno, *Negative Dialectics*, 171.

9. Nagele, "Scene of the Other," 107.

10. Gilles Deleuze, *Foucault* (Minneapolis: Minnesota University Press, 1986), 66.

11. Deleuze, *Foucault*, 74.

12. Edward Said, *After the Last Sky: Palestinian Lives* (New York: Pantheon, 1986), 18. All further references cited within the text as *Last Sky*.

13. Edward Said, *Orientalism* (New York: Vintage, 1979), 12.

14. Theodor Adorno, *Minima Moralia: Reflections from Damaged Life* (London: N.B.L., 1974), 87.

15. Adorno, *Minima*, 87.

Afterword:
Snapshots, the Beginnings of Photography

Robert B. Ray

IN THE LATE TWENTIETH CENTURY, THE UBIQUITY of photography, especially as a document of certain *events*, has engendered a longing for both its earlier invention and its more extensive presence. We now wish that photography had always existed, and that it had been *everywhere*. What did certain things look like *exactly*? The expression on Napoleon's face when Moscow first appeared in the distance? The hands of John Wilkes Booth, in hiding, waiting to assassinate Lincoln? The clothes worn by the Council of Trent? Einstein at the moment of completing the Theory of Relativity? More and more, to have not seen becomes equated with Walter Benjamin's definition of *catastrophe:* "to have missed the opportunity."[1]

Nothing encourages this desire for photographic evidence more than the cinema, which, as Jean-Luc Godard has pointed out, always provides, at the very least, a documentary record of a particular moment's objects and people. As Godard said about his own *Breathless,* "This film is really a documentary on Jean Seberg and Jean-Paul Belmondo."[2] Thus, if we want to know, for example, what Jean Harlow looked like less than a week after her husband Paul Berne was found dead in an apparent suicide, we have only to look at a scene from *Red Dust,* shot on her first day back on the set, but edited without the close-ups which her haggard appearance made unus-

able.[3] In fact, Hollywood's version of the cinema, what Noël Burch calls the Institutional Mode of Representation, dramatically stimulates the desire, and even the expectation, to observe everything.[4] By implicitly guaranteeing its audience the ideal vantage point for every narratively relevant event, by visually underlining (with, for example, close-ups, rack focusing, and camera movements) every important detail or expression, Hollywood's "invisible style" accustoms us to expect photographic accompaniment for everything that might prove significant.

What about the origins of photography itself, its first moments of invention and use? What would they look like on film? What if, by the sheerest chance, we came across a roll of film containing a photographic record of just those things, but produced by a camera whose strange mechanism, an alternative to the lineage of our own, has been lost. Searching for a manual, we fall upon these remarks which will serve as our instructions: "The past has left behind in literary texts images of itself that are comparable to the images which light imprints on a photosensitive plate. Only the future possesses developers active enough to bring these plates out perfectly."[5] Think, then, of each of the following sections as a snapshot of photography's beginnings, developed in terms of our current interests in texts, their ways of producing meaning, and their relation to what we still call "the real."

1.

In the course of his first random stroll through the boulevards and the rue de la Paix, Lucien, like all new-comers to Paris, took more stock of things than of persons. In Paris, it is first of all the general pattern that commands attention. The luxury of the shops, the height of the buildings, the busy to-and-fro of carriages, the ever-present contrast between extreme luxury and extreme indigence, all these things are particularly striking. Abashed at the sight of this alien crowd, the imaginative young man felt as if he himself was enormously diminished.[6]

In the twenty-year period from 1830 to 1850, when the hero of Balzac's *Lost Illusions* arrives in Paris, many of the features associated with "modern life" begin to appear for the first time: the metropolis, the daily newspaper, mass transit, the department store, the democratization of culture. In particular, between 1839 and 1842, three things happen: the word *photography* begins to be used for the first time in English and German,[7] the *physiologies* become the first best-selling mass-market paperback books, and Poe invents the detective story. What connects these three developments?

Dana Brand has argued that modern urban life provoked a crisis of "legibility."[8] As newcomers swarmed into the cities, abandoning their native surroundings which time, size, and tradition had rendered effortlessly comprehensible, anonymity became a condition that almost everyone experienced at some point during the day—in a remote *quartier*, visited for the first time on business; on an unknown street, turned down by mistake; in a neighborhood encountered in the morning rather than the afternoon. Inevitably, this dislocation encouraged crime: "It is almost impossible," Benjamin quotes a Parisian undercover policeman observing, "to maintain good behaviour in a thickly populated area where an individual is, so to speak, unknown to all others and thus does not have to blush in front of anyone."[9] In December 1840, Edgar Allan Poe explicitly connected crime to the illegibility of the anonymous "man of the crowd," who like "a cer-

tain German book . . . does not permit itself to be read."[10] That man, for whom Poe's literate narrator can discover no comforting classification, stands for "the type and the genius of deep crime."[11]

Thus, a proposition: what cannot be read threatens. The first sites of this new anxiety were Paris and London, vast metropolises where people could disappear without a trace, where (as in Balzac and Dickens, the great chroniclers of the potential anonymity haunting all urban identities) credentials, antecedents, and even names became suspect. The first clue connecting this experience to photography is geographical: photography was invented almost simultaneously in France (by Niépce and Daguerre) and in England (by Fox Talbot).

2.

The Count de Lanty was small, ugly, and pockmarked; dark as a Spaniard, dull as a banker.[12]

In *S/Z*, an analysis not only of Balzac's *Sarrasine* (the source of this description of the Count de Lanty) but of all popular narratives, Barthes repeatedly asks, how does Balzac know that Spaniards are dark, bankers dull? Barthes answers by proposing that the realistic novel works precisely to insure that the source for such a sentence "cannot be discerned": "Who is speaking? Is it Sarrasine? the narrator? the author? Balzac-the-author? Balzac-the-man? romanticism? bourgeoisie? universal wisdom? The intersection of these origins creates the writing."[13] Barthes labels these formulaic expressions ("dark as a Spaniard," "dull as a banker") as "cultural codes" or "reference codes" and traces their origin not to reality itself, but to representations of it:

The cultural codes, from which the Sarrasinean text has drawn so many references, will also be extinguished (or at least will emigrate to other texts; there is no lack of hosts. . . . In fact, these citations are extracted from a body of knowledge, from an anonymous Book whose best model is doubtless the School Manual. (205)

For Barthes, of course, the term *School Manual* functions as a metaphor for the imaginary collation of common sense, received ideas, and cultural stereotypes on which the Reference Code relies. In fact, however, something very like actual manuals, guides to the urban scene, did achieve enormous success in Paris between 1840 and 1842: the *physiologies*. The first mass-market, paperback, pocket-sized books, the *physiologies* proved enormously appealing to readers wanting an immediately legible account, however misleadingly simplified, of the cosmopolitan crowd. Roughly 120 different *physiologies* appeared during these three years, each offering what historian Richard Sieburth has called "pseudoscientific portraits of social types": "the Englishman in Paris," "the drinker," "the creditor and the retailer," "the salesgirl," "the deputy," "the stevedore," etc.[14] As books, the *physiologies* were brief, averaging around 120 pages, with thirty to sixty illustrations.[15] While the *physiologies* were not typically comic, their format obviously derived from the same ethos which had spawned the caricature, a form which, in fact, dominated the books' visual style.

Whatever usefulness the *physiologies* purported to have rested on a single, profound faith in the reliability of appearances. As Benjamin observed of these books, "They assured people that everyone was, unencumbered by any factual knowledge, able to make out the profession, the character, the background, and the life-style of passers-by."[16] Dana Brand points out that the plot of Poe's "The Man of the Crowd" turns on the narrator's frustrated desire to "read" the people who pass his coffeehouse window. Having identified (at least to his own satisfaction) noblemen, merchants, attorneys, tradesmen, stockjobbers, clerks, pickpockets, gamblers, "Jew pedlars," professional street beggars, invalids, prostitutes, and "ragged artisans and exhausted laborers of every description," the narrator becomes fascinated by the illegible man to whom none of the readymade categories apply. Sieburth summarizes the *physiologies'* appeal:

> They served to reduce the crowd's massive alterity to proportions more familiar, to transform its radical anonymity into a lexicon of nameable stereotypes, thereby providing their readers with the comforting illusion that the faceless conglomerations of the modern city could after all be read—

and hence mastered—as a legible system of differences.[17]

This "legible system," as *S/Z* shows, is complicit with a culture's world view: in Barthes's words, "If we collect all such knowledge, all such vulgarisms, we create a monster, and this monster is ideology."[18] But a recent *New York Times* article linking the persistence of stereotypes to their "usefulness" concludes that "the new explorations of the cognitive role of stereotypes find them to be a distortion of a process that helps people order their perceptions. The mind looks for ways to simplify the chaos around it. Lumping people into categories is one."[19]

3.

> "We didn't trust ourselves at first to look long at the first pictures he [Daguerre] developed. We were abashed by the distinctness of these human images, and believed that the little tiny faces in the picture could see *us*, so powerfully was everyone affected by the unaccustomed clarity and the unaccustomed truth to nature of the first daguerrotypes."[20]

If the *physiologies* offered to make urban life more comfortable by first making it more legible, photography must initially have seemed part of the same project. Soon after its discovery, the new technology became part of the proliferating systems of registration and surveillance described in Benjamin's *Charles Baudelaire: A Lyric Poet in the Age of High Capitalism*. Fingerprinting, physiological measurements, and photographs recorded identity, enabled its tracking, and circumscribed its possible escape routes into anonymity. After photography, the kind of situation described in *The Return of Martin Guerre*, where a man posing as a long-vanished husband fools an entire town, appeared decisively pre-modern.

Like the *physiologies*, photography had a pseudoscientific basis, particularly in the late eighteenth- and early nineteenth-century rage for classification. But while the new technology seemed the ideal means of gathering the empirical data required by any system, almost immediately the first photographers noticed something going wrong. One historian cites Fox Talbot's surprise at what he found:

And that was just the trouble: fascinating irrelevancy. "Sometimes inscriptions and dates are found upon buildings, or printed placards most irrelevant are discovered upon their walls: sometimes a distant sundial is seen, and upon it—unconsciously recorded—the hour of the day at which the view was taken." To judge from his commentaries, Fox Talbot enjoyed such incidentals. At the same time, though, they were troublesome, for they meant that the instrument was only partially under control, recording disinterestedly in despite of its operator's intentions.[21]

The *physiologies* had subsumed all idiosyncrasies under the rule of the controlling term: "the banker," "the Spaniard." Indeed, their format seemed derived from La Fontaine's dictum, "Nothing more common than the name, nothing rarer than the thing."[22] Photographs, on the other hand, swarming with accidental details unnoticed at the time of shooting, continually evoked precisely what eluded classification—the distinguishing feature, the contingent detail. In doing so, they undercut the *physiologies'* basic project, which photography now revealed to be committed exclusively to language as a way of understanding and ordering the world. What resisted the narrator's efforts to read the man of the crowd?—"the absolute idiosyncrasy of [his] expression."[23]

By showing that every Spaniard was not dark, every banker not dull, photographs effectively criticized all classification systems and insured that any such system attempted in photography (e.g., August Sander's) would inevitably appear not as science but as art. In fact, while the longing for strictly objective, and therefore *exact*, representation had motivated photography's invention, photographs produced the precisely opposite effect—a mute ambiguity that invited subjective revery. Quoting the semiotician Mukarovsky, Paul Willemen has proposed that "the signifying practices having recourse to images can thus be described . . . as 'designed to render things imprecise,' as a movement towards indeterminacy."[24] Thus, photography becomes yet another example of what Edward Tenner has called the "revenge effect" of all technology: a process designed for one purpose turns out not only to subvert that purpose but also to achieve its opposite.[25]

4.

Beyond the obvious facts that he has at some time done manual labour, that he takes snuff, that he is a Freemason, that he has been in China, and that he has done a considerable amount of writing lately, I can deduce nothing else.[26]

That the first detective story (Poe's "The Murders in the Rue Morgue") appeared in 1841, at the height of the *physiologies* craze, and that its author felt obliged to set his tale in Paris, a place he had never been, both suggest the existence of an underlying connection between the two forms. In fact, the detective story represents a transposition of the *physiologies*, an extrapolation from that earlier mode's purely descriptive purposes to narrative. Like the *physiologies*, the detective story offered to make the world, and particularly the urban scene, more legible. To do so, it relied incessantly on the very reference codes the *physiologies* had propagated. Thus, for Sherlock Holmes, physical evidence is always unproblematically indexical: "the writer" will inevitably display a shiny cuff and a worn elbow patch, "the laborer" a muscular hand, "the visitor to China" a particular Oriental tatoo.

Although the detective story arose almost simultaneously with the *physiologies*, it flowered only after their demise. In effect, it was not needed until later when it functioned as an antidote to photography. "Between what matters and what seems to matter," *Trent's Last Case* begins, "how should the world we know judge wisely?"[27] By dramatically increasing the available amount of particularized information, photography not only undercut the *physiologies'* vulnerable, simplistic schema; it insured that in every context where it intervened, distinguishing the significant from the insignificant would become treacherous. "The principal difficulty of your case," Holmes tells his client in "The Naval Treaty," "lay in the fact of there being too much evidence"[28]—precisely the problem, the proliferation of meaning, for which Susan Sontag blames photography.[29] Thus, the first Sherlock Holmes story, "A Scandal in Bohemia," inevitably revises Poe: the new threat, which the detective must find and destroy, is no longer a purloined letter, but an incriminating photograph.

To a certain extent, the detective story differed from its predecessor, replacing the *physiologies'* intolerance for the particular with an insistence on its value. "Singularity," Holmes instructs Watson, "is almost invariably a clue. The more featureless and commonplace a crime is, the more difficult it is to bring home." What neither the detective story nor the *physiologies* can admit, however, is chance, accident, randomness—precisely those properties of all signifying systems which, as Barthes's "Third Meaning" essay shows, photography radically enhances. Every photograph, even the starkly "impoverished"[30] ones favored by advertising and propaganda, can occasion a reading that fixates on contingent details whose precise meaning eludes, at least temporarily, all readily available symbolic systems. The survival of the *physiologies* and the detective story, on the other hand, depends on the *resistance* to the accidental's appeal: if the blond Spaniard has no place in the *physiologies,* the random crime proves fatal to the detective story—and, as Borges's "Death and the Compass" demonstrates, to the detective who wrongly insists on interpreting it. By repudiating the hermeneutic impulse in favor of the accidental, Borges's story marks the triumph of the photographic sensibility and, by implication, its most characteristic incarnation: the candid snapshot. Momentarily overcome, the anxiety to interpret, which had prompted both the *physiologies* and the detective story, returns in *Blow-up,* where it is ironically evoked by exactly such snapshots which now reveal a crime. But while the movie cites the detective story form, it refuses to subordinate images to language, suggesting with its inconclusive ending that the need to explain must ultimately be abandoned.

5.

In the history of films, every great moment that shines is a silent one.

King Vidor[31]

Without its [inner speech's] function of binding subject and text in sociality [some system of shared meanings produced by shared codes], no signification would be possible other than delirium.[32]

At the origins of photography, therefore, an intersection of related problems: the legibility of the surrounding world, the status of the detail, the relationship between image and language. For the *physiologies* and the detective story, rituals of the word's mastery over things, photography represents the other which must be contained. In the twentieth century, this contest finds a new site—the cinema.

Filmmaking has, from the first, been shaped by the answers proposed to a set of fundamental questions: How do we make sense of a film? What happens when we encounter a movie segment for the first time? How do we process cinematic information? During the experimental phase of Soviet cinema, Boris Eikhenbaum suggested, in an especially influential answer, that we accompany our film watching with an "inner speech." In particular, inner speech makes the connection between separate shots. A useful example arises in *Born Free*'s opening scene, which cuts back and forth between a woman washing clothes in a river and a stalking lion, apparently intent on an unseen prey. With the woman and the lion never appearing together in any frame, the sequence culminates in three shots: the lion springs, the woman turns and screams, and the river rushes away, now littered with clothes and a spreading red stain. The scene's meaning is clear: the lion has killed the woman. That meaning, however, while an *effect* of the images, appears nowhere in them. It occurs only in the viewer's mind, whose inner speech responds to the movie's images and sounds with the linguistic formulation, "lion kills woman."

The notion of inner speech reaffirms, in Paul Willemen's words, "the interdependence of the verbal and the visual in cinema."[33] Even the nonverbal is grasped in relation to the verbal, which translates it into our dominant meaning system, language. Significantly, the concept of inner speech arises with silent film and in a genre (propaganda) where unambiguous communication is the goal. In that context, what is most feared is images' capacity to produce not meaning, but what Willemen calls "delirium." Without a verbal soundtrack to anchor the images and constrain their potential drift, and with the continuity rules still inchoate, inner speech had to rely on other visual elements for the verbal formulations that would bind the unrolling pictures into a coherent statement.

Recognizing their images' potential for ambiguity and imprecision, silent-era filmmakers structured their shots around formulaic characters, sequences, and even verbal expressions. The silent cinema, in fact, represents the single most important revival of the *physiologies.* There we again encounter the *physiologies'* basic assumption that every character type has its own unvarying physical embodiment: villains look villainous (with moustaches and squinting eyes), heroines look virtuous (with petticoats and blonde hair), and businessmen look businesslike (with suits and starched shirt-fronts). Very early in the movies' evolution, filmmaking also gravitated to stock actions—the chase, the lovers' meeting, the deathbed vigil. In *S/Z,* Barthes designates such predictable sequences as part of the "proairetic code," that reservoir of generic actions such as "the stroll," "the murder," or "the rendezvous" (Barthes's examples) that trigger ready-made inner speech; indeed, Barthes proposes that this "code of actions principally determines the readability of the text."[34] At its most extreme subservience to language, a silent film's image track would occasionally provide a *visual* translation of a stock phrase: *October*'s juxtaposition of Provisional Dictator Kerensky with a mechanical peacock ("proud as a peacock") is only the most famous example of this device.

Sound moviemaking did not abandon these formulae; it simply relied on newly developed strategies for making them subtler. Most useful were Hollywood's continuity protocols, founded on the two principles of matching and centering, both designed to overcome film's fundamental discontinuity. While the matching rules insured that editing would connect shots by means of certain cinematic grammar, centering guaranteed that all *mise-en-scène* elements (*e.g.,* lighting, framing, shot size) would visually underline narratively important events. To the extent that the continuity rules circumscribed the movies' images, regulated their meaning in terms of a single narrative, and vastly reduced their potential complexity, they became, like the detective story, *a means of policing photography*—and another example of language's control of the image.

While the notion of inner speech arises in film's infancy, Barthes's "third meaning" appears in its maturity. With its insistence on perverse readings that ignore, and indeed refuse, intended or contextually obvious significances, the third meaning disposition clearly descends from surrealist tactics designed to reassert the autonomy and ambiguity of images: think, for example, of Man Ray's habit of watching the screen through his fingers, spread to isolate certain parts of the image; of Breton's advocacy of eating and talking during showings as means for reorienting one's attention to the marginal incident or detail; of Breton's weekend moviegoing:

> When I was "at the cinema age" (it should be recognized that this age exists in life—and that it passes) I never began by consulting the amusement pages to find out what film might chance to be the best, nor did I find out the time the film was to begin. I agreed wholeheartedly with Jacques Vaché in appreciating nothing so much as dropping into the cinema when whatever was playing was playing, at any point in the show, and leaving at the first hint of boredom—of surfeit—to rush off to another cinema where we behaved in the same way.... I have never known anything more *magnetizing;* it goes without saying that more often than not we left our seats without even knowing the title of the film which was of no importance to us anyway. On a Sunday several hours sufficed to exhaust all that Nantes could offer us: the important thing is that one came out "charged" for a few days.[35]

Both Barthes's "third meaning" practice and the surrealist strategies of filmwatching amount to methods of *extraction, fragmentation.* In both, the individual segment, image, or detail is isolated from the narrative that would circumscribe it. "To a certain extent," Barthes proposes, the third meaning "cannot be grasped in the projected film, the film 'in movement,' '*au naturel*,' but only, as yet, in that major artifact which is the still."[36] Like the detective story, Hollywood filmmaking (still the international norm) "arrests the multiplication of meanings," as D. A. Miller argues, "by uniquely privileging one of them"[37]—that set designated "significant" by the unrolling story. In his autobiography, Barthes acknowledged his own "resistance" to the cinema, attributing it to the "statutory impossibility of the fragment" in a continuous, "saturated" medium.[38]

Narrative, in fact, subordinates its images to the linguistic formulations they serve. "The sequence exists," Barthes writes of the action code, "when and because it can be given a name."[39] Thus, encountering a picture offering itself as "a still," we will immediately begin to imagine the missing story. Doing so typically involves a summoning of the received categories stored in inner speech, the "already-done," the "already-read."[40] So we can make this proposition: in late twentieth-century civilization, every image lies surrounded by invisible formulae whose inevitable activation reasserts our stubborn allegiance to language as the only means of making sense.

Artists have begun to play with this situation, implying the traps into which our preference for language leads us. Cindy Sherman's "Film Stills" has become the most famous case, a complex use of photography, disguise, and the word *still* to imply movies which do not in fact exist—and to snare the viewer into "explaining" the photographs in terms of the cinematic conventions (*e.g., film noir,* Antonioni-esque angst, Southern gothic) already available to inner speech. Equally suggestive is Chris Van Allsburg's children's book *The Mysteries of Harris Burdick,* a collection of fourteen captioned images, each purporting to be the single remaining illustration of stories never found.

What is at stake with this relationship between language and image? The research tradition that Jacques Derrida calls "grammatology" posits that different technologies of communication occasion different ways of thinking. An oral culture, for example, relying entirely on human memory to store and retrieve its information, develops conceptual habits that would appear strange to us, inhabitants of a fully alphabetic society. Grammatology further suggests that human history has seen only two major revolutions in communications technology: the first involved precisely this shift from oral to alphabetic cultures; the second, the transition from alphabetic to "electronic" or "cinematic," we are living through now. What are the consequences, characteristics, and modes of an age of photography, film, television, magnetic tape, and computers? How will what we call "thinking" change with this technology?

It will be up to us to decide. And here the matter of language and photography intervenes decisively. To the extent that such deciding will require invention, the persistence of formulae becomes inhibiting. The "already-read" categories of the *physiologies,* the detective story, and inner speech seek to define the new technology (photography, film) in terms of the old (language), and thereby restrict our capacity to admit the full implications of the revolution surrounding us. Roger Cardinal calls this way of dealing with images the "literate mode," derived from "habits of purposeful reading of texts," and assuming that "the artist has centred or signalled his image in accordance with the conventions of representation" so that "the viewer's gaze will be attuned to that focal message and will ignore its periphery." The alternative, "one which focuses less narrowly and instead roams over the frame, sensitive to its textures and surfaces," Cardinal associates with "non-literacy and with habits of looking which are akin to habits of touching."[41] This way of putting the matter seems absolutely consistent with the tradition we might call, following Sontag, "against interpretation." Surrealism, Barthes's "third meaning" essay, and photography itself have all explicitly evoked eroticism as an analogue for a new practice of the image. If that practice involves, as *Blow-up* suggests, a relaxation of the explanatory drive (our version of the will-to-power?), its motto might result from changing one word in the dictum thrown like a knife at the literary establishment almost thirty years ago, ironically by one who has become photography's enemy: in place of a hermeneutics we need an erotics, not of art, but of photography.[42]

NOTES

This essay also appears as chapter two in *The Avant Garde Finds Andy Hardy.*

1. Walter Benjamin, "N [Theoretics of Knowledge; Theory of Progress]," trans. Leigh Hafrey and Richard Sieburth, *The Philosophical Forum* 15, nos. 1–2 (1983–1984): 23.

2. Jean-Luc Godard, "Interview with Yvonne Baby," in *Breathless,* ed. Dudley Andrew (New Brunswick, N.J.: Rutgers University Press, 1987), 166.

3. Samuel Marx and Joyce Vanderveen, *Deadly Illusions: Jean Harlow and the Murder of Paul Berne* (New York: Random House, 1990), 224–25.

4. Noël Burch, "Film's Institutional Mode of Representation and the Soviet Response," *October* 11 (1979): 77–96.

5. Benjamin, "N": 32.

6. Honoré de Balzac, *Lost Illusions*, trans. Herbert J. Hunt (New York: Penguin, 1971), 159.

7. Ian Jeffrey, *Photography: A Concise History* (New York: Oxford University Press, 1981), 240.

8. Dana Brand, "From the *flâneur* to the detective; interpreting the city of Poe," in *Popular Fiction: Technology, Ideology, Production, Reading,* ed. Tony Bennett (London: Routledge, 1990), 220–37.

9. Walter Benjamin, *Charles Baudelaire: A Lyric Poet in the Age of High Capitalism,* trans. Harry Zohn (London: NLB, 1973), 40.

10. Edgar Allan Poe, "The Man of the Crowd," in *The Portable Poe,* ed. Philip Van Doren Stern (New York: Viking, 1945), 107. See Dana Brand's comment on this passage in "From the *flâneur* to the detective," 220–21.

11. Poe, "The Man of the Crowd," 118.

12. Roland Barthes, *S/Z,* trans. Richard Miller (New York: Hill and Wang, 1974), 38.

13. Barthes, *S/Z, 172–73.*

14. Richard Sieburth, "Same Difference: The French Physiologies, 1840–1842," *Notebooks in Cultural Analysis* 1 (1984): 163, 167.

15. Sieburth, "Same Difference": 170.

16. Benjamin, *Charles Baudelaire,* 39.

17. Sieburth, "Same Difference": 175.

18. Barthes, *S/Z,* 97.

19. Daniel Goleman, "'Useful' Modes of Thinking Contribute to the Power of Prejudice," *The New York Times,* 12 May 1987: C10.

20. Walter Benjamin, "A Small History of Photography," trans. Edmund Jephcott and Kingsley Shorter, in *One-Way Street and Other Writings* (London: NLB, 1979), 244.

21. Jeffrey, *Photography,* 12–13.

22. Sieburth, "Same Difference": 184.

23. Poe, "The Man of the Crowd," 112.

24. Paul Willemen, "Cinematic Discourse—The Problem of Inner Speech," *Screen* 22 (1981): 78.

25. Edward Tenner, "Revenge Theory," *Harvard Magazine* (March-April 1991): 26–30.

26. Arthur Conan Doyle, *The Complete Sherlock Holmes* (Garden City, N.Y.: Doubleday, 1927), 177.

27. E. C. Bentley, *Trent's Last Case,* in *Three Famous Murder Novels,* ed. Bennett A. Cerf (New York: Modern Library, 1945), 1.

28. Doyle, *The Complete Sherlock Holmes,* 467.

29. "Because each photograph is only a fragment, its moral and emotional weight depends on where it is inserted. A photograph changes according to the context in which it is seen. . . . And it is in this way that the presence and proliferation of all photographs contributes to the erosion of the very notion of meaning. . . ." Susan Sontag, *On Photography* (New York: Farrar, Straus & Giroux, 1977), 94–95.

30. Roland Barthes, *Mythologies,* trans. Annette Lavers (New York: Hill and Wang, 1972), 125, 127.

31. Quoted in Joseph Cotten, *Vanity Will Get You Somewhere: An Autobiography* (New York: Avon Books, 1987), 106.

32. Willemen, "Cinematic Discourse": 78.

33. Willemen, "Cinematic Discourse": 64.

34. Barthes, *S/Z,* 262.

35. Quoted in *The Shadow and Its Shadow: Surrealist Writings on the Cinema,* ed. Paul Hammond (London: British Film Institute, 1978), 42–43.

36. Roland Barthes, "The Third Meaning," trans. Richard Howard, in *The Responsibility of Forms* (New York: Hill and Wang, 1985), 59.

37. D. A. Miller, "Language of Detective Fiction: Fiction of Detective Language," in *The State of the Language,* ed. Leonard Michaels and Christopher Ricks (Berkeley: University of California Press, 1980), 482.

38. Roland Barthes, *Roland Barthes,* trans. Richard Howard (New York: Hill and Wang, 1977), 54–55.

39. Barthes, *S/Z,* 19.

40. Barthes, *S/Z,* 19.

41. Roger Cardinal, "Pausing over Peripheral Detail," *Framework* [London] 30/31 (1986): 124.

42. Susan Sontag, *Against Interpretation* (New York: Delta, 1966), 14.

About the Contributors

KEVIN G. BARNHURST is author of *Seeing the Newspaper* (1994). He has written essays on such topics as news story layout, social class, and health, published by the Society of Newspaper Design, the *American Scholar*, and *Comment*. Barnhurst is Associate Professor of Graphic Arts at Syracuse University.

MARSHA BRYANT is writing a book on W. H. Auden, documentary, and the 1930s. She was Guest Curator of the exhibit "The Films of Paul Strand" at the Whitney Museum of American Art. Bryant is Assistant Professor of English at the University of Florida.

COREY K. CREEKMUR is coeditor of *Out in Culture: Lesbian, Gay, and Queer Essays on Film and Mass Culture* (1995). He has published essays and reviews in *Wide Angle, Screen,* and *Film Quarterly*. His current work focuses on gender and sexuality in the film Western. Creekmur is Assistant Professor of Film Studies at Wayne State University.

LLOYD DAVIS is author of *Sexuality and Textuality in Henry James: Reading through the Virginal* (1988), and *Guise and Disguise: Rhetoric and Characterization in the English Renaissance* (1993). He is also editor of *Virginal Sexuality and Textuality in Victorian Literature* and a coauthor of *Tools for Cultural Studies: An Introduction* (forthcoming). Davis teaches English and Cultural Studies at the University of Queensland.

JULIA DUFFY has written articles and reviews on Virginia Woolf, Christina Stead, and Australian literature. She now works as a lawyer in Brisbane, Australia.

ROBERT B. RAY is author of *A Certain Tendency of the Hollywood Cinema, 1930–1980* (1985) and *The Avant Garde Finds Andy Hardy* (1995). He has published articles on film and visual theory in *Visible Language, Cinema Journal,* and *Strategies*. Ray is Associate Professor of English and Director of Film Studies at the University of Florida.

CAROL SHLOSS is author of *In Visible Light, Photography and the American Writer: 1840–1940* (1987), and *Gentleman Photographers: The Work of Loring Underwood and William Lyman Underwood* (1987), as well as a book on Flannery O'Connor. Her current book is *Modernism's Daughters: Lucia Joyce, Mary de'Rachewiltz, and Anna Freud*. Shloss is Professor of English at West Chester University.

TIMOTHY SWEET is author of *Traces of War: Poetry, Photography, and the Crisis of the Union* (1990). He has also published articles in *American Literature, Early American Literature,* and *Resources for American Literary Study*. Sweet is Assistant Professor of English at West Virginia University.

MARJA WAREHIME is author of *Brassaï: Images of Culture and the Surrealist Observer* (1995). She has also published essays on literature and the visual arts in *The Yearbook of Interdisciplinary Studies in* the Fine Arts, French Forum, and SubStance. Warehime is Associate Professor of French at the University of South Carolina.

STEPHEN WATT, author of *The Popular Theatres of James Joyce and Sean O'Casey* (1991), has published essays in *PMLA, James Joyce Quarterly,* and *Eire-Ireland.* He is coeditor of *Marketing Modernisms* (forthcoming) and *American Drama: Colonial to Contemporary* (1994). Currently, he is writing *Postmodern/Drama: Rereading the Contemporary Stage.* Watt is Associate Professor of English and Director of Graduate Studies at Indiana University.

Index

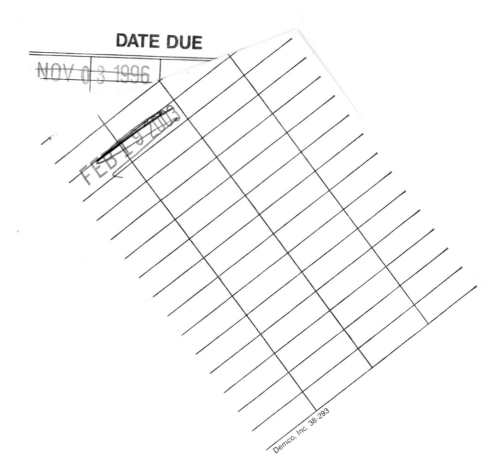

DATE DUE

NOV 0 3 1996

FEB 1 9 2003

Demco, Inc. 38-293